THE GLOSSARY OF
SERVICE
DESIGN

Compiled & Edited By:
Manasi Pathak

Rhythm

Independent
Publication

THE GLOSSARY OF SERVICE DESIGN

Compiled & Edited By:
Manasi Pathak

ISBN:9798862264906

9798862264906

Published by:

Rhythm Independent Publication,

Jinkethimmanahalli, Varanasi, Bengaluru, Karnataka, India - 560036

For all types of correspondence, send your mails to the provided address above.

The information presented herein has been collated from a diverse range of sources, comprehensive perspective on the subject matter.

360-Degree Customer View

A 360-degree customer view is a holistic perspective of a customer's interactions and experiences with a company throughout their entire journey. It encompasses the collection, integration, and analysis of data from multiple touchpoints, such as online platforms, call centers, and in-store purchases, to create a comprehensive understanding of an individual customer. By leveraging data from various sources, a 360-degree customer view enables companies to gain a deeper understanding of their customers' preferences, behaviors, and needs. This comprehensive view allows businesses to tailor their products, services, and marketing strategies to better meet each customer's individual requirements, ultimately enhancing customer satisfaction and driving business growth.

A/B Testing

A/B testing, in the context of service design, refers to a controlled experiment performed to evaluate and compare two different versions of a service, feature, or interface design. The process involves dividing a sample of users into two groups: group A and group B. Group A is exposed to the original or existing version of the service, while group B is exposed to a modified version, which could include changes to the user interface, content, layout, or functionality. The objective of A/B testing is to determine the impact of these changes on user behavior and key performance metrics. By comparing the results from both groups, service designers can gain valuable insights into which version of the service performs better in terms of user engagement, conversion rates, customer satisfaction, and other relevant metrics. To conduct an A/B test, service designers need to define clear objectives and key performance indicators (KPIs) that align with the goals of the service. They also need to carefully plan and execute the test, ensuring that both groups are randomly selected and exposed to the different versions in a consistent and unbiased manner. During the testing phase, data is collected and analyzed to determine the statistical significance of any differences observed between the two versions. This helps in making informed decisions regarding which version of the service should be implemented or further iterated upon. A/B testing can be an iterative process, with multiple rounds of testing conducted to refine and optimize the service. It allows service designers to make data-driven decisions, reducing the risk of implementing changes that may negatively impact the user experience or business outcomes. In conclusion, A/B testing is a valuable technique in service design, allowing service designers to experiment with different versions of a service and make informed decisions based on user behavior and performance metrics.

API Design

API design is a critical element in the process of service design, as it sets the foundation for how different software systems and services communicate and interact with each other. An API, or Application Programming Interface, defines a set of rules and protocols that enable different software applications to connect and exchange data in a standardized and efficient manner.In the context of service design, API design involves the thoughtful and intentional creation of APIs that provide a well-structured and consistent interface for other software components to interact with. It encompasses various aspects such as defining the API endpoints, designing the request and response structures, and establishing the rules and conventions for data exchange and manipulation.

Abductive Reasoning

Abductive reasoning is a critical mode of thinking within the disciplines of Design Thinking. It involves forming plausible hypotheses or interpretations based on the available information and observations. Unlike deductive reasoning, which starts from general principles to arrive at specific conclusions, and inductive reasoning, which builds general principles based on specific observations, abductive reasoning bridges the gap between these two modes of reasoning by generating hypotheses that explain available evidence.

In the context of Design Thinking, abductive reasoning plays a crucial role in the exploration and sense-making stages of the design process. Designers often face complex and ambiguous problems that require them to make sense of diverse and sometimes conflicting information. Through abductive reasoning, designers make educated guesses, create hypotheses, and generate new insights that guide their design decisions.

Accessibility Testing

Accessibility testing in the context of service design refers to the evaluation and assessment of a service to ensure it is usable and accessible to individuals with disabilities. It involves testing the service's design, functionality, and content to identify any barriers or limitations that may prevent people with disabilities from accessing or using the service effectively. The goal of accessibility testing is to ensure that individuals with disabilities, including those with visual, auditory, motor, or cognitive impairments, can navigate, interact with, and benefit from the service. It aims to promote inclusivity and equal opportunities by removing barriers that may hinder or exclude certain user groups from using the service independently and effectively.

Accessibility

Accessibility refers to the design of products, devices, services, or environments that can be used by people with disabilities. It is a key consideration in Design Thinking disciplines, as it aims to ensure that everyone, regardless of their abilities, can have equal access to and use of these designed solutions.

Designing for accessibility involves taking into account various disabilities, such as visual, auditory, physical, and cognitive impairments. This requires understanding the needs and limitations of individuals with disabilities and addressing them through inclusive design strategies.

Adaptive Insights

Adaptive Insights, in the context of Design Thinking disciplines, refers to a software platform that is utilized for financial planning and analysis. It is designed to help businesses in adapting their financial strategies and forecasting in an agile manner.

With its suite of functionalities, Adaptive Insights empowers organizations to collaborate, plan, and make data-driven decisions in order to drive business growth and achieve their financial goals. The software encompasses various modules such as budgeting, forecasting, reporting, and consolidation which assist in streamlining financial operations.

Adaptive Problem Framing

Adaptive Problem Framing refers to the process of defining and shaping the problem statement or challenge within the context of Design Thinking disciplines. It involves understanding and redefining the problem in a way that enables the design team to explore potential solutions and generate innovative ideas.

At the core of Adaptive Problem Framing is the recognition that the initial problem statement may not capture the true essence of the challenge or may limit the potential solutions. The process involves a deep exploration and analysis of the problem space, allowing the design team to gain a deeper understanding of the underlying issues and uncover hidden assumptions.

This iterative process involves multiple steps, such as conducting research, empathizing with the users, defining the problem statement, and reframing it based on new insights. It involves reframing the problem from different perspectives, encouraging the design team to think outside the box and consider alternative angles.

By engaging in Adaptive Problem Framing, design thinkers can uncover new opportunities and reframing the challenge in a way that allows for more innovative and effective solutions. It helps

2

to drive creative ideation and brainstorming sessions, as well as to identify and challenge assumptions that may limit the design process.

In conclusion, Adaptive Problem Framing is a critical component of Design Thinking, enabling designers to redefine the problem statement and approach it from different angles to generate innovative and effective solutions.

Adaptive Problem Solving

Adaptive Problem Solving refers to the iterative and dynamic process of continually identifying, understanding, and resolving complex challenges or open-ended problems within the framework of Design Thinking disciplines. It involves a flexible and responsive approach that recognizes the need to adjust strategies, solutions, and actions based on evolving insights and feedback.

In the context of Design Thinking, Adaptive Problem Solving recognizes that problem-solving is not a linear or rigid process but rather a nonlinear and fluid one. It emphasizes the importance of adaptability, experimentation, and continuous learning in finding innovative and effective solutions that meet the needs of users or stakeholders.

Adaptive Solutions

Adaptive Solutions is a concept within design thinking disciplines that refers to the ability to modify or adjust a solution based on the needs and feedback of users. It entails a flexible and iterative approach to problem-solving, wherein the solution is continuously refined and adapted to ensure it effectively addresses the users' requirements.

The process of developing adaptive solutions involves empathizing with the users to understand their needs and challenges, defining the problem statement, ideating potential solutions, prototyping and testing them, and refining them based on user feedback. This iterative cycle allows designers to gather insights and make informed modifications to the solution, ensuring that it remains aligned with the evolving needs and preferences of the users.

Aesthetics

Aesthetics, in the context of the Design Thinking discipline, refers to the principles and values that inform the visual and sensory aspects of a design solution. It encompasses the inherent beauty, appeal, and harmony of the design, as well as its ability to engage and evoke emotional responses from the users.

Aesthetics plays a crucial role in design thinking as it focuses on creating visually pleasing and engaging experiences that resonate with the target audience. It involves carefully considering factors such as color, form, texture, composition, and overall visual hierarchy to create a harmonious and visually appealing design. Aesthetics also considers the sensory aspects of a design, including how it feels, sounds, or even smells, enhancing the overall user experience.

By paying attention to aesthetics, designers tap into the emotional and psychological aspects of human perception, enhancing the overall usability and desirability of a product or service. Aesthetically pleasing designs have the power to captivate, inspire, and create meaningful connections with users.

Aesthetics is intertwined with other core principles of design thinking, such as empathy and iteration. By understanding the needs and desires of the users, designers can create aesthetically pleasing solutions that resonate with their preferences and emotions. Additionally, aesthetics often undergo iterations and refinements throughout the design thinking process, as designers incorporate user feedback and insights to continuously improve the visual and sensory aspects of the design.

Affinity Clustering

Affinity clustering is a key technique used in Design Thinking disciplines to facilitate the organization and categorization of ideas, insights, and information. It is a methodical process that helps teams identify and group related concepts, enabling deeper analysis and synthesis.

In essence, affinity clustering involves gathering a diverse range of input and then sorting it into logical groups based on shared themes or relationships. It provides a visual representation of the collective knowledge and perspectives, making it easier for teams to explore patterns, uncover insights, and make connections that may not have been immediately apparent.

Affinity Diagram

An affinity diagram is a method used in service design to organize and consolidate large amounts of data or ideas into meaningful categories or themes. It is a visual tool that helps to make sense of complex information and identify patterns, relationships, and insights. The process of creating an affinity diagram typically involves the following steps: 1. Data collection: Gather all relevant data, such as user research findings, customer feedback, observations, and any other input that is relevant to the problem or challenge being addressed. 2. Data analysis: Review and analyze the collected data to identify common themes or patterns. Look for similarities, connections, or relationships between different pieces of data. 3. Idea generation: Generate ideas or insights based on the analyzed data. Encourage brainstorming and creative thinking to generate a range of possible solutions or opportunities. 4. Affinity mapping: Organize the generated ideas or insights into categories or groups. Look for similarities or relationships between different ideas and cluster them together. 5. Labeling: Assign a label or a heading to each category or group to describe the common theme or idea that it represents. Use clear and concise labels that capture the essence of each category. 6. Sense-making: Step back and review the affinity diagram as a whole. Look for higher-level patterns, overarching themes, or insights that emerge from the categorization and grouping of ideas. The affinity diagram can be used as a collaborative tool in workshops or design sessions, where multiple stakeholders can contribute their perspectives and insights. It helps to create a shared understanding and consensus among team members, facilitates decision-making, and guides the design process. In conclusion, an affinity diagram is a powerful method in service design for organizing and making sense of large amounts of data or ideas. It helps to uncover patterns, insights, and relationships that can inform the design process and lead to better solutions.

Affinity Diagramming Apps

An affinity diagramming app is a digital tool used in the discipline of Design Thinking to organize and make sense of large amounts of information or ideas. It helps teams or individuals categorize and group related ideas or themes into meaningful clusters, allowing for easier analysis and decision-making.

In the context of the Design Thinking process, affinity diagramming is often used in the early stages of problem-solving and ideation. It encourages collaboration and promotes a deeper understanding of the problem space by providing a visual representation of the collected information or ideas.

The app typically provides a virtual canvas where users can input their ideas or data as individual sticky notes or cards. These digital notes can be easily moved, rearranged, and grouped together based on their similarities or relationships. By visually clustering and organizing the ideas, patterns or insights can emerge, helping to uncover connections and potential solutions.

Furthermore, affinity diagramming apps often offer additional features such as the ability to add labels or tags to the grouped items, allowing for further categorization or filtering. This enables users to dive deeper into specific themes or subtopics within the overall dataset.

Overall, affinity diagramming apps are invaluable tools in the Design Thinking discipline as they facilitate collaborative sense-making and help teams or individuals organize and analyze complex information or ideas, ultimately leading to better problem-solving and decision-making.

Affinity Diagramming Software

An affinity diagramming software is a digital tool used in Design Thinking disciplines to organize and consolidate ideas and data collected during the research and exploration stages of a project. It allows interdisciplinary teams to collaborate and make sense of large amounts of qualitative or quantitative information gathered through interviews, surveys, observations, or other research methods.

The software enables the creation of virtual sticky notes, which can be easily moved, grouped, and rearranged according to patterns or similar themes identified in the data. This process, known as affinity diagramming, helps to identify key insights, connections, and trends that might not be immediately apparent when looking at the information in its raw form.

Affinity Diagramming

Affinity diagramming is a service design technique used to organize and categorize ideas, insights, observations, and data in a visual and collaborative manner. It helps to identify common themes, patterns, and connections, facilitating the generation of meaningful insights and the development of design solutions.During the affinity diagramming process, a diverse group of stakeholders or participants come together to collectively brainstorm ideas or contribute their individual perspectives. Each idea or piece of data generated is captured on a separate sticky note or card. These notes are then openly displayed on a wall or board, making them visible to all participants.Once all ideas have been shared, the next step involves organizing and grouping the notes based on their inherent similarities or relationships. Participants collaboratively move the notes around, clustering related ideas together. These clusters can be easily adjusted or rearranged as needed, ensuring that the emerging groupings accurately represent the underlying connections.After all the notes have been organized into clusters, the process continues with an additional round of discussion and refinement. Participants collectively analyze each cluster to identify overarching themes, patterns, or insights that emerge. This helps to make sense of the collective data, uncovering deeper insights and understanding of the problem or opportunity at hand.The affinity diagramming technique promotes collaboration and inclusivity, as it allows all participants to actively contribute to the categorization and analysis process. Through the visual representation of ideas and the physical engagement of moving and rearranging notes, it helps to foster a shared understanding and ownership of the design challenge.By employing affinity diagramming, service designers can harness the power of collective intelligence, overcoming biases and limitations that may arise from individual perspectives. It enables the identification of common pain points, opportunities, and user needs, supporting the development of user-centered design solutions that address the underlying complexities of a service system.

Affinity Diagrams

A short formal definition of Affinity Diagrams in the context of Design Thinking disciplines is as follows: Affinity Diagrams are a visual tool used in the ideation phase of the Design Thinking process to organize a large amount of unstructured data into meaningful and related groups. This method enables teams to uncover patterns, themes, and relationships among different ideas or concepts. Affinity Diagrams help in synthesizing diverse perspectives and input from participants, fostering collaboration, and gaining insights that can inform the design process. The process of creating an Affinity Diagram involves the following steps: 1. Brainstorming: The team generates a large number of ideas, opinions, or observations related to a specific problem or question. Each idea is written on a sticky note or a small piece of paper. 2. Grouping: The team starts to organize the ideas into different groups based on shared characteristics or themes. Similar ideas are placed together. 3. Labeling: Each group is given a label or heading that represents the shared theme or concept. These labels help in providing a clear overview of the clusters. 4. Arranging: The groups are arranged visually, usually in a hierarchical manner, to show the relationships between different clusters. 5. Analysis: As the diagram takes shape, the team reflects on the patterns and connections that emerge. This analysis helps to identify key insights and make informed decisions. Affinity Diagrams serve as a powerful sensemaking tool by structuring and organizing complex information in a way that is understandable and meaningful to the design team. They offer a visual representation of the collective knowledge and understanding, enabling teams to move forward with a shared perspective and a solid foundation for the next steps in the design process.

Affinity Mapping

Affinity mapping is a technique used in the context of Design Thinking disciplines to organize and make sense of large amounts of data, ideas, or observations. It involves grouping related information into categories or clusters based on their inherent connections or similarities. By visually mapping these connections, designers and teams are able to analyze and synthesize the collected information more effectively, leading to insights and potential design opportunities.

In the affinity mapping process, data is typically represented on sticky notes or cards, and participants collaborate to identify patterns, themes, or relationships among the collected items. The mapping is done in a collaborative and iterative manner, allowing for flexibility and modifications based on emerging insights. Through this collaborative exploration, the team can uncover patterns that may have been hidden or overlooked when the data was viewed in isolation.

Affordances

Affordances in the context of service design refer to the perceived possibilities and actions that users can take based on the design and characteristics of a service. Originally coined by psychologist James Gibson, affordances are a fundamental concept in human-computer interaction and design. They help shape user behavior and interactions, guiding users to understand how they can engage with and utilize a service.

Agile Development

Agile Development is a project management approach that focuses on delivering services through iterative and incremental processes. It emphasizes flexibility, collaboration, and continuous improvement. In the context of service design, Agile Development allows for a customer-centric and responsive approach to creating and enhancing services. It emphasizes the importance of understanding the needs and expectations of customers, and seeks to deliver valuable services that meet those needs in a timely manner. Unlike traditional development approaches that follow a sequential and rigid process, Agile Development enables service designers to respond to changing requirements, priorities, and feedback throughout the service design lifecycle.

Agile Methodology

Agile Methodology, in the context of service design, refers to a flexible and iterative approach to project management and development that emphasizes collaboration, adaptability, and continuous improvement. It is a customer-centric approach that aims to deliver value by prioritizing the needs and requirements of the end users. Agile Methodology focuses on breaking down projects into smaller, manageable tasks or features called user stories. These user stories are then prioritized based on their value and complexity. The development team works on these user stories in short iterations or sprints, usually lasting from one to four weeks. At the end of each sprint, a potentially shippable product increment is delivered, allowing for early feedback and validation. The key principles of Agile Methodology are transparency, inspection, and adaptation. Transparency ensures that all stakeholders have a clear understanding of the project objectives, progress, and potential challenges. Inspection involves continuous monitoring and evaluation of the project to identify areas for improvement. Adaptation allows for flexibility in changing requirements or priorities based on emerging insights or changing market conditions. Agile Methodology promotes collaboration and cross-functional teamwork. The project team, including designers, developers, and stakeholders, work closely together throughout the project lifecycle. Regular meetings and discussions, such as daily stand-ups and sprint reviews, enable effective communication and alignment of objectives. One of the core values of Agile Methodology is customer collaboration over contract negotiation. This means that customer involvement and feedback are prioritized over strict adherence to initial project requirements. Agile teams embrace change and aim to deliver a product that meets the evolving needs and expectations of the users. In conclusion, Agile Methodology in service design is an iterative and collaborative approach to project management that focuses on delivering value to the end users. It emphasizes flexibility, transparency, and continuous improvement to ensure customer satisfaction and successful project outcomes.

Agile Service Development

Agile Service Development refers to a methodology that focuses on delivering efficient and effective services through iterative and collaborative processes. It is a service design approach that embraces flexibility, adaptability, and continuous improvement. In Agile Service Development, the emphasis is on breaking down projects into smaller, manageable tasks called user stories. These user stories are prioritized based on their value and complexity, allowing the team to work on the most crucial aspects first. The approach encourages frequent feedback and collaboration between cross-functional teams, including designers, developers, and stakeholders. One of the key principles of Agile Service Development is the concept of sprints, which are time-bound iterations typically lasting from one to four weeks. During each sprint, the team works on a set of user stories, ensuring that working prototypes or service increments are developed at the end of each iteration. This iterative approach allows for early validation of ideas, detection of issues, and incorporation of user feedback, resulting in quicker and more accurate solutions. Agile Service Development also promotes a customer-centric approach, where the needs and preferences of users are considered throughout the design and development process. Regular user testing and feedback sessions help refine and improve the service design, ensuring that it meets the expectations and requirements of the intended audience. Another important aspect of Agile Service Development is the continuous refinement and adaptation of services. With each iteration, the team learns from previous experiences, making adjustments and enhancements to the service design. This approach allows for agility in responding to changing market conditions, user needs, and technological advancements.

Agile Sprint

An Agile Sprint is a time-boxed iteration within the Agile service design process, where a cross-functional team collaborates to complete a set of predefined tasks or user stories. During an Agile Sprint, the team follows a set of Agile principles and methodologies to deliver value to the end users and stakeholders. The Sprint typically lasts for a fixed duration, commonly two weeks, but can vary depending on the specific project and team dynamics. At the beginning of each Sprint, the team identifies and selects a subset of tasks or user stories from the product backlog – a prioritized list of requirements or desired features. This subset of work is referred to as the Sprint backlog and forms the basis for the Sprint's objectives. Once the Sprint begins, the team collaboratively works on the selected tasks, dividing the work among themselves based on their skills and expertise. Daily stand-up meetings are conducted to synchronize efforts, provide updates on progress, and identify any obstacles or challenges that might be hindering the team's progress. The team continuously reviews and refines its work throughout the Sprint, ensuring that the design solutions are aligned with the needs of the end users and stakeholders. Regular sprint reviews and feedback sessions are conducted to gather insights and validate the design decisions made by the team. At the end of the Sprint, the team delivers a potentially shippable increment of the service or product, which can be tested, evaluated, and potentially released to the end users or stakeholders. A Sprint retrospective is then held to reflect on the Sprint process, identify areas for improvement, and make adjustments for the next Sprint. By employing Agile Sprints, service design teams can iteratively and incrementally develop and refine their services, ensuring that each Sprint contributes to the overall improvement and optimization of the service. This iterative approach allows for flexibility, adaptability, and responsiveness to changing requirements and feedback, resulting in a service that is more customer-centric and effective in meeting user and stakeholder needs.

Algorithmic Thinking

Algorithmic Thinking is a problem-solving approach within the discipline of Design Thinking that involves breaking down complex problems into smaller, more manageable parts and developing a step-by-step procedure or sequence of actions to solve them. It is a systematic way of thinking that focuses on constructing a set of logical and sequential instructions, or algorithms, to address specific challenges or achieve desired outcomes.

Algorithmic Thinking in Design Thinking involves carefully analyzing and understanding the problem at hand, identifying the key variables and constraints, and then devising a clear and structured plan to tackle the problem. This approach emphasizes the importance of defining clear objectives, considering various possible solutions, and iteratively refining and improving the solution through frequent evaluation and testing.

Ambidextrous Innovation

Ambidextrous innovation refers to the ability of individuals or organizations to simultaneously pursue both exploitative and exploratory approaches to innovation. It is a concept that originated from the fields of organizational theory and strategic management, and it has gained recognition in the context of design thinking disciplines.

In design thinking, ambidextrous innovation entails the development and implementation of strategies that balance both incremental improvement of existing products or services (exploitation) and the exploration of new ideas and possibilities (exploration).

Ambidextrous Thinking

Ambidextrous thinking in the context of design thinking disciplines refers to the ability to balance and integrate both analytical and creative thinking approaches. It involves being able to think critically and objectively, while also embracing a more intuitive and imaginative mindset.

Design thinking typically involves a user-centered and iterative approach to problem-solving, which requires both logical analysis and creative ideation. Ambidextrous thinking allows designers to effectively navigate these various stages of the design process.

Ambiguity Tolerance

Ambiguity tolerance refers to the ability of an individual or a team within the context of Design Thinking disciplines to tolerate, navigate, and effectively manage ambiguity and uncertainty that arises during the design process.

In the field of design, it is common for designers to encounter situations where the problem at hand is ill-defined, the data or information is incomplete or unclear, and there are multiple possible solutions or approaches. Ambiguity tolerance involves the capacity to embrace and engage with such situations without feeling overwhelmed or uncertain.

Analogous Inspiration

Analogy refers to drawing similarities between two different things in order to understand and gain insights from one thing by looking at the other. Inspiration, on the other hand, is the process of stimulating creativity, motivation, or admiration in an individual or group. In the context of service design, analogous inspiration involves finding inspiration for designing new services, improving existing services, or solving service-related problems by drawing analogies from unrelated domains or sources. It is a method that leverages the power of lateral thinking and encourages designers to explore ideas from unexpected places.

Analogous Thinking

Analogous thinking in the context of design thinking disciplines refers to the process of drawing parallels and making connections between seemingly unrelated ideas, concepts, or experiences. It involves using these connections to gain new insights, generate innovative solutions, and make informed design decisions. Analogous thinking encourages designers to explore different domains and disciplines, looking for inspiration and ideas outside of their immediate field of expertise. By examining and studying diverse sources, such as nature, technology, art, and culture, designers can uncover patterns, principles, and approaches that can be applied to their own design challenges. This way of thinking allows designers to break free from traditional thought patterns and established conventions, fostering creativity and originality in their work. By combining and synthesizing ideas from different contexts, designers can generate fresh perspectives and unique solutions that address complex problems in a meaningful and effective way. Analogous thinking is a central pillar of design thinking methodologies, as it encourages designers to think critically and divergently. By actively seeking out and making connections between ideas, designers can cultivate a mindset that embraces ambiguity, uncertainty, and complexity. This mindset enables designers to approach design problems with an open and exploratory attitude, leading to breakthrough insights and innovative solutions. Overall, analogous thinking plays a crucial role in design thinking disciplines by allowing designers to leverage the power of interdisciplinary insights, enhance their creative problem-solving abilities, and ultimately create more impactful and meaningful designs.

Anthropocentrism

Anthropocentrism is the philosophical perspective that places human beings at the center of all considerations and values. In the context of Design Thinking disciplines, anthropocentrism refers to the approach of focusing on human needs, desires, and behaviors when designing products, services, or systems.

Design Thinking is a human-centered approach to problem-solving that seeks to understand and address the needs, aspirations, and behaviors of the users or customers. By adopting an anthropocentric perspective, designers aim to create solutions that are tailored to the specific needs and preferences of human beings.

Anthropological Research

Anthropological research in the context of service design refers to the systematic study of human behavior, culture, and social interaction in order to gain insights and understandings that can inform the design of services. It involves applying anthropological methods and theories to investigate how people engage with and make sense of various service experiences. Service design is a multidisciplinary approach that aims to create meaningful and user-centered service experiences. It involves understanding the needs, desires, and expectations of users in order to design and improve services that effectively meet their requirements. Anthropological research plays a crucial role in this process by providing in-depth insights into the cultural and social dimensions of user experiences.

Anthropology

Anthropology, in the context of Design Thinking disciplines, refers to the study of human behavior, beliefs, and cultures. It involves the analysis and understanding of how people perceive, interact, and interpret their surroundings.

Anthropology in Design Thinking focuses on observing and comprehending the needs, desires, and motivations of individuals and communities to create meaningful and impactful designs. It involves conducting ethnographic research, gathering qualitative data, and employing various anthropological methods to gain deep insights into people's lives.

Anticipatory Design

Anticipatory Design is a concept within the field of Design Thinking that focuses on creating products or solutions that anticipate and address users' needs and expectations before they arise. It involves using data, research, and insights to predict user behaviors and future trends, allowing designers to proactively design experiences that are intuitive, efficient, and delightful.

The core principle of anticipatory design is to reduce cognitive load for users by minimizing decision-making and automating tasks whenever possible. By leveraging artificial intelligence, machine learning, and other advanced technologies, designers can develop intelligent systems that learn from users' actions and adapt to their preferences over time. This not only enhances usability but also creates personalized experiences that cater to individual needs and preferences.

Anticipatory design also emphasizes the importance of empathy and understanding of users' contexts, desires, and pain points. Through user research and feedback, designers gain insights into users' goals, motivations, and challenges, enabling them to design solutions that truly resonate. This approach enables designers to create products and experiences that empathetically address users' needs, increasing engagement and satisfaction.

In summary, anticipatory design is a key aspect of Design Thinking that focuses on designing products and solutions that proactively address users' needs, predict future behavior, and minimize cognitive load. By leveraging data, research, and insights, designers can create intuitive and personalized experiences that anticipate and exceed user expectations.

Anticipatory Innovation

Anticipatory Innovation refers to the proactive identification and creation of innovative solutions to address future needs and challenges. Rooted in the principles of Design Thinking, it involves a forward-thinking approach that aims to anticipate and shape the future rather than merely reacting to it.

In the context of Design Thinking disciplines, anticipatory innovation involves leveraging a deep understanding of users, their needs, and the context in which they operate to identify emerging trends and anticipate future demands. It goes beyond the traditional problem-solving mindset and focuses on envisioning and creating new possibilities.

Anticipatory Thinking

Anticipatory thinking, as applied within the context of Design Thinking disciplines, refers to the cognitive ability to envision and prepare for potential future scenarios and their implications. It involves adopting a forward-thinking mindset and utilizing various techniques and tools to anticipate and address future challenges or opportunities.

Anticipatory thinking plays a crucial role in the design process, as it helps designers to proactively consider the long-term effects of their solutions and make informed decisions. By adopting a proactive approach, designers can develop innovative and sustainable solutions that not only meet immediate needs but also align with future requirements.

Assumption Mapping

Assumption mapping, in the context of service design, refers to the process of identifying and visualizing the underlying assumptions that exist within a service or system. It is a method used to uncover hidden beliefs and biases that can influence the design and delivery of services. By mapping out assumptions, service designers can gain a deeper understanding of the factors that shape the design and implementation of a service. This process helps to challenge and validate these assumptions, enabling designers to make more informed decisions and create more effective and user-centered services.

Assumption Testing

Assumption testing is a critical aspect of the design thinking process that involves evaluating and validating the underlying assumptions made during the problem-solving and solution development phases. It is an iterative and systematic approach to challenging and questioning the assumptions to mitigate potential risks and increase the chances of success.

In design thinking, assumptions are often considered as the beliefs or hypotheses about the users, customers, context, or problem that guide the design and development process. These assumptions can be based on limited information, previous experiences, or certain biases.

The purpose of assumption testing is to minimize the impact of false assumptions and ensure that the design solution is founded on accurate and reliable insights. It involves conducting research, gathering data, and conducting experiments to validate or invalidate the assumptions. This iterative process allows teams to identify any disconnect between the assumed understanding and the reality.

The methods used for assumption testing may vary depending on the nature of the assumption and the available resources. Some common approaches include user interviews, surveys, observation, prototyping, and data analysis. By actively seeking evidence to validate or challenge assumptions, design thinking teams can make informed decisions and pivot their strategies if necessary.

Backcasting

Backcasting is a strategic planning tool commonly used in service design to envision a desired future state and work backwards to determine the necessary steps to achieve that future state. In the context of service design, backcasting involves identifying a long-term goal or vision for a service and then carefully examining the conditions and necessary actions required to bring that vision to life. Unlike forecasting, which predicts future outcomes based on past and current data, backcasting takes a future-oriented approach by starting with the desired outcome and working backwards to identify the necessary actions and changes needed to achieve that outcome.

Balance Of Qualitative And Quantitative

Balance of Qualitative and Quantitative in the context of Design Thinking disciplines refers to the harmony between subjective, human-centered insights (qualitative) and objective, data-driven analysis (quantitative).

Qualitative research involves collecting and interpreting non-numerical data such as observations, interviews, and user feedback. It seeks to understand the motivations, emotions, and behaviors of users, helping to uncover their unmet needs and challenges. Qualitative methods like empathy maps, user personas, and journey mapping provide rich, context-specific insights into user experiences and can fuel creative problem-solving.

On the other hand, quantitative research involves collecting and analyzing numerical data using statistical techniques. It provides measurable and replicable information about user behavior, preferences, and patterns. Quantitative methods such as surveys, analytics, and A/B testing help designers validate hypotheses, make data-driven decisions, and measure the impact of design solutions.

Both qualitative and quantitative approaches have their strengths and limitations. Qualitative research brings depth and empathy, allowing designers to uncover the underlying needs and motivations of users. Quantitative research, with its objectivity and precision, provides statistical evidence and allows for scalability and generalization. By balancing the two, designers can gain a comprehensive understanding of the problem space, generate innovative ideas, and evaluate their impact effectively.

A successful Design Thinking process integrates qualitative and quantitative methods at different stages. It starts with qualitative research to empathize with users, define the problem, and ideate solutions. Quantitative research then helps designers prototype, test, and refine their ideas based on valid metrics. This iterative approach ensures that decisions are grounded in both human insights and empirical evidence, leading to more effective, user-centered design outcomes.

Behavior Mapping

Behavior mapping is a critical component of the Design Thinking discipline. It involves the systematic observation and analysis of human behavior in order to gain insights and inform the design process. By understanding how people behave, think, and feel in specific contexts, designers are able to create solutions that are more user-centered and meet their needs effectively.

The process of behavior mapping typically begins with in-depth research and observation of individuals or target users. Designers immerse themselves in the environment or situation where the behavior of interest occurs, documenting what they see and hear. These observations are then analyzed to identify patterns, trends, and underlying motivations that drive the observed behavior.

Behavior mapping goes beyond simply recording what people do. It seeks to uncover the reasons behind their actions and to understand their underlying needs, desires, and emotions. This deeper understanding of human behavior enables designers to develop empathetic insights and generate ideas that address unmet user needs.

The insights gained from behavior mapping are used to inform the design process, guiding the creation of user-centric solutions. By aligning the design with users' behavior and desires, designers can ensure that the final product or service is intuitive, engaging, and meaningful.

Behavioral Analysis Platforms

A behavioral analysis platform is a tool or software that enables designers and researchers in the field of Design Thinking to collect, analyze, and interpret data related to human behavior.

These platforms assist in understanding and predicting users' actions, preferences, and motivations, which in turn enables designers to create more effective and user-centered solutions.

Design Thinking is a human-centered approach to problem-solving that requires a deep understanding of user needs, wants, and behaviors. By employing a behavioral analysis platform, designers can gather quantitative and qualitative data on how users interact with a product, service, or experience. This data can include user actions, such as clicks and scrolls, as well as subjective feedback, such as surveys and interviews.

The platform enables designers to track and analyze user behavior over time, uncover patterns and trends, and identify areas for improvement or innovation. By conducting behavioral analysis, designers can gain insights into user preferences, pain points, and motivations. With this knowledge, they can make informed decisions and implement design changes that better align with users' needs and goals.

In addition to data collection and analysis, behavioral analysis platforms often offer collaboration and visualization features. Design teams can work together to make sense of the data, share insights, and communicate their findings to stakeholders. Visualization tools can help designers present data in a meaningful and compelling way, facilitating the understanding and adoption of design recommendations.

Behavioral Design

Behavioral design is a discipline within the field of Design Thinking that focuses on understanding and influencing human behavior in order to design products, services, and experiences that effectively meet user needs and goals. It leverages insights from psychology, cognitive science, and behavioral economics to inform the design process.

By applying the principles of behavioral design, designers can create interventions that encourage desired behaviors and discourage undesired ones. This involves analyzing the factors that drive human behavior, such as motivations, beliefs, and biases, and using that knowledge to design solutions that align with these drivers. Through careful consideration of the user's context and psychology, designers can optimize the chances of a successful outcome.

Behavioral Economics

Behavioral economics, in the context of service design, is a field of study that combines principles from psychology and economics to understand how individuals make choices and decisions in the service environment. It aims to analyze and predict human behavior by examining cognitive biases, heuristics, and social influences that impact decision-making processes. By incorporating insights from behavioral economics, service designers can better understand and cater to the needs and preferences of their target users. This approach acknowledges that individuals do not always make rational decisions and that their behavior is influenced by various factors.

Behavioral Insights Dashboards

Behavioral Insights Dashboards are visual representations of data that are designed to provide insight into human behavior and decision-making. These dashboards are a tool used within the framework of Design Thinking disciplines to inform and guide the design process.

By aggregating and displaying data related to user behavior, preferences, and motivations, Behavioral Insights Dashboards enable designers to better understand their target audience and make more informed design decisions. These dashboards typically include quantitative and qualitative data, such as user surveys, interviews, observations, and analytics data, presented in a visually digestible format.

Behavioral Insights Platforms

A Behavioral Insights Platform in the context of Design Thinking disciplines refers to a system or tool that incorporates psychological and behavioral principles to understand human behavior and decision-making processes. The platform utilizes data analytics, experimentation, and user research to gain insights into individual and collective behaviors, motivations, and biases.

By using a Behavioral Insights Platform, designers and researchers can uncover patterns, trends, and cognitive biases that influence user preferences and actions. The platform enables the collection and analysis of both qualitative and quantitative data, facilitating a deep understanding of users' needs, desires, and pain points.

Behavioral Insights

Behavioral insights, in the context of service design, refer to the use of psychological and behavioral principles to understand and influence user behavior in order to improve the design and delivery of services. By incorporating knowledge from fields such as psychology, behavioral economics, and social sciences, behavioral insights provide a framework for understanding how people think, make decisions, and behave in real-world situations. This understanding can then be applied to service design to create more user-centered and effective experiences.

Behavioral Mapping

Behavioral mapping, in the context of Design Thinking disciplines, refers to a technique used to observe and analyze human behavior within a specific context or environment. It involves carefully documenting and visually representing the activities, interactions, and emotions of individuals or groups to gain insights into their needs, preferences, and pain points.

The process of behavioral mapping typically consists of direct observation and recording of behaviors and events as they occur, without interfering or influencing the participants. The observations are captured through various means, such as notes, sketches, photographs, or videos, depending on the context and resources available. These observations are then analyzed and synthesized to identify patterns, trends, and underlying motivations.

Behavioral Patterns

A behavioral pattern, in the context of Design Thinking disciplines, refers to recurring actions, reactions, or responses exhibited by individuals or groups within a given context or environment. These patterns are observed through the study of human behavior, including their thoughts, emotions, and actions.

By understanding behavioral patterns, Design Thinkers can gain insights into user needs, preferences, and motivations, enabling them to develop more effective solutions and create experiences that resonate with users. This understanding can also help identify barriers or challenges that users may face, allowing for the design of more inclusive and user-centric solutions.

Behavioral Prototyping

Behavioral prototyping in the context of service design involves creating a tangible representation or simulation of a service experience to understand and test user behavior and interactions. It is a method used to gain insights into how users might interact with a service and how it may fit into their daily lives. Behavioral prototyping helps service designers and stakeholders identify potential pain points, understand user needs, and refine service concepts. It allows designers to study the impact of different design choices on user behavior and to make informed decisions based on these observations.

Behavioral Psychology

Behavioral psychology, within the context of Design Thinking disciplines, refers to the study of human behavior and its influence on the design process. It focuses on understanding how individuals think, feel, and act in order to create more effective and user-centered designs.

Design Thinking is a problem-solving approach that emphasizes empathy and human-centeredness. By adopting principles from behavioral psychology, designers can gain insights into user needs, motivations, and preferences. This understanding enables them to design products, services, or experiences that are tailored to meet these needs and enhance user satisfaction.

Benchmarking

Benchmarking is a strategic process used in the context of service design to measure and compare the performance of a service against industry best practices or competitors. It involves analyzing various aspects of a service, such as quality, efficiency, and customer satisfaction, and comparing them with similar services in the market. The primary purpose of benchmarking is to identify opportunities for improvement and to set performance goals for the service being evaluated. By understanding how other successful services operate and achieve positive outcomes, organizations can identify gaps in their own service and develop strategies to bridge those gaps.

Bias Reduction

The term "Bias Reduction" refers to the practice of minimizing or eliminating the influence of unconscious biases and preconceived notions in the design thinking process. It involves adopting a more open-minded and empathetic approach in order to generate inclusive and unbiased design solutions.

In the context of design thinking disciplines, bias reduction is crucial as it promotes the creation of designs that truly meet the needs and preferences of diverse user groups. By acknowledging and addressing biases, designers are able to create solutions that are more inclusive, considerate, and fair.

Bias Toward Action

Bias Toward Action, in the context of Design Thinking, refers to the inclination or preference to take action and experiment in order to generate insights and solutions. It is a mindset that encourages designers and problem solvers to quickly prototype, test, and iterate their ideas in order to learn from real-world feedback.

This bias is based on the understanding that a bias towards action allows for a more rapid and iterative approach to problem-solving. Instead of spending extensive time on analysis and planning, designers focus on taking small, tangible steps towards creating and testing ideas. By doing so, they are able to gather practical knowledge and insights that can inform the design process.

Blue Ocean Strategy

Blue Ocean Strategy refers to a strategic framework for creating new opportunities and uncontested market space in service design. It involves shifting the focus from competing in existing markets (red ocean) to creating new markets or delivering unique services in untapped customer segments (blue ocean). Blue Ocean Strategy encourages service designers to break away from the traditional industry boundaries and explore new value propositions that meet the unmet needs of customers. This often requires a shift in thinking from a product-centric approach to a customer-centric approach.

Blue Sky Thinking

Blue sky thinking is a concept commonly used within the discipline of Design Thinking. It refers to the process of generating innovative and out-of-the-box ideas without any constraints or limitations. This approach encourages individuals to think beyond traditional boundaries and explore creative possibilities that may seem unconventional or unrealistic at first glance.

Blue sky thinking is characterized by an open-minded and imaginative mindset that allows for the exploration of fresh ideas and perspectives. It encourages individuals to challenge existing assumptions, break away from established norms, and consider unconventional solutions to problems. By abandoning preconceived notions and embracing a 'anything is possible' attitude, blue sky thinking can stimulate creativity and lead to truly innovative design solutions.

Blueprinting

Blueprinting is a service design method that visually represents the customer experience and service delivery process. It provides a detailed blueprint of the entire service journey, highlighting the different touchpoints and interactions between customers, employees, and other elements involved in the service. The primary purpose of blueprinting is to identify opportunities for improvement and to create a seamless and satisfying customer experience. It allows service designers to have a holistic view of the service from the customer's perspective, understanding their needs, expectations, and pain points throughout their journey.

Boundary Crossing

Boundary Crossing in the context of Design Thinking refers to the process of transcending traditional boundaries and exploring diverse perspectives, disciplines, and contexts to drive innovation and problem-solving. It involves breaking down silos and engaging with individuals who possess different knowledge, experiences, and backgrounds in order to gain fresh insights and generate novel ideas.

Design Thinking emphasizes a multidisciplinary approach, recognizing that solutions to complex problems often lie at the intersection of various disciplines and domains. Boundary Crossing encourages designers to look beyond their respective fields and collaborate with experts from other areas, such as technology, engineering, social sciences, arts, and business. By doing so, they can leverage a diverse range of skills, perspectives, and approaches to approach challenges holistically and develop more effective solutions.

Boundary Objects

Boundary Objects are conceptual or physical artifacts that serve as a bridge between different stakeholders and facilitate communication and collaboration in the context of service design. These objects help to overcome language barriers and different interpretations of concepts and meanings, allowing diverse parties to work together towards a common understanding. In service design, boundary objects act as a means of aligning perspectives, consolidating information, and fostering mutual learning among various stakeholders. They provide a shared platform where different voices, expertise, and interests can come together and interact. By enabling the exchange of knowledge, ideas, and perspectives, boundary objects promote collaboration and enable the co-creation of services.

Boundary Spanning

Boundary spanning in the context of Design Thinking disciplines refers to the process of bridging the gap and actively engaging with various stakeholders, teams, and disciplines to explore different perspectives, gather insights, and facilitate collaboration.

Design Thinking is a multidisciplinary approach that involves understanding users' needs and solving complex problems through creative and iterative processes. However, in order to effectively address these challenges, designers must go beyond their own domain and interact with individuals and groups that may have different expertise, knowledge, and perspectives.

Brainstorming Sessions

A brainstorming session is a collaborative exercise within the field of design thinking disciplines where a group of participants come together to generate ideas, explore possibilities, and solve complex problems. It is a creative and non-judgmental process that encourages open dialogue and free thinking.

During a brainstorming session, participants are encouraged to share their thoughts, ideas, and perspectives without fear of criticism or rejection. The focus is on quantity rather than quality, with the goal of generating a large number of ideas in a short amount of time.

The session typically begins with a clearly defined problem statement or challenge. Participants then engage in a rapid-fire exchange of ideas, building upon and expanding upon each other's contributions. There are no wrong answers or bad ideas in a brainstorming session, as the emphasis is on generating novel and diverse solutions.

Facilitators play a crucial role in guiding the session, ensuring that all participants have an equal opportunity to contribute and that the discussion stays focused. They may use various techniques such as mind mapping, visualization exercises, or random word stimulation to spark creativity and encourage new perspectives.

At the end of the session, the generated ideas are typically further evaluated and refined through additional design thinking processes such as prototyping, user testing, and iteration. Brainstorming sessions are an essential tool in the design thinking toolkit, as they promote collaboration, creativity, and innovation.

Brainstorming

Service design is a formal methodology used to create and improve services in a systematic and user-centered manner. It involves the planning, organizing, and implementation of various elements to ensure that the service provided meets the needs and expectations of the users. Service design utilizes a multidisciplinary approach, integrating insights from various fields such as design, management, and customer experience. It involves understanding the user's perspective, identifying their pain points and desires, and then designing and delivering services that effectively address those needs.

Brand Experience

A brand experience is a holistic and multi-sensory interaction that customers have with a brand throughout their entire customer journey. It encompasses the sum of all touchpoints, both physical and digital, that contribute to shaping the overall perception and impression of a brand in the minds of its customers. At its core, a brand experience is about creating meaningful and memorable connections between a brand and its customers. It goes beyond just delivering products or services; it is about curating an experience that aligns with the brand's values, purpose, and promise to customers. Service design plays a crucial role in shaping and optimizing the brand experience. It involves understanding the needs, desires, and pain points of customers and designing services that not only meet their functional requirements but also evoke positive emotions and create a strong brand connection. Service designers employ various methods and tools to craft a brand experience that resonates with customers. They conduct extensive user research, map customer journeys, and design touchpoints that create a seamless and delightful experience. This may involve designing intuitive user interfaces for digital interactions, creating visually appealing and functional physical spaces, or developing engaging and personalized communication strategies. By focusing on the brand experience, service designers can help organizations differentiate themselves from competitors, build customer loyalty, and drive customer advocacy. A positive and consistent brand experience across all touchpoints fosters trust, strengthens brand affinity, and ultimately leads to increased customer satisfaction and loyalty.

Brand Strategy

Brand strategy refers to a comprehensive plan that outlines how a company positions and differentiates its brand in the market. It involves the identification of the company's target audience, the communication of its brand values and messaging, and the development of a cohesive brand identity across all touchpoints. When applied to service design, brand strategy is the process of shaping the customer experience to align with the company's brand. It involves understanding the core attributes and values of the brand and translating them into tangible service elements and interactions. This includes defining the desired customer journey, designing service touchpoints, and ensuring that every aspect of the service reflects the brand's values and resonates with its target audience.

Brand Touchpoints

Brand touchpoints refer to the various interactions that customers have with a brand throughout their customer journey. These touchpoints shape the overall customer experience and help to build and maintain the brand's identity and reputation. In the context of service design, it is crucial to identify and map out the different brand touchpoints to ensure a seamless and consistent experience for customers at every stage of their interaction with the brand. By understanding these touchpoints, companies can optimize and enhance the customer experience to meet their needs and expectations.

Business Canvas Model

A Business Canvas Model is a visual framework that is used to describe, analyze, and design a business model for a service. It provides a structured approach for understanding how different components of a business interact and contribute to its overall success. The Business Canvas Model is commonly used in service design to help organizations create or improve their services in a systematic and strategic way.The Business Canvas Model consists of nine key building blocks that represent different aspects of a service: 1. Customer Segments: Identifies the targeted groups of customers or users who will benefit from the service. 2. Value Proposition: Describes the unique value or benefit that the service provides to the customers. 3. Channels: Specifies the various channels through which the service is delivered or accessed by the customers. 4. Customer Relationships: Defines the nature and type of relationships that the service provider intends to establish and maintain with its customers. 5. Revenue Streams: Identifies the different sources of revenue for the service provider, including pricing models and payment methods. 6. Key Activities: Outlines the crucial tasks and activities that are necessary to deliver the service. 7. Key Resources: Represents the resources, both physical and intangible, that are required to support the provision of the service. 8. Key Partnerships: Identifies the external organizations or entities that are essential for the successful execution of the service. 9. Cost Structure: Details the costs associated with operating the service and generating revenue.By mapping out these building blocks on the Business Canvas Model, service designers can gain a holistic understanding of how each component contributes to the overall value proposition of the service. This visual representation also allows for the identification of potential gaps or areas for improvement, enabling organizations to make informed decisions in their service design process.

Business Case

A business case, in the context of service design, refers to a detailed document or presentation that outlines the justification for a particular business initiative or project. It presents a compelling argument for why an organization should invest resources into a specific service design effort. The purpose of a business case is to demonstrate the potential value and benefits that can be gained from implementing a new service or improving an existing one. It typically includes an analysis of the current service situation, identifies the problem or opportunity that the proposed service design initiative aims to address, and outlines the project objectives and expected outcomes. Additionally, the business case provides an estimation of the required resources, such as time, budget, and personnel, needed to execute the service design project.

Business Ecosystem Mapping

Business ecosystem mapping is a strategic tool used in service design to identify and analyze the complex relationships, dependencies, and interactions between various stakeholders and actors within a specific industry or market. It aims to visualize and understand how different entities, such as companies, customers, suppliers, and competitors, interact with each other and influence the overall dynamics of the ecosystem in which they operate. The process of business ecosystem mapping involves gathering and analyzing data from a wide range of sources, including market research, competitor analysis, customer insights, and industry trends. This information is then organized and presented in a visual format, often in the form of a diagram or network map, to illustrate the interconnectedness of different stakeholders and their roles within the ecosystem. By mapping out the business ecosystem, service designers can gain a holistic view of the market landscape and identify key trends, opportunities, and challenges. It allows them to identify potential gaps or inefficiencies in the current ecosystem, as well as potential areas for innovation and collaboration. Moreover, business ecosystem mapping enables organizations to better understand their own position within the ecosystem and how they can leverage their strengths and capabilities to create value for both their customers and other ecosystem stakeholders. It can help organizations identify potential partners or collaborators and develop strategies to strengthen their competitive advantage. In summary, business ecosystem mapping is a valuable tool in service design that helps organizations gain a comprehensive understanding of the complex relationships and dynamics within a specific industry or market. It provides insights into the interconnectedness of different stakeholders and their roles within the ecosystem, facilitating strategic decision-making and innovation.

Business Impact Analysis

A Business Impact Analysis (BIA) is a structured process used in service design to assess and understand the potential consequences of a disruption or loss of key business functions and processes. It allows organizations to identify and prioritize critical services and resources, evaluate their vulnerabilities, and develop effective strategies for mitigating risks and ensuring business continuity. During a service design process, the BIA helps organizations to analyze and quantify the potential impacts that could result from various types of disruptions, including natural disasters, cyber attacks, equipment failures, or human error. By understanding the potential consequences, organizations can make informed decisions and allocate resources to protect and recover critical business functions and processes. The BIA typically involves the following steps: 1. Identification of critical functions and processes: The first step of the BIA is to identify and prioritize the most critical functions and processes that are essential for the organization's operations and delivery of services. This includes assessing the dependencies and interdependencies between different functions and processes. 2. Impact assessment: Once the critical functions and processes are identified, an impact assessment is conducted to evaluate the potential consequences of their disruption. This includes considering the financial, operational, reputational, legal, and regulatory impacts that could occur. 3. Vulnerability analysis: The BIA also involves assessing the vulnerabilities and risks associated with each critical function and process. This includes identifying single points of failure, weaknesses in infrastructure and systems, and potential threats and risks. 4. Recovery strategies: Based on the impact assessment and vulnerability analysis, organizations can develop appropriate strategies for recovering and restoring critical functions and processes. This may involve implementing backup systems, redundancy measures, contingency plans, or alternative work arrangements. By conducting a BIA, organizations can have a comprehensive understanding of their critical functions and processes, the potential impacts of their disruption, and the necessary strategies for minimizing risks and ensuring business continuity. This enables organizations to be better prepared and respond effectively to disruptions, ultimately safeguarding their reputation, customer satisfaction, and overall business performance.

Business Model Canvas

A Business Model Canvas is a strategic management tool used to describe, design, challenge, and ultimately explore and communicate an organization's service value proposition. It provides a visual representation of how a service provider can create, deliver, and capture value for its customers. The canvas is divided into nine key building blocks that encompass the main components of a service business: 1. Customer Segments: Identifying and understanding the target customer groups the service is catered to. 2. Value Proposition: Defining the unique value that the service offers to address the needs and solve the problems of the target customers. 3. Channels: Determining the distribution and communication channels through which the service will be delivered to customers. 4. Customer Relationships: Establishing the types of relationships that will be cultivated with customers to ensure satisfaction and loyalty. 5. Revenue Streams: Identifying the sources of revenue and how the service will be monetized. 6. Key Resources: Identifying the critical assets, capabilities, and infrastructure required to deliver the service. 7. Key Activities: Defining the primary actions that need to be performed to deliver the service. 8. Key Partnerships: Identifying the strategic alliances and collaborations necessary to enhance the service delivery. 9. Cost Structure: Evaluating the structure of costs incurred in delivering the service and ensuring profitability. This systematic approach helps organizations evaluate and refine their service design by facilitating a comprehensive analysis of how different elements interact and contribute to the success of the business. By visualizing the service model on a single canvas, it becomes easier for stakeholders to understand, discuss, and make informed decisions regarding the service's design and implementation. The Business Model Canvas can be used in the development phase of a new service, as well as for assessing and improving existing services. It allows organizations to align their operational activities with the desired customer experience, optimize resource allocation, and identify potential areas for innovation and growth. Overall, the Business Model Canvas serves as a powerful tool for service design, enabling organizations to systematically analyze and plan their service offerings, ultimately leading to increased value creation, customer satisfaction, and business success.

Business Model Generation

The Business Model Generation is a strategic tool used in service design to describe, analyze, and create innovative business models. It provides a framework for understanding and visualizing how a company creates, delivers, and captures value. A business model represents the logic and structure of a company's strategy, including its key elements and relationships. The process of Business Model Generation involves identifying and defining the following elements: - Customer Segments: The different groups or types of customers that a company aims to serve. - Value Proposition: The unique combination of products, services, and experiences that create value for a specific customer segment. - Channels: The methods by which a company reaches and interacts with its customers to deliver the value proposition. - Customer Relationships: The types of relationships a company establishes and maintains with its customers. - Revenue Streams: The ways in which a company generates revenue from its customer segments. - Key Resources: The assets, infrastructure, and capabilities required to deliver the value proposition. - Key Activities: The actions and processes a company must perform to deliver the value proposition. - Key Partnerships: The strategic relationships and alliances a company forms to leverage its resources and capabilities. - Cost Structure: The costs and expenses incurred to operate the business model. By systematically analyzing and designing each of these elements, the Business Model Generation framework helps service designers identify opportunities for innovation and improvement. It encourages a holistic approach to business strategy and fosters collaboration and creativity in developing new models. The resulting business model canvas, a visual representation of the elements, allows teams to communicate and align their understanding of the business model. Overall, Business Model Generation is a powerful tool that enables service designers to create and refine business models that are innovative, customer-centric, and strategically aligned.

Business Model Innovation

Business Model Innovation refers to the process of creating and implementing new strategies, structures, and systems in order to deliver value to customers and differentiate a company from its competitors. This approach involves rethinking and redesigning various components of a company's business model, such as its value proposition, revenue streams, customer segments, key activities, resources, and partnerships. Service design plays a crucial role in the context of business model innovation. It involves designing the delivery of services in a way that addresses the needs and wants of customers, while also aligning with the overall business strategy. By focusing on the customer experience and understanding their preferences, service design can help identify new opportunities for improving the value proposition and creating a competitive advantage.

Business Process Redesign

Business Process Redesign (BPR) is a critical aspect of service design aimed at improving and optimizing existing business processes to enhance efficiency, effectiveness, and customer satisfaction. It involves the complete rethinking and restructuring of processes to achieve significant improvements in performance and achieve strategic objectives. In the context of service design, BPR focuses on evaluating and redesigning the processes involved in delivering a service to customers. It aims to eliminate unnecessary steps, redundancies, and inefficiencies that can hinder the overall customer experience and business performance.

Business Process Reengineering (BPR)

Business Process Reengineering (BPR) is a fundamental redesign and restructuring of an organization's processes to achieve dramatic improvements in performance. It is the radical rethinking and redesigning of business processes to achieve significant enhancements in critical measures of performance, such as cost, quality, service, and speed. The primary objective of BPR is to enable organizations to become more efficient and effective by eliminating non-value-added activities and streamlining processes. BPR aims to align an organization's processes with its strategic goals and customer needs, resulting in improved customer satisfaction and increased competitive advantage. BPR involves analyzing and rethinking every aspect of a business process, including its inputs, outputs, activities, and information flow. It requires a cross-functional approach, involving employees from different departments and levels within an organization, to identify opportunities for process improvement and innovation. During the BPR process, organizations critically examine their existing processes and challenge traditional assumptions and practices. They seek to identify bottlenecks, inefficiencies, and areas of waste in order to develop new, streamlined processes that are more customer-focused and value-driven. Key steps in BPR include: - Identifying the scope and objectives of the reengineering initiative. - Mapping and analyzing the current processes to identify areas for improvement. - Designing and developing new processes that align with the organization's strategic goals and customer needs. - Implementing and testing the new processes, including any necessary changes to technology, systems, and organizational structure. - Monitoring and evaluating the performance of the new processes, making adjustments as needed. Successful BPR initiatives require strong leadership, effective change management, and the involvement and commitment of all stakeholders. It is important to communicate the purpose and benefits of BPR to gain support and overcome resistance. In conclusion, Business Process Reengineering is a systematic approach to improving organizational performance by rethinking and redesigning processes. It aims to eliminate waste, improve efficiency, and meet customer needs more effectively. BPR is a powerful tool for organizations seeking to enhance their competitive advantage and achieve sustainable growth.

Card Sorting

Card sorting is a service design method used to understand and organize information, ideas, or content in a way that aligns with users' mental models. It is a user-centered approach that involves participants categorizing and prioritizing information using physical or digital cards. During a card sorting session, participants are presented with a set of cards that represent different pieces of information or concepts related to a particular topic or subject. The participants are then asked to group these cards based on similarities, relationships, or any other criteria they deem appropriate. This activity helps to uncover patterns and insights about how users naturally perceive and organize information. Card sorting is typically conducted in a controlled environment, such as a usability lab or through remote online platforms. The process can be moderated or unmoderated, depending on the goals and resources of the project. In a moderated session, a facilitator guides the participants through the activity, providing instructions and answering any questions that may arise. In an unmoderated session, participants complete the activity independently, following predefined instructions. The data collected from card sorting sessions can be analyzed to identify common groupings or themes. This analysis helps designers make informed decisions about the information architecture or content structure of a product, service, or website. It can also inform the development of navigation menus, search filters, or other interactive elements that support users in finding the information they need. Card sorting can be applied in various contexts, such as website design, content organization, menu structuring, or information hierarchy. It is particularly useful when designing products or services that involve complex information or multiple categories. By involving users in the sorting process, designers gain valuable insights into users' mental models, which can lead to more intuitive and user-friendly designs. In conclusion, card sorting is a valuable service design method that allows designers to understand how users naturally categorize and prioritize information. Through this method, designers can create more user-centered and intuitive designs that align with users' mental models.

Case-Based Reasoning

Case-Based Reasoning is a problem-solving approach that uses previous experiences, called cases, as a foundation for making decisions or solving new problems. In the context of service design, Case-Based Reasoning involves the utilization of past experiences and knowledge to design and improve services. Service design is a process of creating and delivering services that meet the needs and expectations of users. It involves understanding the users, identifying their pain points, and designing solutions to address those issues. Case-Based Reasoning can be applied in service design to leverage existing knowledge and experiences in order to come up with more effective and efficient solutions.

Challenge Assumptions

Challenge Assumptions, in the context of Design Thinking disciplines, refers to the process of questioning and critiquing the underlying beliefs, notions, and expectations that are commonly taken for granted or accepted as true. This practice encourages individuals and teams to disregard preconceived notions and explore alternative perspectives and possibilities.

By challenging assumptions, Design Thinkers aim to overcome cognitive biases and uncover potential opportunities, hidden biases, or flawed assumptions that may hinder the problem-solving process or limit creative thinking. It involves reevaluating the existing assumptions about the user, the problem, and the solution to discover new insights and perspectives that can lead to innovative solutions and designs.

Change Agent Roles

Change Management

Change Management in the context of service design refers to the structured approach of planning, implementing, and managing changes to services, processes, systems, or technologies within an organization. It involves the coordination and communication of these changes across different stakeholders, departments, and teams to ensure the successful integration and adoption of the new service or process. The purpose of Change Management in service design is to minimize the negative impact of the changes on the organization, while maximizing the benefits that can be derived from the new service or process. It aims to minimize disruptions, conflicts, and resistance that may arise from the change, and instead promote a smooth and efficient transition.

Channel Mapping

Channel mapping, in the context of service design, refers to the process of visually representing and organizing the various touchpoints and channels through which a service is delivered to its users or customers. It involves mapping out the different channels, such as physical stores, websites, mobile apps, call centers, social media platforms, and any other medium or communication channel used to interact with customers. Channel mapping is an essential step in service design as it helps identify and analyze the different touchpoints and channels that users or customers interact with throughout their journey with a service. By visually representing these channels, service designers can gain a better understanding of the user experience and the potential gaps or areas for improvement.

Churn Rate

Churn rate, in the context of service design, refers to the rate at which customers or users discontinue using a particular service or product over a given period of time. It is a key metric that helps businesses understand and quantify the number of customers they are losing and the efficiency of their retention strategies. Churn rate is typically calculated by dividing the number of customers who have cancelled or unsubscribed from the service by the total number of customers at the beginning of the time period. This calculation provides a percentage that represents the proportion of customers lost during that period.

Circular Economy

A circular economy is a regenerative system that aims to keep products, materials, and resources in continuous use for as long as possible by reducing waste, minimizing resource consumption, and maximizing value creation. In the context of service design, a circular economy approach focuses on designing services that promote sustainability and minimize the negative environmental impact. It involves rethinking the traditional linear "take-make-dispose" model and instead adopting a more holistic approach that encompasses the entire lifecycle of a service.

Co-Creation Workshops

Co-Creation Workshops in the context of service design refer to collaborative sessions where stakeholders, designers, and users come together to ideate, innovate, and co-design solutions for a particular service or experience. These workshops are typically facilitated by trained professionals and aim to foster creativity, inclusivity, and user-centricity in the design process. The primary objective of Co-Creation Workshops is to gather diverse perspectives and harness collective intelligence to create meaningful and impactful experiences for users. By bringing together individuals with different expertise, backgrounds, and roles, these workshops enable cross-pollination of ideas and contribute to the development of holistic, user-centered solutions.

Co-Creation

Co-creation in the context of service design refers to the collaborative process of designing and delivering services, where both the service providers and the service users actively participate in the creation and development of services. It is a method that involves bringing together various stakeholders, including customers, employees, designers, and other relevant parties, to collectively contribute their knowledge, expertise, and ideas to shape and improve the service experience. This approach recognizes that service providers do not have all the knowledge and insights needed to create and deliver successful services, and that involving service users in the process is crucial for creating services that meet their needs and expectations.

Co-Creative Ideation

Co-creative ideation refers to the collaborative process of generating and developing ideas in the context of Design Thinking disciplines. It involves the active participation of multiple stakeholders, including designers, users, and other relevant individuals or groups.

This process seeks to foster a shared understanding and ensure diverse perspectives are considered, in order to generate innovative and meaningful solutions to complex problems. Co-creative ideation acknowledges that the best ideas often emerge from the collective intelligence and creativity of a group, rather than relying solely on the expertise of an individual designer.

Co-Design Sessions

Co-Design Sessions refer to collaborative workshops in the context of service design where stakeholders, designers, and end-users come together to collectively ideate, prototype, and co-create solutions for a particular service or experience. These sessions aim to break down silos, foster empathy, and leverage the collective expertise of all participants to generate innovative and user-centric ideas. During Co-Design Sessions, participants engage in various activities and exercises such as brainstorming, mind mapping, storytelling, role-playing, visualizing, and prototyping. These activities encourage active participation, open communication, and creative thinking, allowing different perspectives to be explored and integrated into the design process. The key objectives of Co-Design Sessions are: 1. Collaboration: Co-Design Sessions promote collaboration among stakeholders, including designers, end-users, and other relevant parties. By involving all key stakeholders in the design process, it ensures that different viewpoints, needs, and expectations are considered, resulting in more inclusive and effective solutions. 2. Empathy: Co-Design Sessions create opportunities for participants to empathize with each other's experiences, challenges, and aspirations. By understanding each other's perspectives, participants can develop a deeper sense of empathy, which helps in generating design solutions that truly address the needs and desires of the end-users. 3. Innovation: Co-Design Sessions foster a culture of innovation by providing a space for participants to explore, experiment, and think outside the box. Through collaborative ideation and prototyping, participants can challenge existing assumptions and envision new and imaginative possibilities for the service or experience being designed. 4. User-centricity: Co-Design Sessions prioritize the needs and preferences of the end-users. By involving end-users in the design process, it ensures that their voices are heard, their insights are valued, and that the final solution is tailored to their specific requirements. This approach leads to more user-friendly and relevant services. Overall, Co-Design Sessions play a critical role in the service design process as they enable diverse perspectives to converge, facilitate co-creation, and drive innovation. By involving all relevant stakeholders, these sessions help in shaping services that are truly user-centric, inclusive, and aligned with the needs and aspirations of the people they aim to serve.

Cognitive Bias

A cognitive bias refers to a systematic pattern of deviation from rationality or objective thinking, which affects the design thinking process. It is a mental shortcut or a preconceived notion that leads to a distorted understanding, judgment, or decision-making. These biases can limit our ability to generate creative solutions, empathize with users, and adopt an open-minded approach to problem-solving. It is crucial to recognize and address these biases to ensure an effective design thinking process.

Cognitive biases can manifest at different stages of the design thinking process. During the empathize phase, confirmation bias may lead designers to seek information that confirms their existing assumptions, while neglecting contradictory evidence. Anchoring bias can influence the ideation phase by causing designers to seize onto the first idea that comes to mind, limiting exploration of other potential solutions. The availability bias may also impact the prototyping phase, as designers tend to rely on readily available information or examples rather than exploring new possibilities.

Cognitive Diversity

Cognitive Diversity is the concept of including individuals with different cognitive abilities, perspectives, and thinking styles in the design thinking process. It recognizes that people with varying ways of perceiving, understanding, and solving problems can contribute unique insights and ideas that lead to more innovative and effective solutions.

In the context of design thinking disciplines, cognitive diversity is crucial for promoting creativity, critical thinking, and empathy. Design thinking is a human-centered approach to problem-solving that involves understanding users' needs, generating ideas, prototyping solutions, and testing and refining them. By incorporating individuals with diverse cognitive abilities, such as those who excel in analytical thinking, intuitive thinking, big-picture thinking, or detailed-oriented thinking, design thinking teams can benefit from a wider range of perspectives and increase the likelihood of generating innovative and relevant solutions.

Cognitive Ergonomics

Cognitive Ergonomics refers to the design and optimization of services to enhance human cognitive abilities, comfort, and effectiveness in performing tasks within a given context. In the context of service design, cognitive ergonomics focuses on understanding and improving the cognitive processes involved in the delivery and reception of services. It aims to design services that are intuitive, easy to use, and supportive of users' cognitive capabilities. By considering the mental workload, attention span, memory, decision-making, and problem-solving abilities of users, cognitive ergonomics seeks to minimize cognitive load and maximize performance and satisfaction.

Cognitive Flexibility

Cognitive flexibility in the context of Design Thinking disciplines refers to the ability to adapt and shift thinking patterns in order to generate creative solutions to complex problems. It involves being open-minded, embracing ambiguity, and being willing to explore different perspectives and approaches.

Design Thinking is a problem-solving approach that emphasizes empathy, creativity, and collaboration. It involves a series of iterative steps such as empathizing with users, defining the problem, ideating potential solutions, prototyping, and testing. Throughout this process, cognitive flexibility plays a crucial role in challenging assumptions, generating new ideas, and refining solutions.

Cognitive Load Analysis Kits

Cognitive Load Analysis Kits refer to a set of tools and methods used in the field of Design Thinking disciplines to assess and manage the cognitive load of users during the interaction with a product, service, or system.

The term "cognitive load" refers to the amount of mental effort and resources required for an individual to process and understand information. In the context of Design Thinking, understanding and optimizing cognitive load is crucial for creating user-centered designs that enhance usability and user experience.

The Cognitive Load Analysis Kits are typically comprised of various techniques and artifacts, such as observation protocols, surveys, questionnaires, and cognitive load measurement tools. These kits are used by designers and researchers to identify the cognitive demands and challenges faced by users during different stages of interaction with a design.

By employing the Cognitive Load Analysis Kits, designers can gather quantitative and qualitative data to assess the cognitive load imposed on users during tasks, identify areas of high cognitive demand that can lead to errors or user frustration, and iteratively improve the design to reduce cognitive load and enhance usability. These kits also enable designers to understand users' mental models, cognitive strategies, and information processing capabilities, which can inform the design decisions and aid in creating intuitive and seamless user experiences.

Cognitive Load Analysis Software

Cognitive Load Analysis Software refers to a specialized tool used in the context of Design Thinking disciplines that helps analyze and manage cognitive load during the design process.

Cognitive load refers to the mental effort exerted by individuals when presented with information or tasks. In design thinking, managing cognitive load is crucial as it directly impacts the user experience and the effectiveness of the design solution.

The Cognitive Load Analysis Software captures and analyzes various aspects of cognitive load, such as the complexity of the design task, the information processing requirements, and the user's cognitive capacity. By examining these factors, the software allows designers to optimize the design process and ensure that the resulting solutions are user-friendly and efficient.

This software provides designers with valuable insights into the cognitive demands placed on users throughout the design process. By identifying potential areas of high cognitive load, designers can proactively find ways to streamline the user experience, simplify instructions, or reduce information overload. Additionally, the software can help identify areas where additional support or training may be required for users to successfully interact with the design solution.

In summary, Cognitive Load Analysis Software in Design Thinking provides a systematic approach to understanding and managing cognitive load during the design process. By using this software, designers can optimize their designs to minimize the mental effort required from users, ultimately leading to improved usability and user satisfaction.

Cognitive Load Analysis Tools

Cognitive Load Analysis Tools refer to a set of tools and techniques used in the field of Design Thinking disciplines to understand and evaluate the mental effort or cognitive load imposed on individuals during a particular task or activity. These tools are designed to measure and analyze the mental workload, information processing capacity, and cognitive resources required by individuals to perform a specific task effectively and efficiently.

Cognitive load is the amount of mental effort or processing capacity that individuals need to complete a task or process information. It is influenced by factors such as the complexity of the task, the available resources, the individual's prior knowledge and experience, and the information presentation format. Cognitive Load Analysis Tools help designers and researchers gain insights into individuals' cognitive load during tasks, allowing them to identify potential bottlenecks, optimize the task design, and enhance overall user experience.

Cognitive Load Management

Cognitive Load Management in the context of Design Thinking disciplines refers to the practice of reducing mental effort and maximizing learning by effectively managing the cognitive load imposed on individuals during the design process.

Design Thinking involves a complex and iterative problem-solving approach that requires individuals to navigate through various stages, such as understanding the problem, generating ideas, prototyping, and testing. This process can generate a significant cognitive load on designers, potentially overwhelming their cognitive capacity and hindering their ability to think creatively and effectively.

The management of cognitive load in Design Thinking involves several strategies. One important strategy is chunking, which involves breaking down complex tasks into smaller, more manageable parts. By dividing the design process into smaller steps or subtasks, designers can focus their attention on specific aspects and prevent cognitive overload.

Another strategy is providing clear and concise information. Designers often need to process large amounts of information, including user research data, market trends, and technical constraints. To reduce cognitive load, it is crucial to present information in a structured and organized manner, highlighting the most relevant details and minimizing irrelevant or redundant information.

Additionally, cognitive load can be managed through the use of external aids and tools. For example, designers can utilize visual representations, such as diagrams or sketches, to offload cognitive processing and enhance understanding. Collaboration and teamwork are also essential, as they can distribute the cognitive load among team members and facilitate shared decision-making.

In conclusion, Cognitive Load Management in Design Thinking disciplines involves the deliberate effort to minimize mental effort and maximize learning by effectively managing the cognitive load imposed on individuals during the design process. By employing strategies such as chunking, providing clear information, and utilizing external aids, designers can optimize their cognitive resources and enhance their creative problem-solving abilities.

Cognitive Load Theory

Cognitive Load Theory is a framework used in the field of Design Thinking disciplines to understand and optimize the mental effort or load imposed on individuals during problem-solving and learning activities. It aims to improve the effectiveness of these activities by managing and reducing cognitive overload, which occurs when the demands on an individual's working memory exceed its capacity.

According to Cognitive Load Theory, there are three types of cognitive load: intrinsic, extraneous, and germane. Intrinsic cognitive load is inherent to the complexity of the task and is difficult to modify. However, extraneous cognitive load refers to unnecessary or inefficient ways of presenting information or structuring activities that can be eliminated or reduced through effective design. Germane cognitive load, on the other hand, is associated with the mental effort required for meaningful learning and problem solving.

By understanding and applying Cognitive Load Theory, designers in Design Thinking disciplines can optimize the learning and problem-solving experiences of their users. They can do this by carefully considering the organization and presentation of information, minimizing irrelevant or distracting elements, providing clear and concise instructions, and utilizing instructional techniques that promote deeper understanding. This can result in improved user engagement, comprehension, and problem-solving performance.

Cognitive Load

Cognitive load refers to the amount of mental effort or capacity required to process information and perform cognitive tasks. In the context of Design Thinking disciplines, cognitive load plays a crucial role in the design and development of products, services, or experiences.

When designing a solution, it is important to consider the cognitive load on the end-users. High cognitive load can overwhelm users and hinder their ability to understand, learn, or use the product effectively. On the other hand, a well-designed solution should aim to minimize cognitive load and make the user experience more intuitive and seamless.

Cognitive Mapping Software

Cognitive Mapping Software refers to a digital tool used in the context of Design Thinking disciplines to visually represent and organize complex information and ideas. It helps in understanding various elements and relationships within a system or problem space, facilitating effective decision-making.

Using this software, users can create maps or diagrams that visually depict their thought processes, allowing them to analyze and explore the connections between different concepts, variables, and components. These maps can range from simple to intricate, depending on the complexity of the problem being addressed.

Cognitive Psychology

Cognitive Psychology can be defined as a branch of psychology that focuses on studying the mental processes involved in perception, thinking, problem-solving, memory, and decision-making. It aims to understand how individuals acquire, process, and use information to make sense of the world around them.

In the context of Design Thinking disciplines, cognitive psychology plays a crucial role in understanding the human mind and its cognitive abilities, which are essential in shaping the design process.

By studying cognitive psychology, designers gain insights into how individuals perceive and interpret information, how they think and reason, and how they make decisions. This knowledge helps designers create user-centered designs that resonate with the target users.

Designers who apply cognitive psychology principles in their work can optimize the user experience by designing interfaces that minimize cognitive load, maximize usability, and enhance information processing. They can create intuitive designs that align with users' mental models and make complex tasks more manageable.

Furthermore, cognitive psychology helps designers understand how memory works and can be utilized to improve user engagement and retention. Designers can employ techniques like chunking, repetition, and meaningful associations to enhance information retention and recall.

In summary, cognitive psychology provides valuable insights into the human mind, which designers can leverage to create exceptional user experiences. By understanding the cognitive processes underlying perception, thinking, and decision-making, designers can design products and interfaces that are intuitive, efficient, and enjoyable to use.

Cognitive Walkthrough

A cognitive walkthrough is a usability evaluation method used in service design to systematically evaluate how users interact with a digital system or service. It aims to identify any potential issues or barriers users may face when using the system and provide insights for improvement. During a cognitive walkthrough, evaluators put themselves in the shoes of users and step through the system's interactive tasks. They follow a predefined set of scenarios and tasks, considering the system's design and features from a user's perspective. The evaluation focuses on four main aspects: visibility, understanding, prediction, and control. Visibility refers to how well users can perceive the available options or actions at each stage of the interaction. Evaluators assess the clarity of visual cues and navigational elements, ensuring that users can easily identify where to go or what actions to take. Understanding examines how well users can comprehend the system's instructions, prompts, or messages. Evaluators assess the clarity and simplicity of the language used, ensuring that instructions are easy to understand and follow. Prediction assesses whether users can accurately anticipate the system's response to their actions. Evaluators consider how consistent and predictable the system's reactions are to user inputs, ensuring that users can make informed decisions and expect logical outcomes. Control evaluates the degree of user control over the system's actions and behaviors. Evaluators assess the flexibility and responsiveness of the system, ensuring that users can navigate through the service smoothly and have control over their interactions. Throughout the cognitive walkthrough, evaluators document any potential issues or challenges users may encounter. These findings serve as valuable insights to inform iterative service design improvements. By identifying and addressing usability issues early in the design process, service providers can enhance user satisfaction, reduce user errors, and improve overall user experience. In conclusion, cognitive walkthroughs play a vital role in service design by providing a systematic approach to evaluate the usability of digital systems or services. By analyzing the visibility, understanding, prediction, and control aspects, service providers can identify and address potential issues, leading to enhanced user experiences.

Cognitive Walkthroughs

A cognitive walkthrough is a usability evaluation method used in the context of Design Thinking disciplines to assess the effectiveness and efficiency of a digital or physical product from a user's perspective. It involves a step-by-step analysis of a user's cognitive processes and interactions with the product, with the aim of identifying potential usability issues and areas for improvement.

During a cognitive walkthrough, a team of evaluators imagines themselves as a typical user and performs specific tasks or scenarios using the product. They systematically assess each step of the interaction, considering the user's goals, knowledge, and experience. The evaluation is based on four key cognitive factors:

1. The user's understanding of the system's state: Evaluators assess whether users can accurately infer the current state of the product and understand the implications of their actions.

2. The user's decision-making process: Evaluators analyze whether the product provides sufficient information or feedback for users to make informed decisions at each step.

3. The visibility of the system's status: Evaluators consider whether the product effectively communicates its status and progress to users, helping them navigate through the interaction.

4. The ability to reach a desired outcome: Evaluators evaluate whether users can successfully complete their goals using the product, examining the ease of use and efficiency of the required actions.

A cognitive walkthrough provides valuable insights into the user experience, highlighting usability challenges and informing iterative design iterations. By identifying potential obstacles early in the design process, designers can make informed decisions to enhance the product's usability and user satisfaction.

Collaboration With End Users

Collaboration with end users, within the context of Design Thinking disciplines, refers to the active involvement and engagement of the intended users or customers throughout the design process. It is a fundamental approach that emphasizes empathy, understanding, and co-creation between designers and the people for whom the design is intended.

End users, also known as stakeholders or participants, play a crucial role in shaping the final outcome of a design solution. Their valuable insights, perspectives, and experiences are integrated into the design process to ensure that the end result effectively meets their needs and desires.

By collaborating with end users, designers are able to gather firsthand knowledge and understanding of their specific contexts, pain points, and motivations. This process involves a range of methods such as interviews, observational studies, surveys, and interactive workshops that encourage open dialogue and participation.

Collaboration with end users enables designers to move beyond assumptions and biases, gaining authentic and actionable insights. It fosters a deep sense of empathy and allows designers to uncover latent needs and design opportunities that might have been overlooked otherwise.

In addition to the benefit of understanding users, collaboration also fosters a sense of ownership and buy-in from the end users themselves. By involving them in the design process, designers ensure that the final solution is not only relevant and usable but also meaningful and satisfying to the people it is designed for.

Collaboration With Experts

Collaboration with experts plays a crucial role in the practice of Design Thinking disciplines. It involves actively engaging and working together with individuals who possess deep knowledge and expertise in various domains to generate innovative and effective solutions to complex problems.

By collaborating with experts, Design Thinkers gain valuable insights and perspectives that can inform their design process. These experts may come from diverse fields such as engineering, psychology, anthropology, or business, and their expertise can contribute to a more comprehensive understanding of the problem at hand. They bring specialized knowledge and skills that can help identify hidden opportunities, challenge assumptions, and offer alternative viewpoints.

Collaboration

Collaboration is a key aspect of Design Thinking disciplines, encompassing the collective effort of individuals working together towards a common goal. It involves the active participation, exchange of ideas, and shared decision-making among team members with diverse backgrounds, skills, and perspectives.

In the context of Design Thinking, collaboration fosters the generation of innovative and effective solutions to complex problems. By encouraging open communication and collaboration, the discipline enables individuals to leverage their collective knowledge and expertise, leading to the development of creative and user-centric solutions.

Collaborative Creativity

Collaborative creativity, within the framework of Design Thinking disciplines, refers to the collective and participatory generation of ideas, solutions, and innovations through a collaborative and iterative process. It emphasizes the importance of diverse perspectives, collaboration, and co-creation among individuals with different backgrounds and expertise.

In this approach, creativity is not limited to the individual genius but rather is nurtured and enhanced through the collective effort of a multidisciplinary team. It recognizes that diverse perspectives bring in a wider range of ideas, insights, and approaches, leading to more innovative and effective solutions.

Collaborative Design Platforms

A collaborative design platform refers to a digital tool or software that enables teams to work together remotely and concurrently on the design thinking process. It provides a space where designers, stakeholders, and other team members can collaborate, share ideas, and contribute to the overall design solution.

These platforms typically incorporate various features that facilitate collaboration, such as real-time editing, commenting, version control, and task management. By using a collaborative design platform, teams can overcome geographical barriers and time constraints, allowing for an efficient and inclusive design thinking process.

Collaborative Design Workspaces

Collaborative design workspaces in the context of Design Thinking disciplines refer to physical or virtual environments that foster collaboration and creative problem-solving among multidisciplinary teams. These workspaces are specifically designed to support the iterative and dynamic nature of the Design Thinking process, where diverse perspectives are brought together to generate innovative solutions.

In a collaborative design workspace, team members from various disciplines, such as designers, engineers, marketers, and users, work together in a fluid and interactive manner. The space is organized to encourage open communication, knowledge sharing, and co-creation. This could be a physical office space with movable furniture, writable surfaces, and informal meeting areas, or it could be a virtual platform that allows for remote collaboration and real-time sharing of ideas and prototypes.

Collaborative design workspaces enable teams to engage in key Design Thinking activities, such as empathy research, ideation, prototyping, and testing, in a collaborative and participatory manner. By bringing together different perspectives and skillsets, these workspaces facilitate the exploration of a wide range of ideas, rapid experimentation, and learning through iteration.

Furthermore, collaborative design workspaces foster a sense of ownership, pride, and accountability among team members as they collectively work towards a shared goal. They promote a culture of collaboration, trust, and support, where individuals feel empowered to contribute their unique insights and skills. Ultimately, collaborative design workspaces enhance the effectiveness of Design Thinking by creating an environment that nurtures creativity, unlocks collective intelligence, and drives innovation.

Collaborative Ideation Apps

Collaborative Ideation Apps refer to digital platforms or tools designed to facilitate the collaborative process of generating and developing ideas within the context of Design Thinking disciplines.

These apps enable individuals or groups to engage in ideation activities such as brainstorming, concept development, and idea evaluation in a collaborative and interactive manner. By providing a space for users to contribute and iterate on ideas together, these apps promote the principles of inclusivity, diversity, and openness that are central to Design Thinking.

Collaborative Ideation Kits

Collaborative Ideation Kits are tools used in the context of Design Thinking disciplines to facilitate and enhance the ideation process within a collaborative team setting. These kits are typically physical or digital collections of various tools, materials, and resources that are specifically designed to stimulate creativity, encourage active participation, and foster collaboration among team members.

The purpose of Collaborative Ideation Kits is to provide a structured framework and set of activities that enable teams to generate and explore a wide range of ideas and potential solutions to a given design challenge. These kits often include tools such as brainstorming cards, idea mapping templates, sketching materials, prototyping supplies, and other resources that help teams to visualize and communicate their ideas effectively.

By utilizing Collaborative Ideation Kits, teams are able to overcome common ideation challenges such as idea stagnation, lack of participation, or a limited range of ideas. These kits promote a more inclusive and dynamic ideation process by providing a variety of techniques and resources that cater to different thinking styles and preferences. They encourage teams to think outside the box, challenge assumptions, and explore unconventional approaches to problem-solving.

Furthermore, by engaging in collaborative activities facilitated by these kits, teams are able to leverage the collective intelligence and diverse perspectives of the group, fostering collaboration and co-creation. Collaborative Ideation Kits also promote a culture of experimentation and iteration, as teams are encouraged to prototype and refine their ideas based on feedback and insights gained through the ideation process.

Collaborative Ideation Platforms

Collaborative Ideation Platforms are digital tools and platforms designed to facilitate the generation and exchange of ideas in the context of Design Thinking disciplines. These platforms enable individuals or teams, irrespective of geographical limitations, to contribute ideas, insights, and feedback, thereby fostering a collaborative environment for ideation and problem-solving.

The key objective of Collaborative Ideation Platforms is to promote inclusiveness and maximize the diversity of perspectives during the ideation process. The platforms typically provide a structured framework or framework templates, such as design challenges or problem statements, to guide participants through the ideation process.

Through these platforms, participants can employ various ideation techniques, such as brainstorming, mind mapping, or card sorting, to generate and capture ideas. The platforms often facilitate real-time collaboration, allowing multiple individuals to contribute ideas simultaneously and allowing participants to comment, build upon, or offer feedback on each other's ideas.

Collaborative Ideation Platforms also provide functionalities for organizing and filtering ideas to enable efficient evaluation and analysis. Participants can vote or rate ideas based on their viability, feasibility, or desirability, helping to identify and prioritize the most promising concepts for further development and implementation.

In summary, Collaborative Ideation Platforms leverage digital technologies to enable remote and collaborative ideation within the framework of Design Thinking disciplines. By providing a structured and inclusive environment for idea generation, these platforms facilitate the exploration of diverse perspectives and ultimately support the development of innovative solutions to complex challenges.

Collaborative Ideation Workspaces

A collaborative ideation workspace is a physical or virtual environment that is specifically designed to facilitate the creative and collaborative process of generating and developing ideas. It is an essential component of the Design Thinking disciplines, which are used to solve complex problems and drive innovation.

Within a collaborative ideation workspace, individuals or teams can come together to brainstorm ideas, share knowledge and insights, and explore potential solutions. The environment is intentionally designed to promote open communication, trust, and a sense of psychological safety, which are crucial for fostering creativity and encouraging participants to think outside the box.

Physical collaborative ideation workspaces often feature flexible furniture arrangements, such as movable tables and chairs, whiteboards or chalkboards for visualizing ideas, and plenty of wall space for displaying and organizing information. These spaces may also include various tools and materials, such as sticky notes, markers, and prototyping materials, to support the ideation process.

Virtual collaborative ideation workspaces, on the other hand, are digital platforms or applications that allow individuals or teams to collaborate remotely. These platforms typically provide features such as virtual whiteboards, chat functionalities, and document sharing capabilities. Remote participants can contribute ideas, provide feedback, and collaborate in real time, regardless of their physical location.

Collaborative Ideation

Collaborative Ideation is a key component of the Design Thinking process. It refers to the collaborative generation and exploration of ideas within a group or team. The goal of Collaborative Ideation is to foster creativity and innovation by leveraging the collective knowledge, perspectives, and experiences of all participants.

During Collaborative Ideation, individuals come together to brainstorm, share ideas, and build upon each other's thoughts. This process encourages active collaboration and cross-pollination of ideas, leading to the development of diverse and novel solutions to complex problems. It involves creating a safe and inclusive space where everyone's ideas are valued, and no judgment or criticism is allowed.

The Collaborative Ideation process typically involves various techniques and activities, such as brainstorming sessions, mind mapping, rapid prototyping, and design studios. These methods help stimulate creativity, break down silos, and promote a culture of open-mindedness and curiosity.

Collaborative Ideation is effective because it harnesses the power of collective intelligence. By bringing together individuals with different backgrounds, expertise, and perspectives, it maximizes the chances of generating breakthrough ideas and insights. It also encourages participants to build on each other's ideas, leading to the emergence of more refined and robust solutions.

In summary, Collaborative Ideation is a fundamental aspect of Design Thinking that emphasizes active collaboration, inclusiveness, and the exploration of diverse ideas. By leveraging the collective intelligence of a group, it helps unlock creative solutions and drive innovation.

Collaborative Innovation Platforms

A collaborative innovation platform, in the context of Design Thinking disciplines, refers to a digital tool or software that facilitates and supports the collaborative process of generating ideas, problem-solving, and implementing innovative solutions. It provides a virtual space for individuals, teams, or even organizations to come together, share their perspectives, and work collectively towards a common goal.

These platforms typically incorporate various features and functionalities, such as virtual brainstorming tools, ideation boards, project management tools, and communication channels. They allow for real-time collaboration, enabling multiple users to contribute and build upon each other's ideas and insights. By providing a centralized and accessible platform, these tools promote cross-functional collaboration and enhance the effectiveness of Design Thinking methodologies.

Collaborative Innovation

Collaborative innovation, in the context of Design Thinking disciplines, refers to the process of bringing together diverse individuals with different skills, backgrounds, and perspectives to collectively generate innovative solutions to complex problems. It emphasizes the power of collaboration, co-creation, and shared decision-making in driving creative and meaningful outcomes.

Design Thinking, as an approach to problem-solving, recognizes the value of involving multiple stakeholders throughout the innovation process. By fostering a collaborative environment, it allows for the exploration of various perspectives, insights, and expertise, leading to more holistic and user-centered solutions.

Collaborative Problem Solving

Collaborative Problem Solving in the context of Design Thinking disciplines can be defined as a process that involves multiple individuals working together to identify, understand, and address complex problems or challenges. It is a collaborative approach that encourages diverse perspectives, encourages free-flowing communication, and embraces iterative problem-solving.

Collaborative Problem Solving in Design Thinking begins with a shared understanding of the problem at hand. This involves gathering insights from various stakeholders and users through methods such as interviews, observations, or surveys. Through empathizing with the target audience and identifying their needs, the team gains a deeper understanding of the problem they are trying to solve.

Once the problem is defined, the collaborative team engages in ideation, generating a wide range of creative solutions without judgment. This divergent thinking allows for a rich exploration of possibilities and enables the team to think outside the box. Through these brainstorming sessions, the team combines their unique expertise and experiences to uncover innovative ideas.

After the ideation phase, the team moves into the convergence phase. Here, they narrow down the generated ideas and select the most promising ones based on feasibility, desirability, and viability. Through open and constructive conversations, the team debates and discusses the merits of each idea before making a collective decision.

The final step in Collaborative Problem Solving is prototyping and testing. The team creates quick prototypes to visualize and test their solutions, gathering feedback from users, stakeholders, or experts. This iterative process allows for continuous refinement and improvement based on real-world insights, ultimately leading to a more effective and user-centric solution.

Collaborative Problem-Solving Apps

A collaborative problem-solving app is a digital tool that facilitates teamwork and collaboration among individuals or groups in the context of the Design Thinking disciplines. These apps are specifically designed to support the process of problem-solving by implementing the principles of collaborative thinking and leveraging the power of technology to enhance teamwork and creativity.

These apps provide a platform for users to work together, brainstorm ideas, analyze problems, and propose solutions in a collaborative and systematic manner. They often incorporate various features such as real-time collaboration, digital whiteboards, virtual sticky notes, and interactive visualization tools to facilitate the exchange of ideas and foster effective communication among team members.

By using collaborative problem-solving apps, teams can overcome geographical barriers and work together efficiently regardless of their physical location. These apps enable remote teams to collaborate effectively and ensure that all team members have equal opportunities to contribute and participate in the problem-solving process.

The key benefits of using collaborative problem-solving apps include improved team communication, enhanced creativity, increased productivity, and the ability to capture and record ideas and insights in a digital format. These apps also promote inclusivity and diversity by allowing individuals from different backgrounds and perspectives to contribute and collaborate on problem-solving tasks.

In summary, collaborative problem-solving apps are powerful digital tools that empower individuals and teams to work together in a structured and collaborative manner. They promote effective communication, foster creativity, and facilitate the generation of innovative solutions in the context of the Design Thinking disciplines.

Collaborative User Research

Collaborative user research is a critical component of the Design Thinking process, which involves multidisciplinary teams working together to gain a comprehensive understanding of users and their needs. It is a methodical approach that brings together different perspectives and expertise to generate insights that inform the design and development of innovative solutions.

During collaborative user research, cross-functional teams collaborate in conducting research activities such as interviews, observations, and surveys to gather rich qualitative and quantitative data about users. This collaborative approach ensures that different team members can contribute different insights and interpretations of the collected data, resulting in a holistic understanding of users and their context.

The collaborative nature of this research method also promotes empathy and fosters an inclusive and participatory environment. It encourages team members to actively listen to each other's perspectives, challenge assumptions, and collectively make sense of the research findings. This collaborative process helps to uncover deep insights, uncover latent needs, and ideate potential solutions that address the identified user problems.

The insights gained from collaborative user research serve as a foundation for the iterative design process, enabling teams to create user-centered solutions that resonate with real user needs and expectations. By involving diverse team members in the research process, organizations can leverage a variety of skills, experiences, and perspectives to ultimately create more innovative and impactful products and services.

Collaborative Whiteboarding Tools

Collaborative whiteboarding tools are digital platforms that enable teams to visually ideate, brainstorm, and collaborate in real-time during the design thinking process. These tools facilitate the sharing and creation of ideas, concepts, and solutions through an interactive virtual whiteboard.

Designed specifically for the design thinking disciplines, collaborative whiteboarding tools aim to enhance the collaboration and creativity of multidisciplinary teams. These tools allow team members to contribute their thoughts, concepts, and drawings on a shared canvas, promoting collective understanding and co-creation. The virtual whiteboard often replicates the experience of a physical whiteboard, providing a familiar interface for participants.

With collaborative whiteboarding tools, teams can overcome the limitations of physical whiteboards by working together remotely and asynchronously. These tools offer features such as sticky notes, drawing tools, shapes, text boxes, and color options to facilitate the expression of ideas. Additionally, participants can leverage features like commenting, voting, and annotation to provide feedback and refine concepts.

The real-time collaboration aspect of these tools allows team members to see each other's contributions instantly, fostering a sense of engagement, motivation, and accountability. This instant feedback loop accelerates the design thinking process, enabling teams to iterate and refine their ideas more efficiently.

In conclusion, collaborative whiteboarding tools are essential for design thinking disciplines as they empower teams to collaboratively ideate, visualize, and refine their concepts. By leveraging these tools, teams can enhance their creativity, communication, and overall problem-solving capabilities, regardless of physical location or time constraints.

Competitor Benchmarking

Competitor Benchmarking is a strategic process in service design that involves evaluating and comparing the performance, capabilities, and offerings of a company's competitors. It is a systematic analysis that helps businesses understand their position in the market and identify opportunities for improvement and differentiation. The goal of competitor benchmarking is to gather information and insights about the competitors' strategies, products, services, customer experiences, and operational practices. By analyzing these factors, companies can gain a comprehensive understanding of the competitive landscape and identify areas where they can capitalize on their strengths and address weaknesses.

Concept Development

Concept Development in the context of service design refers to the process of creating and refining ideas, strategies, and solutions for the design of a service. It involves developing a clear understanding of the problem or opportunity at hand, and then generating and exploring a range of possible concepts to address it. The goal of concept development is to create innovative and effective solutions that meet the needs and expectations of the service users, while also considering the capabilities and constraints of the service provider. It is a collaborative and iterative process that involves input from various stakeholders, such as service designers, service users, and other relevant parties.

Concept Ideation

Concept Ideation is a process within Design Thinking disciplines that involves generating and developing new ideas and concepts to address a specific problem or challenge. It is a collaborative and iterative process that encourages divergent thinking to explore a wide range of possibilities and potential solutions.

The goal of Concept Ideation is to generate a variety of creative and innovative ideas that go beyond conventional thinking. This process involves brainstorming, prototyping, and testing ideas to identify the most feasible and effective solutions. It encourages a multidisciplinary approach, bringing together individuals with different perspectives and expertise to contribute to the ideation process.

During Concept Ideation, a diverse range of techniques and tools are used to stimulate creative thinking and facilitate idea generation. These may include mind mapping, sketching, role-playing, and storyboarding. By utilizing these methods, participants are able to break free from traditional constraints and explore unconventional solutions.

It is important to note that Concept Ideation is not focused on finding a single "right" answer, but rather on generating a variety of potential solutions and ideas. The emphasis is on quantity rather than quality during the initial stages, as this allows for a greater range of possibilities to be explored.

Once a range of concepts has been generated, they are evaluated based on various criteria such as feasibility, desirability, and viability. This evaluation process helps to refine and narrow down the concepts to the most promising ideas that can be further developed and implemented.

In conclusion, Concept Ideation is a crucial stage within Design Thinking disciplines that fosters creativity and innovation. By encouraging diverse thinking and exploring unconventional ideas, it enables the development of unique solutions to complex problems.

Concept Mapping Software

Concept mapping software is a digital tool used within the context of Design Thinking disciplines to visually depict, organize, and connect complex ideas and concepts. It provides a platform for individuals or teams to structure their thoughts, brainstorm ideas, and create a visual representation of the relationships between different concepts.

By allowing users to create diagrams, maps, or flowcharts, concept mapping software aids in the exploration, analysis, and synthesis of concepts, facilitating the process of problem-solving and design ideation. It serves as a means to visually represent the connections and hierarchies between ideas in a non-linear format, promoting a holistic view of the problem or design challenge at hand.

Concept Mapping

Concept mapping is a visual tool used in service design to identify and organize key concepts, ideas, and relationships. It is a graphical representation that enables designers to map out and connect various components of a service, such as user needs, service touchpoints, and stakeholder interactions. At its core, concept mapping helps service designers clarify their understanding of a problem or challenge and align various stakeholders around a shared understanding. By visually representing the interdependencies between different aspects of a service, concept mapping helps designers identify gaps, inconsistencies, and potential areas for improvement. Concept mapping is typically created using a diagramming tool or software. The diagram starts with a central theme or main concept, which is then connected to sub-concepts and related ideas. These connections can be represented through lines, arrows, or other visual elements, indicating the relationships between concepts. The key benefit of using concept mapping in service design is its ability to foster collaboration and facilitate communication among stakeholders. It provides a shared language and mental model that allows everyone involved to contribute their perspectives and insights. Through this collaborative process, designers can gain a comprehensive understanding of the service ecosystem and identify opportunities to enhance the overall service experience. Concept mapping also aids in identifying potential challenges and risks associated with implementing a service. By visually mapping out the various components and interactions, designers can anticipate bottlenecks, points of failure, or areas of confusion for users. This enables them to proactively address these issues during the design process, resulting in a more seamless and effective service. In conclusion, concept mapping is a valuable tool in service design that enables designers to visually represent and organize key concepts, ideas, and relationships. By providing a shared language and mental model, it enhances collaboration and communication among stakeholders, resulting in a more comprehensive understanding of the service ecosystem. Moreover, concept mapping helps identify potential challenges and risks, allowing designers to proactively address them, leading to an improved and more user-centered service experience.

Concept Refinement

Design Thinking is a problem-solving approach that involves a deep understanding of users' needs and requirements, combined with iterative ideation and prototyping, to create innovative solutions. It is a discipline that encompasses various methods and tools to foster creativity and collaboration, ultimately leading to human-centered designs.

At its core, Design Thinking focuses on empathizing with users to gain insights into their experiences and challenges, defining the problem at hand, and brainstorming ideas to address those problems. This process is characterized by an iterative and non-linear nature, where designers continuously gather feedback, refine their solutions, and iterate on their ideas.

Concept Testing Platforms

Concept testing platforms refer to digital tools or platforms that facilitate the evaluation and validation of new ideas, concepts, or designs during the design thinking process. These platforms are designed to gather feedback from the target audience or users, allowing designers to iterate and refine their concepts based on the feedback received.

The primary purpose of concept testing platforms is to help designers assess the viability, desirability, and feasibility of their concepts before investing significant resources in their development and implementation. By soliciting user feedback and opinions, designers can gain valuable insights and make informed decisions about the further direction of their designs.

Concept Testing

Concept testing, in the context of service design, refers to the evaluation and validation of a potential service concept before it is fully developed and implemented. It aims to gather feedback and insights from users, stakeholders, and experts in order to assess the viability and desirability of the proposed service. The process of concept testing typically involves presenting the service concept to a representative sample of the target audience or user group. This can be done through various research methods such as surveys, interviews, focus groups, or prototype testing. The main objective is to understand how the target audience perceives and understands the service concept, and to identify any potential gaps or areas for improvement. By conducting concept testing, service designers can gain valuable insights into the users' needs, preferences, and expectations. This information allows designers to iterate and refine the service concept early on, before significant resources are invested in implementation. It helps to minimize the risk of designing and launching a service that does not meet the users' needs or align with their expectations. During concept testing, participants may be asked to provide their feedback, opinions, and suggestions regarding various aspects of the service concept, such as its value proposition, features, user interface, pricing, or overall user experience. The feedback collected helps designers to identify potential improvements or modifications that can enhance the appeal and usability of the service. In addition to gathering feedback from users, concept testing also involves seeking input from other stakeholders such as industry experts, regulators, or business partners. Their perspectives can provide valuable insights and validation from a broader perspective, helping to identify any potential risks or opportunities associated with the proposed service concept. Overall, concept testing plays a critical role in the service design process as it allows designers to refine and validate their ideas before investing resources into full-scale implementation. By gathering feedback and insights, designers can ensure that they are creating services that effectively meet the needs and expectations of their target audience, leading to increased user satisfaction and business success.

Concept Visualization Tools

Concept visualization tools are digital or physical aids used in the context of Design Thinking disciplines to visually represent and communicate abstract ideas and concepts. These tools enable designers and other stakeholders to collaboratively explore, refine, and articulate their

35

thoughts and visions during the creative process.

By leveraging concept visualization tools, design thinkers can effectively express complex ideas, enhancing their understanding and increasing the likelihood of successful outcomes. These tools provide a visual medium for sharing ideas, allowing for easier comprehension and engagement by all involved parties.

Conceptual Development

Conceptual Development refers to the process of generating and refining ideas, concepts, and solutions in the context of Design Thinking disciplines. It involves the exploration and development of concepts and their underlying principles to address a specific problem or challenge.

Conceptual Development typically begins with problem identification and research, where designers aim to understand the user's needs, behaviors, and motivations. Through empathizing with the users, designers gain insights and identify opportunities for improvement or innovation. This phase often involves conducting interviews, observations, and research to gather data and information.

Once designers have a deep understanding of the problem, they move on to the ideation phase in which they generate a wide range of ideas and concepts. This can be done through brainstorming sessions, sketching, or other creative techniques. The emphasis in this phase is on quantity and diversity, allowing for the exploration of different perspectives and possibilities.

Following ideation, designers enter the refinement phase where they select the most promising ideas and concepts and further develop them. This involves evaluating the feasibility, desirability, and viability of the concepts, considering technical, economic, and user-centric factors. Iterative cycles of testing, prototyping, and feedback are often employed to refine and improve the concepts.

Conceptual Development is an iterative and collaborative process, involving input and feedback from users, stakeholders, and interdisciplinary teams. It is essential for designers to embrace open-mindedness and creativity, as well as the ability to think critically and analytically. The goal is to create innovative, human-centered solutions that address the underlying needs and challenges identified during the initial research phase.

Conceptual Exploration

Design thinking is a human-centered approach that focuses on understanding and solving complex problems in creative and innovative ways. It is a discipline that combines empathy, experimentation, and collaboration to develop meaningful solutions.

At its core, design thinking is about shifting the focus from product-centric to human-centric. It involves understanding the needs and desires of the end users and designing solutions that meet those needs effectively and efficiently. Design thinking promotes a deep understanding of the user's context, motivations, and pain points, which forms the foundation for creating solutions that truly resonate with the users.

Design thinking follows a structured and iterative process, typically consisting of five stages: empathize, define, ideate, prototype, and test. The empathize stage involves immersing oneself in the user's world, gaining insights through observations and interviews. The define stage involves synthesizing the gathered information to identify the core problem that needs to be solved. In the ideate stage, diverse and multidisciplinary teams brainstorm and generate a wide range of ideas. These ideas are then refined and transformed into tangible prototypes in the prototype stage. Finally, in the test stage, the prototypes are tested with real users to gather feedback and iterate on the design.

Design thinking encourages a culture of experimentation and learning from failure. It embraces an iterative approach, where solutions are constantly refined and improved based on user feedback. Design thinkers embrace ambiguity and uncertainty, recognizing that the best solutions often emerge through a non-linear and exploratory process.

In summary, design thinking is a human-centered and iterative approach to problem-solving that emphasizes understanding the user, generating diverse ideas, and prototyping and testing solutions. It is a mindset and a set of tools that empower individuals and teams to create innovative and meaningful solutions to complex problems.

Conceptual Frameworks

A conceptual framework in the context of Design Thinking disciplines is a structured system of ideas, principles, and concepts that guide the design process, providing a framework for understanding, organizing, and solving complex design problems. It serves as a foundation for designers to navigate through the different stages of the design thinking process, from problem identification to solution implementation.

The key components of a conceptual framework include problem definition, user empathy, ideation, prototyping, and testing. It helps designers gain a deep understanding of the users' needs, motivations, and pain points by employing research methods such as interviews, observations, and surveys. This user-centric approach ensures that the design solutions address real problems and resonate with the users.

The framework also encourages ideation and brainstorming to generate innovative and creative solutions. It promotes divergent thinking, enabling designers to generate a wide range of ideas without judgment or evaluation. These ideas are then refined through convergent thinking, where designers evaluate and select the most promising solutions for further development.

Prototyping and testing are integral parts of the conceptual framework, as they allow designers to iterate and refine their solutions based on user feedback. Through rapid prototyping, designers can quickly create tangible representations of their ideas, which can be tested and validated with users. This iterative process helps designers uncover potential flaws, identify areas for improvement, and refine their designs to meet user needs effectively.

Conceptualization

Conceptualization in the context of Design Thinking disciplines refers to the process of generating ideas and developing a deep understanding of the problem or challenge at hand. It involves exploring various perspectives, analyzing user needs and expectations, and envisioning potential solutions.

During the conceptualization phase, designers aim to define the problem statement clearly and identify the underlying issues. This requires them to conduct extensive research, gather relevant data, and analyze user insights to gain a comprehensive understanding of the problem's context and complexities.

Once designers have gathered all the necessary information, they can begin ideating and generating potential solutions. This involves brainstorming sessions, sketching out ideas, and prototyping to explore and evaluate different possibilities. The goal is to encourage a wide range of ideas and perspectives while considering feasibility and desirability.

Throughout the conceptualization process, designers iterate and refine their ideas based on feedback and insights gained through user testing and evaluation. By continuously iterating, designers can develop a deeper understanding of the problem space and identify the most effective solutions.

Concurrent Prototyping

Concurrent Prototyping in the context of Design Thinking disciplines refers to the simultaneous creation and development of multiple prototypes during the design process. It involves designing and building multiple versions of a product or solution to explore different ideas, generate multiple options, and gather feedback from users and stakeholders.

Concurrent Prototyping recognizes that design is an iterative process and that it is important to explore multiple possibilities before committing to a final design. By creating and testing multiple prototypes in parallel, designers can quickly validate or invalidate ideas, identify potential issues or improvements, and iterate on their designs more efficiently.

Conjoint Analysis

Conjoint analysis is a powerful research technique used in service design to understand consumer preferences and decision-making processes. It involves presenting consumers with different combinations of product or service attributes and asking them to make choices or rank their preferences. This allows service designers to determine the relative importance of different attributes and how they contribute to overall consumer satisfaction. Conjoint analysis is based on the principle that consumers make trade-offs between different attributes when making decisions. By systematically varying the levels of attributes such as price, quality, responsiveness, and convenience, service designers can identify the optimal combination of attributes that will maximize customer satisfaction. There are two main types of conjoint analysis: choice-based and rating-based. In choice-based conjoint analysis, consumers are presented with multiple profiles or scenarios and asked to choose their preferred option. This helps service designers understand the relative importance of different attributes and how they influence consumer choice. In rating-based conjoint analysis, consumers are asked to rate their preferences for different attribute levels on a numerical scale. This provides more detailed information about the relative importance of different attribute levels and allows for a more fine-grained analysis. Conjoint analysis can be conducted using various methods such as surveys, interviews, or experiments. The data collected from conjoint analysis is typically analyzed using statistical techniques such as regression analysis or maximum likelihood estimation. This allows service designers to quantitatively determine the impact of different attributes on consumer preferences and make informed decisions about service design and marketing strategies. Overall, conjoint analysis is a valuable tool in service design as it helps service designers understand customer preferences and make data-driven decisions about service attributes. By identifying the optimal combination of attributes that will maximize customer satisfaction, service designers can design services that meet customer needs and differentiate themselves from competitors in the market.

Consistent And Coherent

Consistent in the context of Design Thinking disciplines refers to maintaining a uniformity or stability in the elements, principles, and goals throughout the design process. It is essential to ensure that the decisions, actions, and outputs are aligned with the overall objective and don't conflict with each other. Consistency helps in creating a unified and seamless experience for users or stakeholders.

Coherent, on the other hand, means that the different parts of the design solution are logically connected and make sense as a whole. It implies that there is a clear and logical flow between the different stages, concepts, or components of the design. Cohesion ensures that the design is rational, understandable, and meaningful to the users or recipients.

Constraints As Catalysts

Constraints as Catalysts refer to the use of limitations or restrictions as a driving force for creativity, innovation, and problem-solving within Design Thinking disciplines. In this context, constraints are not seen as obstacles, but rather as opportunities to push the boundaries and explore new possibilities.

In Design Thinking, constraints can come in various forms, such as budget limitations, time constraints, technical constraints, or even social and cultural constraints. Rather than viewing these constraints as limitations that hinder the design process, they are used as catalysts to inspire innovative solutions.

Constraints As Opportunities

Constraints as Opportunities refers to the mindset and approach in Design Thinking disciplines that views limitations or constraints as valuable opportunities for creativity, innovation, and problem-solving. Instead of perceiving constraints as obstacles or hindrances, this perspective sees them as catalysts for unlocking new possibilities and finding elegant solutions.

Design Thinking is a human-centered problem-solving methodology that involves iterative processes of understanding the needs and challenges of users, ideating potential solutions, prototyping and testing them, and implementing the most effective solution. Within this framework, constraints play a crucial role in shaping the design process and outcomes.

Constructive Critique

Design Thinking is a problem-solving approach that is centered around understanding and empathizing with users, generating creative ideas, and iterating through a cycle of prototyping and testing to develop innovative solutions. It is a discipline that combines analytical and creative thinking to tackle complex problems and uncover new opportunities. Design Thinking is characterized by a human-centered focus, which means that the needs, desires, and behaviors of the end-users are at the forefront of the design process. Through thorough research and observation, designers aim to deeply understand the users' perspectives and experiences to gain valuable insights. This empathetic understanding enables designers to identify pain points, challenges, and unmet needs, which then serve as foundations for problem statements and design opportunities. The next phase of Design Thinking involves ideation, where designers generate a multitude of ideas to address the identified problem or challenge. This step encourages divergent thinking, as designers explore a wide range of possible solutions without judgment or limitation. By embracing ambiguity and pushing boundaries, designers aim to come up with innovative and creative concepts that can potentially disrupt existing paradigms. Following the ideation phase, designers move on to prototyping and testing. Here, they create tangible representations of their ideas, such as physical models, wireframes, or interactive prototypes. These prototypes are then evaluated and tested with potential users to gather feedback and insights. Through this iterative process, designers refine and improve their solutions based on the feedback received, continuously striving for user-centric designs. Design Thinking's interdisciplinary approach encourages collaboration among individuals with diverse backgrounds, expertise, and perspectives. It fosters a culture of continuous learning, adaptation, and user-centered innovation. Design Thinking can be applied to a wide range of contexts and challenges, including product design, service design, experience design, organizational design, and social innovation. In conclusion, Design Thinking is a problem-solving approach that prioritizes user empathy, creative ideation, prototyping, and testing. It combines analytical thinking with a deep understanding of human needs and desires to develop innovative solutions. It is a discipline that encourages collaboration, iteration, and continuous improvement to create impactful and meaningful designs.

Content Auditing

A content audit is a systematic process that involves evaluating and analyzing the existing content of a service or website. It aims to identify the strengths, weaknesses, and gaps in the content to determine how effectively it meets the needs and goals of the users and the business. The content auditing process begins by defining the objectives and criteria for evaluating the content. This includes understanding the target audience, their expectations, and the business goals of the service. It then involves inventorying and organizing the content, categorizing it based on various factors such as type, relevance, and quality. This allows for a comprehensive overview of the content available. The next step in the content auditing process is assessing the quality of the content. This involves analyzing the content against the defined criteria, such as accuracy, clarity, and readability. It helps to identify content that is outdated, redundant, or in need of improvement. Content gaps, where there is a lack of relevant information, can also be identified during this step. Once the content has been assessed, the findings are documented and recommendations are made for improvement. This includes updating, rewriting, or removing content that is deemed ineffective or outdated. The recommendations are based on improving user experience, ensuring that the content aligns with user needs and business goals, and enhancing overall service design. Content auditing plays a crucial role in service design as it helps to optimize the user experience and ensure that the content meets the needs of the users and the business. By identifying gaps and areas for improvement, it allows for a more strategic approach towards content creation and management. Regular content audits can also help to maintain the quality and relevance of the content over time.

Content Strategy

Content strategy in the context of service design refers to the planning, creation, and management of content that is used to support and enhance the overall user experience and align with the goals and objectives of a service. At its core, content strategy involves strategic thinking and decision-making regarding the content that is presented to users throughout the different touchpoints of a service. It includes determining what types of content are needed, how it should be structured and organized, and how it should be delivered to users in a way that is relevant, engaging, and useful to their needs.

Contextual Adaptation

Contextual Adaptation refers to the process of designing and adapting a solution to meet the specific needs and constraints of a particular context or user group. It is an essential element of the Design Thinking methodology, which focuses on understanding and empathizing with users, and developing innovative solutions that address their unique challenges and requirements.

The process of Contextual Adaptation involves gathering deep insights about the users and their context through research and observation. This includes understanding their behaviors, preferences, and the environmental factors that influence their interactions and experiences. By immersing themselves in the users' world, designers gain a comprehensive understanding of the challenges they face and the opportunities for improvement.

Once the user insights are gathered, designers use this knowledge to generate and refine ideas for potential solutions. These ideas are then adapted and tailored to the specific context, taking into account the cultural, societal, and technological factors that may impact the effectiveness and usability of the solution.

Throughout the design process, designers continuously test and iterate their solutions in collaboration with the users, using feedback to refine and adapt the design to better match the users' needs and expectations. This iterative approach ensures that the final solution is a result of a deep understanding of the users and their context, and is optimized to provide maximum value and impact.

Contextual Analysis

Contextual analysis is a method used within the discipline of Design Thinking to gather insights and understand the context in which a problem or challenge exists. It involves examining the broader environment, including the social, cultural, economic, and technological factors that may impact the problem at hand.

By conducting a contextual analysis, designers can gain a deeper understanding of the users they are designing for and the constraints they may face in their particular context. This understanding helps designers generate more meaningful and relevant solutions that address the real needs and behaviors of the users. Through observation, interviews, and research, designers can uncover important insights about the users' preferences, motivations, values, and goals.

Contextual Awareness

Contextual Awareness refers to the deep understanding of the overall context in which a design problem exists, including the environment, circumstances, users, and their needs. In Design Thinking disciplines, this concept is crucial for creating effective and meaningful solutions.

Designers practicing Contextual Awareness employ various research methods such as direct observation, interviews, and immersion in order to gain insights and empathy towards the end users. They seek to identify the specific needs, motivations, and behaviors of the users, as well as the broader social, cultural, and environmental factors that may influence the problem or solution.

Contextual Design Tools

Contextual design tools are a set of techniques and methods used in the field of design thinking disciplines to gain a deeper understanding of users' needs, behaviors, and experiences in order to design products, services, or systems that effectively meet those needs.

These tools are essential in the design process as they enable designers to uncover key insights and translate them into actionable design decisions. They help designers bridge the gap between user requirements and design solutions, ensuring that the final product not only solves the problem at hand but also resonates with the users on a meaningful level.

Contextual Design

Contextual Design is an approach to service design that focuses on understanding user needs and preferences while considering the specific context in which a service is used. It involves gathering detailed information about users, their goals, and the environment in which they interact with the service, and using this information to inform the design process. Contextual Design consists of several key steps. First, the design team engages in fieldwork to observe users in their natural environment, gathering data through methods such as interviews and site visits. This allows the team to gain a deep understanding of users' needs, motivations, and challenges. Next, the team creates an affinity diagram to organize and analyze the gathered data, identifying patterns and themes. This helps to uncover common needs and pain points, which can then inform the design of the service. Once the data has been analyzed, the design team develops personas to represent different user types. Personas are fictional characters that embody the characteristics and needs of specific user groups. They serve as a tool to help the team empathize with users and make design decisions that meet their needs. Based on the insights gained from fieldwork and the personas, the design team creates a set of design ideas and prototypes. These prototypes are then tested with users, allowing for iterative refinement of the service design. This user-centered approach ensures that the final design is relevant, usable, and meaningful to users. Overall, Contextual Design is a holistic and iterative approach to service design that places a strong emphasis on understanding users and their context. By gathering rich data, analyzing it, and involving users throughout the design process, Contextual Design enables the creation of services that are practical, effective, and aligned with user needs.

Contextual Empathy

Contextual empathy is a key component of Design Thinking, a problem-solving approach that emphasizes the user's needs and experiences. It involves understanding and relating to the user's context, including their emotions, behaviors, and physical environment. By empathizing with the user's specific situation and gaining deep insights into their needs and challenges, designers can create more meaningful and effective solutions.

Contextual empathy requires designers to adopt a non-judgmental and open mindset, actively seeking to understand the user's perspective and experiences. It involves conducting research and gathering data through various methods such as interviews, observations, and immersion in the user's environment. By immersing themselves in the user's world, designers can gain a holistic understanding of their needs, motivations, and pain points.

Designers practicing contextual empathy integrate these insights into their design process to inform their decisions and problem-solving strategies. They use their understanding of the user's context to generate innovative ideas and develop solutions that truly meet their needs. Through continuous iteration and feedback, designers can refine and improve their solutions, ensuring they are both desirable and feasible.

By employing contextual empathy, designers can create solutions that are user-centered, intuitive, and meaningful. It allows them to design products, services, and experiences that resonate with the user's emotions, values, and aspirations. This approach helps to build empathy and trust between the user and the designer, leading to better design outcomes and increased user satisfaction.

Contextual Inquiry

A contextual inquiry in the context of service design is a research method that aims to gain a deep understanding of the user's needs, motivations, and behaviors in relation to a specific service. It involves observing users in their natural environment and asking them open-ended questions to gather rich qualitative data. The purpose of a contextual inquiry is to uncover insights about how users currently interact with a service, identify pain points and opportunities for improvement, and inform the design process. By observing users in their real-life context, designers can gain a holistic understanding of their experiences and challenges, enabling them to create more meaningful and effective services.

Contextual Inspiration

Contextual inspiration refers to the process of gathering relevant information and insights from the surrounding environment, in order to inform the design thinking process. It involves observing, listening, and engaging with the people, places, and situations that are directly related to the problem or challenge at hand.

Design thinking disciplines, which encompass various stages such as empathizing, defining, ideating, prototyping, and testing, rely heavily on contextual inspiration to generate innovative and human-centered solutions. By immersing themselves in the context, designers are able to gain a deep understanding of the needs, wants, and behaviors of the people they are designing for, as well as the larger social, cultural, and environmental factors that influence the problem.

Contextual Sensitivity

Contextual sensitivity refers to the ability of a designer to understand and respond to the specific context in which a design challenge or problem exists. Context includes not only the physical environment in which a design will be implemented, but also the social, cultural, and economic factors that influence it.

In the realm of Design Thinking disciplines, contextual sensitivity is a critical skill as it allows designers to create solutions that are not only visually and aesthetically pleasing but also functional and meaningful to the end users. It requires a deep understanding of the target audience, their needs, and the unique challenges they face within their specific context.

Contextual Understanding

Contextual Understanding is a critical component of Design Thinking disciplines that involves gaining in-depth knowledge and insights about the specific context in which design problems and challenges are situated. It refers to the process of observing, researching, and empathizing with the people, environments, and systems that will be affected by the design solution.

By developing contextual understanding, designers are able to identify the needs, desires, and aspirations of the users or stakeholders involved. This understanding illuminates the complexities and nuances of the problem space and helps designers to uncover underlying issues, constraints, and opportunities that could inform the design process.

Continuous Improvement

Continuous Improvement refers to an ongoing, systematic process in the field of service design that focuses on identifying, analyzing, and implementing enhancements to a service to achieve better results. It is a proactive and systematic approach that involves making incremental improvements to a service over time, with the goal of continuously meeting and exceeding customer expectations. In the context of service design, continuous improvement requires a disciplined approach to collect and analyze data, identify areas of improvement, generate ideas, and implement changes. It involves monitoring key performance indicators (KPIs) to track the effectiveness of the service and identify opportunities for enhancement. Continuous improvement initiatives are typically driven by customer feedback, market trends, technological advancements, and operational efficiency goals. The process of continuous improvement typically follows a cycle known as the Plan-Do-Check-Act (PDCA) cycle or the Deming Cycle. In the planning phase, the service design team identifies the goals and objectives for improvement, collects data, and analyzes the current performance of the service. Based on the analysis, the team then develops improvement plans and strategies. In the doing phase, the team implements the planned changes and carefully monitors their impact on the service. Data is collected, and performance indicators are measured to assess the effectiveness of the changes. In the checking phase, the team analyzes the data collected during the doing phase and evaluates the results against the predefined goals and objectives. This analysis helps to determine the success of the changes and whether further improvements are required. Finally, in the acting phase, the team takes action based on the results of the analysis. If the changes were successful, they are integrated into the service design. If not, the team refines the plans and strategies and repeats the PDCA cycle until the desired level of improvement is achieved. Continuous improvement is a key element in service design as it allows organizations to adapt and evolve in response to changing customer needs, market dynamics, and technology advancements. By constantly seeking ways to enhance the service, organizations can stay ahead of competitors, increase customer satisfaction, and drive business growth.

Convergent Discovery

Convergent Discovery is a critical step in the Design Thinking process that involves narrowing down the possible solutions to a problem by systematically evaluating and selecting the most promising ideas. It focuses on converging and consolidating key findings and insights gained through the divergent exploration phase.

In this phase, design thinkers analyze and synthesize the multitude of information and ideas generated during the earlier stages. They sift through the diverse perspectives, opinions, and potential solutions to tease out the most relevant and feasible options. By applying various evaluation criteria, such as desirability, feasibility, and viability, they gradually converge on a smaller set of ideas or concepts that have the greatest potential for success.

This convergent decision-making process is often supported by tools and techniques that help visualize and compare different options objectively. These might include methods like decision grids, concept scoring, or SWOT analysis. By organizing and structuring their thinking, design thinkers can objectively assess the strengths and weaknesses of each potential solution and make informed decisions about which ones to pursue further.

Ultimately, the goal of Convergent Discovery is to distill a large range of possibilities into a manageable set of solutions that have the highest likelihood of addressing the identified problem. This focused selection allows design thinkers to move forward with more confidence, as they have intentionally narrowed down their options based on rational assessments and prioritization of their ideas.

Convergent Problem Solving

Convergent problem solving is a key aspect of the Design Thinking methodology, which aims to find innovative solutions to complex challenges. It is a disciplined approach that involves narrowing down options and making decisions based on a systematic evaluation of possibilities.

In the context of Design Thinking, convergent problem solving involves the synthesis and analysis of various ideas, insights, and concepts generated through the earlier stages of the design process, such as empathizing and defining the problem. It requires the team to converge their focus on a select few ideas or solutions that have the greatest potential for addressing the problem at hand.

Convergent Thinking

Convergent thinking is a critical aspect of Design Thinking, which refers to the process of bringing together different ideas, perspectives, and data to arrive at a single, optimal solution to a given problem or challenge. This approach promotes focused and systematic thinking aimed at reaching a consensus on the most suitable solution.

In the context of Design Thinking disciplines, convergent thinking involves narrowing down and refining a wide range of potential solutions generated during the earlier stages of the design process. This is achieved through careful evaluation, analysis, and comparison of ideas, considering various criteria such as feasibility, desirability, and viability.

Convergent thinking requires teams to converge their collective knowledge and expertise, fostering collaboration and interdisciplinary thinking. It involves synthesizing information, identifying patterns, and prioritizing essential aspects to make informed decisions that align with user needs and project goals.

By employing convergent thinking, designers can avoid getting stuck in an endless sea of possibilities and make progress towards a feasible, practical solution. It helps to overcome ambiguity and uncertainty, eventually leading to a refined and well-defined concept that can be converted into a tangible product, service, or experience.

Conversation Mapping

Conversation mapping is a technique used in service design to visually map out the interactions and conversations that occur between individuals or groups within a service ecosystem. It provides a way to understand the flow and dynamics of conversations, helping designers gain insights into the experiences, needs, and pain points of different stakeholders. By mapping out conversations, designers can identify gaps or inefficiencies in communication and collaboration, leading to improved service experiences. The process involves capturing the key moments, touchpoints, and information exchanged during conversations, as well as the emotions and intentions of the participants.

Conversion Rate Optimization (CRO)

Conversion Rate Optimization (CRO) is a process that aims to enhance the efficiency and effectiveness of a website or digital service design by increasing the percentage of visitors who take a desired action. It involves utilizing various data-driven techniques and insights to understand user behavior and make informed design modifications to improve conversion rates. CRO is based on the principle that every interaction with a website or digital service presents an opportunity to convert a user into a customer or achieve a specific goal. By analyzing user interactions and conducting experiments, CRO aims to identify friction points, optimize conversion funnels, and create a seamless user experience that encourages desired actions.

Cooperative Design

Cooperative Design is a collaborative approach within the discipline of Design Thinking that involves multiple stakeholders working together to create innovative solutions. It focuses on inclusivity and active participation, ensuring that all voices are heard and considered during the design process.

In Cooperative Design, the goal is to harness the collective intelligence and diverse perspectives of the participants to understand the problem at hand and generate creative solutions. This approach recognizes that no single individual has all the answers and that collaborative efforts yield more robust and effective outcomes.

Creative Collaboration

Creative collaboration is a central component of Design Thinking disciplines, which focuses on the collaborative process of generating innovative and user-centered solutions to complex problems. It involves the collective effort of a diverse group of individuals with different backgrounds, perspectives, and skill sets coming together to collaboratively ideate, iterate, and refine ideas.

In a creative collaboration, participants engage in open and constructive dialogue, fostering an environment that encourages the sharing of diverse viewpoints and facilitates the exploration of new possibilities. This approach helps to challenge assumptions, break down silos, and promote a mindset of curiosity and experimentation.

Creative Confidence

HTML stands for Hypertext Markup Language, and it is the standard markup language used for creating and structuring web pages. It consists of various elements and tags that are used to define the structure and content of a web page. Within the context of Design Thinking disciplines, Creative Confidence can be defined as the ability to trust in one's own creative capabilities and to approach problem-solving and innovation with a sense of courage and resilience. It involves being open to taking risks, embracing failure as a learning opportunity, and having the belief that creativity is a skill that can be developed and nurtured. Creative Confidence is an essential mindset when practicing Design Thinking because it encourages individuals to think beyond conventional boundaries and explore multiple perspectives in order to identify innovative solutions to complex problems. It encourages the exploration of new ideas and the willingness to challenge the status quo, all while fostering a spirit of collaboration and co-creation. By embracing Creative Confidence, individuals are empowered to overcome fear and self-doubt, enabling them to unleash their full creative potential. This mindset allows for the development of empathetic design solutions that address the needs and desires of end-users, generating meaningful and impactful outcomes. In conclusion, Creative Confidence is a fundamental aspect of Design Thinking disciplines, as it fuels the discovery and creation of innovative and user-centered solutions.

Creative Constraints Frameworks

A creative constraints framework is a tool used in the context of Design Thinking disciplines to stimulate innovative thinking and guide the design process. It provides a structured approach for designers to work within predefined boundaries, challenges, or limitations that can inspire creative solutions.

By imposing limitations or constraints, such as budget restrictions, time constraints, technological limitations, or specific user needs, designers are forced to think more critically and find unique and inventive solutions within these boundaries. The framework encourages designers to explore unconventional ideas, rethink assumptions, and push the boundaries of what is possible.

Creative Constraints Platforms

A creative constraints platform is a tool or platform that facilitates the application of creative constraints in the context of Design Thinking disciplines. Design Thinking is an iterative problem-solving approach used to generate innovative solutions that address users' needs and preferences.

Creative constraints are limitations or restrictions that are intentionally imposed on a design project to stimulate creativity and encourage innovative thinking. These constraints can be related to time, budget, resources, technology, or specific design requirements. By imposing constraints, designers are forced to think outside the box, explore alternative approaches, and come up with unique solutions.

A creative constraints platform provides a structured framework for designers to define and implement constraints throughout the design process. It typically includes features such as constraint definition, ideation tools, collaboration capabilities, and evaluation mechanisms. These platforms enable designers to explore different constraints and experiment with various techniques and methodologies to stimulate creativity.

The purpose of using a creative constraints platform is to foster innovation by challenging and stretching designers' creative abilities. It helps teams break free from conventional thinking and generate unique ideas that may not have emerged in the absence of constraints. By providing a systematic approach to implementing constraints, these platforms enable designers to effectively channel their creativity and develop inventive solutions that meet users' needs in novel and unexpected ways.

Creative Constraints Workshops

Creative Constraints Workshops are a method used within the Design Thinking disciplines to generate innovation and problem-solving solutions by imposing limitations or constraints on the design process. The purpose of these workshops is to encourage creativity and out-of-the-box thinking by challenging participants to work within a set of restrictions.

During the workshops, participants are given a creative problem or challenge to solve, along with a set of constraints that limit their options or resources for finding a solution. These constraints can include limitations on time, budget, materials, technology, or any other relevant factor. By imposing these limitations, the workshops aim to push participants to think creatively and find innovative solutions that they may not have considered if given unlimited resources.

Creative Constraints

Creative Constraints, in the context of Design Thinking disciplines, refer to intentional limitations or boundaries that are imposed on the design process to inspire innovation and encourage out-of-the-box thinking.

These constraints are not restrictions, but rather catalysts for creativity, promoting a focused and efficient ideation process. By defining specific limitations, such as budget, time, resources, or technical specifications, designers are forced to think creatively and strategically to find optimal solutions within these boundaries.

Creative Experimentation

Design Thinking is a problem-solving approach that emphasizes creative experimentation in order to generate innovative solutions. This discipline integrates various techniques and processes from diverse areas to tackle complex problems and develop user-centered designs.

At its core, creative experimentation in Design Thinking refers to the iterative process of generating and testing multiple ideas and concepts. It involves a willingness to take risks, think outside the box, and explore uncharted territories to arrive at novel solutions. Through this approach, designers are able to challenge assumptions, uncover new insights, and unlock innovative possibilities.

Creative Exploration

Design Thinking is a problem-solving methodology that uses a human-centric approach to tackle complex issues and find innovative solutions. It is a discipline that combines analytical thinking, creativity, and empathy to understand and address the needs of users or customers.

The process of Design Thinking typically involves five stages: Empathize, Define, Ideate, Prototype, and Test. During the Empathize stage, designers immerse themselves in the users' or customers' world to gain a deep understanding of their needs, emotions, and aspirations. The Define stage involves synthesizing the gathered information to identify the core challenges or opportunities that need to be addressed.

In the Ideate stage, designers generate a wide range of ideas to solve the defined problem, without judgment or criticism. The focus is on quantity rather than quality at this stage. These ideas are then narrowed down to a few promising concepts during the Prototype stage, where tangible representations of the potential solutions are created. These prototypes can be physical or digital, depending on the nature of the problem.

Finally, in the Test stage, the prototypes are evaluated and refined based on feedback from the users or customers. This iterative process allows designers to learn from failures, make necessary improvements, and eventually arrive at an optimal solution. Throughout the Design Thinking process, collaboration, iteration, and user-centricity are essential elements that enable designers to create meaningful and effective solutions.

Creative Expression

Design Thinking is a disciplined approach to problem-solving and innovation that incorporates human-centered design principles. It is a process-driven methodology that focuses on understanding the needs and wants of users, generating creative ideas, prototyping and testing solutions, and iterating until a successful outcome is achieved.

At its core, Design Thinking is about empathy, collaboration, and iteration. It starts by gaining a deep understanding of the people for whom we are designing, their experiences, and the context in which they operate. This empathetic understanding allows designers to uncover hidden insights and identify unmet needs and opportunities.

The collaborative nature of Design Thinking encourages cross-functional teams to come together and work collectively to generate a wide range of ideas. By involving diverse perspectives, expertise, and experiences, Design Thinking promotes the generation of innovative and unique solutions.

Finally, Design Thinking is iterative in nature, meaning that it is an ongoing process of learning and improvement. Designers create prototypes to quickly test and gather feedback on their ideas. This allows for rapid learning and refinement of solutions, leading to more effective and user-centric outcomes.

In conclusion, Design Thinking is a disciplined and process-driven approach to problem-solving and innovation. By focusing on empathy, collaboration, and iteration, it enables designers to create solutions that are truly human-centered and address the needs and wants of users.

Creative Problem Solving

Creative problem solving in the context of service design refers to the process of generating innovative and effective solutions to complex problems or challenges faced by service providers or users. It involves a structured approach that encourages the exploration of different perspectives, ideas, and possibilities. By leveraging a combination of analytical and creative thinking, creative problem solving aims to break free from traditional or conventional approaches and discover new ways of solving problems. It encourages individuals or teams to think outside the box and consider multiple viewpoints, exploring various potential solutions before settling on the most suitable one.

Critical Analysis

Design Thinking is a problem-solving approach that emphasizes empathy, collaboration, and iteration to create innovative solutions. It is a set of principles and practices rooted in the field of design that can be applied to various disciplines.

At its core, Design Thinking is characterized by a human-centered approach. It starts by understanding the needs, desires, and challenges of the people who will be using a product or service. This empathy-driven understanding helps to uncover insights and identify opportunities for improvement.

The collaboration aspect of Design Thinking involves bringing together individuals from diverse backgrounds and expertise to work together towards a common goal. By leveraging the diverse perspectives and knowledge of the team members, Design Thinking encourages multidisciplinary problem-solving and fosters creativity and innovation.

However, Design Thinking is not a linear process. It is iterative and encourages experimentation and learning from failures. Prototyping and testing are essential components of Design Thinking, as they allow ideas to be quickly validated and refined based on user feedback. This iterative approach ensures that the final solution is user-centric and meets the needs of the target audience.

Overall, Design Thinking is a mindset and a methodology that can be applied to a wide range of challenges. It promotes a holistic and user-centric approach to problem-solving, encourages collaboration and creativity, and fosters a culture of experimentation and learning.

Critical Incident Technique

The Critical Incident Technique (CIT) is a qualitative research method commonly used in service design to gather and analyze data about specific incidents or interactions that have had a significant impact on the customer experience. The technique involves collecting detailed accounts from individuals who have recently encountered a service failure or success, aiming to identify the key factors that contributed to these critical incidents. By focusing on specific incidents, the CIT allows designers to gain a deeper understanding of the customer's perspective and their emotional reactions throughout the service journey. This information can then be used to inform the design and improvement of services, ensuring that customer needs and expectations are met. The CIT helps to uncover both positive and negative critical incidents, providing valuable insights for service providers to develop strategies for enhancing customer satisfaction and loyalty.

Critical Inquiry

Critical Inquiry is a fundamental component of Design Thinking disciplines. It refers to the systematic and objective evaluation of ideas, concepts, and solutions in order to identify strengths, weaknesses, and potential improvements. Through critical inquiry, designers and teams can gain a deeper understanding of their design challenges and make informed decisions throughout the design process.

Critical inquiry involves asking probing questions, challenging assumptions, and exploring different perspectives. It requires the ability to analyze information, identify biases, and draw logical conclusions. This process helps designers to uncover hidden problems, discover innovative solutions, and refine their designs.

Critical Reflection

Critical reflection, within the context of Design Thinking disciplines, refers to the process of actively analyzing, evaluating, and questioning one's own thoughts, assumptions, and actions in order to gain deeper insights and improve future design solutions.

It involves a conscious and deliberate examination of the problem-solving process, considering alternative perspectives, and challenging established beliefs and assumptions. Critical reflection encourages designers to reflect on their own cognitive biases, preconceived notions, and personal and cultural influences that may impact their design decisions.

This practice is crucial in Design Thinking as it helps designers to identify potential limitations, biases, or blind spots that could hinder the effectiveness of their design process. By engaging in critical reflection, designers are able to gain a more comprehensive understanding of the problem at hand and develop innovative and inclusive design solutions.

Furthermore, critical reflection also enables designers to learn from their design failures and successes, allowing them to continuously improve their design thinking skills. It promotes a culture of continuous learning and growth within design teams, encouraging open-mindedness, adaptability, and creativity.

Critical Thinking

Critical thinking in the context of Design Thinking disciplines refers to the ability to analyze, evaluate, and synthesize information and ideas to make informed and rational design decisions.

It involves questioning assumptions, exploring multiple perspectives, and examining evidence to gain a deeper understanding of the design problem or challenge at hand. Critical thinking in design thinking is about being open-minded and curious, and being willing to challenge existing beliefs, preconceived notions, and established solutions.

Cross-Functional Teams

Cross-Functional Teams, in the context of service design, refer to groups of individuals from different functional areas or departments within an organization who come together to collaborate on solving a specific problem or delivering a specific service. These teams typically consist of members with diverse skillsets and expertise, representing various disciplines such as marketing, design, operations, finance, and customer service.The primary goal of cross-functional teams in service design is to ensure that all aspects of a service are taken into consideration and optimized for a seamless customer experience. By incorporating multiple perspectives and areas of expertise, these teams can identify potential challenges, explore new opportunities, and develop creative solutions to enhance service quality and meet customer needs.

Cultural Context Guides

Cultural Context Guides refer to the resources or tools that help designers understand and navigate the cultural aspects and nuances of a particular context when practicing Design Thinking. Design Thinking is a human-centered approach to problem-solving that involves empathy, experimentation, and collaboration.

When designers work on projects that involve different cultures or target specific cultural groups, it is crucial to consider the cultural context in order to create effective and meaningful solutions. Cultural Context Guides provide designers with insights, knowledge, and understanding of the cultural norms, values, beliefs, and practices that are relevant to the project at hand.

Cultural Context Workshops

A cultural context workshops refer to a collaborative and interactive session conducted within the framework of design thinking disciplines to understand and analyze the cultural aspects that influence the design process and final outcome. These workshops aim to deepen the designers' understanding of the target users' cultural background, values, beliefs, and preferences, enabling them to align their design solutions more effectively with the users' needs and expectations.

During cultural context workshops, designers engage in various activities such as interviews, observations, and group discussions to gain insights into the cultural nuances and context of the specific user community. These workshops often involve the participation of diverse stakeholders, including ethnographers, anthropologists, sociologists, and community representatives, who provide valuable input and perspectives.

Cultural Context

Cultural context in the discipline of Design Thinking refers to understanding and considering the cultural background, beliefs, values, and practices of individuals and communities during the design process. It involves recognizing and respecting the diverse perspectives and experiences that shape people's perceptions, behaviors, and needs.

By taking cultural context into account, designers can create solutions that are more inclusive, relevant, and effective. It allows designers to gain insights into the specific needs, preferences, and challenges of different cultural groups, and tailor their designs to better meet those diverse needs.

Cultural Probes

Cultural Probes are a method used in service design to gather in-depth insights and understandings about the cultural context, values, and experiences of users. They are a set of carefully designed and thought-provoking tools, presented to users as a means of self-expression, used to elicit personal responses and reflections. The main goal of Cultural Probes is to go beyond surface-level information and uncover the underlying attitudes, beliefs, and motivations of users. By providing users with open-ended and creative tasks, Cultural Probes encourage them to explore and express their thoughts and feelings about a particular service or context. This can include their desires, aspirations, frustrations, and everyday practices. Typically, Cultural Probes consist of a set of prompts or instructions, accompanied by a range of materials such as disposable cameras, diaries, postcards, maps, or questionnaires. Users are asked to interact with these materials over a specific period of time, usually a few days or weeks. They are encouraged to document aspects of their lives, experiences, and interactions that are relevant to the service being studied. The collected data from Cultural Probes is often rich and varied, providing designers with valuable insights into the unspoken needs, desires, and aspirations of their users. It helps designers gain a more holistic understanding of the cultural, social, and emotional aspects that influence the experience of a service. This deeper understanding enables designers to identify opportunities for improvement and innovation, ensuring that their service aligns with the values and expectations of users. Cultural Probes are particularly useful in service design as they foster empathy and engagement between designers and users. They allow users to express themselves in a way that is personal and meaningful to them, leading to more authentic and accurate insights. By encouraging users to become active participants in the design process, Cultural Probes empower them and give them a voice in shaping the services that affect their lives.

Cultural Probing

Cultural probing is a research method employed in the discipline of Design Thinking that involves immersing oneself in a specific culture or community to gain a deeper understanding of its beliefs, values, behaviors, and needs. It is a technique used to gather rich insights and empathize with the target audience, enabling designers to design innovative solutions that resonate with the culture they are designing for.

Unlike traditional market research methods that rely on surveys and interviews, cultural probing focuses on direct observation and engagement with the target culture. It involves spending time within the community, observing their daily routines, engaging in conversations, participating in activities, and documenting personal experiences. By immersing oneself in the culture, designers can gain a holistic and nuanced understanding of the target audience's context, preferences, challenges, and aspirations.

Cultural probing enables designers to uncover deep-seated cultural norms, values, and rituals that may not be easily expressed through traditional research methods. It helps generate meaningful insights that can inspire innovative design solutions tailored to the unique needs and aspirations of the target culture.

Overall, cultural probing is a powerful tool in the Design Thinking process as it empowers designers to approach their work with cultural sensitivity, empathy, and a deep understanding of the target audience. By gaining insights into the culture they are designing for, designers can create solutions that not only meet functional needs but also resonate with the cultural fabric of the community they serve.

Cultural Sensitivity Guides

Cultural sensitivity guides in the context of Design Thinking disciplines refer to frameworks or principles that aim to promote awareness, understanding, and respect for diverse cultural perspectives and practices.

These guides are designed to assist designers in creating inclusive and culturally appropriate solutions to problems and challenges. They emphasize the importance of considering the cultural context in which a product, service, or experience will be used or consumed.

Cultural Sensitivity

Cultural sensitivity refers to the ability to understand, appreciate, and respect the values, beliefs, and customs of different cultures. It is an important aspect of the design thinking discipline that aims to create inclusive and user-centered solutions.

In the context of design thinking, cultural sensitivity plays a vital role in ensuring that designs address the needs and preferences of diverse user groups. By considering cultural factors, such as language, symbols, and social norms, designers can create products, services, and experiences that are relevant and meaningful to a wide range of users.

Cultural Understanding

Cultural understanding refers to the ability to recognize, respect, and appreciate the diverse beliefs, values, customs, practices, and behaviors of different cultures. In the context of design thinking disciplines, cultural understanding plays a crucial role in creating inclusive and effective design solutions.

By understanding the cultural contexts in which a design solution will be implemented, designers can ensure that their creations are relevant, accessible, and meaningful to the intended users. This involves conducting research, engaging with diverse communities, and actively listening to the needs and perspectives of different cultural groups.

Curiosity

Design Thinking is an iterative problem-solving approach that combines empathy, creativity, and rationality to generate innovative solutions to complex challenges.

It is rooted in understanding and addressing the needs and desires of end-users through extensive research and user-centered design principles. Design Thinking involves a systematic process of discovery, interpretation, ideation, experimentation, and implementation, with a strong emphasis on collaboration and iteration.

Customer Acquisition Cost (CAC)

Customer Acquisition Cost (CAC) is a metric used in service design to determine the amount of money a company spends in order to acquire a new customer. It is an important measure for businesses as it helps in evaluating the effectiveness and efficiency of their marketing and sales activities. CAC is calculated by dividing the total expenses incurred for acquiring customers, including marketing and sales costs, by the number of new customers acquired during a specific time period. The formula for calculating CAC is: CAC = (Total Marketing and Sales Expenses) / (Number of New Customers Acquired) The marketing and sales expenses included in the calculation of CAC may include various costs such as advertising, promotional activities, sales team salaries, commission, and other related expenses. These costs are attributed to the acquisition of new customers and not to the retention or servicing of existing customers. The CAC metric provides valuable insights into the cost-effectiveness of different customer acquisition channels and strategies. By comparing the CAC for different channels or campaigns, companies can identify the most efficient and cost-effective methods of acquiring new customers. This information can be used to make informed decisions about resource allocation and budget planning. For example, if a company finds that their CAC is higher than the expected lifetime value (LTV) of a customer, it indicates that their customer acquisition efforts are not efficient or cost-effective. In such cases, the company may need to reassess its marketing strategies and tactics to reduce CAC and improve overall profitability. Monitoring CAC over time also helps businesses assess the impact of changes in their marketing and sales activities. If the CAC starts increasing, it may signify that the company's customer acquisition efforts are becoming less efficient or that the market conditions are changing. This allows businesses to make necessary adjustments and optimize their resources to maintain or improve customer acquisition efficiency.

Customer Advisory Boards

Customer Advisory Boards (CABs) are structured forums or groups comprised of selected customers who provide valuable insights and feedback to organizations in order to shape their service design. CABs are an essential component of user-centered service design, as they enable organizations to better understand customer needs, expectations, and preferences. CABs typically consist of a diverse group of customers from different segments or demographics. These customers are chosen based on their knowledge, experience, and their ability to provide constructive feedback. The number of members in a CAB can vary depending on the organization's size, scope, and objectives. The primary role of a CAB is to act as a bridge between the organization and its customers. It serves as a platform for customers to express their opinions, share their ideas, and discuss their experiences with the organization's services. This valuable feedback allows organizations to gain deeper insights into their customers' needs and desires, facilitating the design of more customer-centric services. During CAB meetings, which can be held on a regular basis, members are provided with opportunities to engage in open and candid discussions with the organization's representatives. These discussions can cover a wide range of topics, including service quality, innovation, problem resolution, and overall customer experience. CAB members are encouraged to share their perspectives, provide suggestions, and challenge existing assumptions, enabling organizations to gain fresh perspectives and identify areas for improvement. The feedback gathered through CABs serves as a critical input for organizations' service design processes. It helps identify areas where the organization's services are falling short and where improvements are required. CAB insights also contribute to the development of new service offerings, enhancements to existing services, and the implementation of innovative solutions that better meet customers' evolving needs. In summary, Customer Advisory Boards are structured and diverse customer forums that enable organizations to gain invaluable insights and feedback. By actively involving customers in the service design process, organizations can enhance their understanding of customer expectations and design services that truly meet their customers' needs, resulting in improved customer experiences and greater customer satisfaction.

Customer Archetypes

A customer archetype is a representation or model of a specific type of customer that is typically encountered in the context of service design. It helps designers understand and empathize with different types of customers in order to design better experiences and cater to their specific needs and expectations. Customer archetypes are created based on common characteristics, behaviors, and preferences observed in a specific group of customers. These archetypes are not meant to represent every individual customer, but rather serve as a general framework to guide the design process.

Customer Effort Score (CES)

The Customer Effort Score (CES) is a metric used in service design to measure the ease with which customers can interact with a company or complete a specific task. It is a quantitative measure that helps organizations evaluate the level of effort required by customers to navigate their products or services. CES is typically assessed through surveys or feedback forms that ask customers to rate their experience based on the level of effort they had to exert. The questions are designed to capture specific interactions or scenarios that customers may encounter during their journey, such as finding information, resolving issues, or making a purchase. The main objective of CES is to understand the customer's perspective and identify pain points or areas of improvement in the user experience. By measuring the level of effort required, organizations can assess the effectiveness of their service design and identify opportunities to reduce friction and enhance customer satisfaction. The CES metric is often represented on a scale, with respondents selecting a score that reflects their perception of effort. The scale can vary depending on the survey design, with options ranging from numerical scales (e.g., 1-5) to descriptive scales (e.g., easy to difficult). Organizations can analyze the CES data by segmenting it based on different customer profiles or touchpoints. This allows them to identify specific areas that require attention and allocate resources accordingly. For example, if a certain customer segment consistently reports high levels of effort when interacting with customer support, the organization can focus on improving the support process and training their agents to reduce friction. The CES metric is valuable for service designers as it provides actionable insights to enhance the user experience and improve customer loyalty. By reducing customer effort, organizations can increase customer satisfaction and loyalty, ultimately leading to higher retention rates and positive word-of-mouth recommendations.

Customer Empathy Maps

A Customer Empathy Map is a visual tool used in service design to help organizations gain a better understanding of their customers' needs, motivations, and experiences. It provides a holistic view of the customer by capturing both their thoughts and emotions in various stages of their interaction with the service. The empathy map is divided into four quadrants, each representing a different aspect of the customer's experience: 1. Seeing & Hearing: This quadrant captures the sensory inputs that the customer receives during their interaction with the service. It encompasses the physical environment they are in, the people they come into contact with, and the information they receive through various channels. By understanding what the customer sees and hears, organizations can identify opportunities to enhance the visual and auditory aspects of their service delivery. 2. Saying & Doing: This quadrant focuses on the customer's actions and verbal expressions. It explores what the customer says and does during their interaction with the service. It helps organizations understand the customer's behaviors and attitudes towards the service, enabling them to align their offerings with the customer's expectations. 3. Thinking & Feeling: This quadrant delves into the customer's thoughts and emotions throughout their journey. It captures their concerns, desires, and motivations, as well as any pain points or moments of delight they may experience. By understanding what the customer thinks and feels, organizations can design experiences that resonate with the customer on an emotional level. 4. Pains & Gains: This quadrant highlights the customer's pain points and areas of gain during their interaction with the service. It helps organizations identify the obstacles and challenges that customers face and the opportunities to create value for them. By addressing the customer's pain points and providing solutions to their problems, organizations can enhance the overall customer experience and build long-lasting relationships.

The Customer Empathy Map is a powerful tool that fosters empathy within organizations, enabling them to design customer-centric services. It provides a deeper understanding of the customer by capturing their needs, motivations, and experiences. By using the empathy map, organizations can identify opportunities to improve their service delivery and create more meaningful and relevant experiences for their customers.

Customer Empathy Tools

Customer Empathy Tools are instruments or techniques used in the context of Design Thinking disciplines to gain a deep understanding of customers' needs, desires, and emotions, in order to develop meaningful and impactful solutions. These tools enable designers and researchers to empathize with customers by stepping into their shoes, so as to uncover hidden insights and generate innovative ideas.

Design Thinking is a human-centered approach to problem-solving that emphasizes understanding and addressing the needs of the end-users. Customer Empathy Tools are essential for designers to go beyond surface-level understanding and to truly connect with customers on an emotional level. By empathizing with customers, designers can identify pain points, desires, values, and motivations that are often unspoken or subconscious.

Some examples of Customer Empathy Tools include:

- User Interviews: Conducting open-ended interviews with customers to understand their experiences, preferences, and challenges.

- Observational Research: Actively observing and documenting customers' behaviors and interactions in real-life situations, to uncover deeper insights.

- Empathy Maps: Creating visual representations of customers' thoughts, feelings, actions, and needs, to better understand their perspectives.

- Personas: Developing fictional character profiles based on research data, representing different types of customers, to personalize the design process.

- Journey Mapping: Mapping out the customer's entire experience, from initial touchpoints to end goals, to identify opportunities for improvement.

Overall, Customer Empathy Tools play a crucial role in Design Thinking by helping designers gain a deep understanding of customers and their needs. By uncovering and addressing these needs, designers can develop solutions that are truly user-centered and create meaningful impact.

Customer Empathy

Customer empathy is a key concept in the discipline of Design Thinking. It refers to the ability of designers to understand and truly connect with the thoughts, emotions, and experiences of the customers they are designing for. It is about putting oneself in the shoes of the customers, and truly seeing the world from their perspective.

This empathy is crucial in the design process as it allows designers to gain deep insights into the needs, desires, and challenges of the customers. By truly understanding the customers, designers are able to create solutions that truly meet their needs and provide them with a great user experience.

Customer Experience (CX)

Customer Experience (CX) in the context of service design refers to the overall interaction and perception a customer has with a company or brand throughout their entire journey across multiple touchpoints. It encompasses all the emotions, thoughts, and behaviors that a customer experiences before, during, and after engaging with a company's products or services. The goal of designing customer experiences is to create meaningful and memorable interactions that exceed customer expectations, build loyalty, and drive customer satisfaction. It involves understanding and addressing customer needs, desires, and preferences throughout every step of the customer journey. A successful CX design takes into consideration various factors, such as user interface design, usability, accessibility, branding, and communication. It involves understanding the target audience, their motivations, and pain points, and then designing an experience that not only meets their needs but also evokes positive emotions and leaves a lasting impression. Service design plays a crucial role in shaping the customer experience. It involves designing and optimizing all the touchpoints and channels through which customers interact with a company, including physical spaces, digital platforms, customer support systems, and any other point of contact. Service design aims to ensure that each touchpoint is seamless, relevant, and aligned with the company's brand values and customer expectations. Furthermore, service design also involves considering the entire customer journey as a holistic experience, rather than focusing only on individual touchpoints. This approach ensures that every interaction is connected and consistent, enabling customers to navigate effortlessly and receive consistent quality of service across all touchpoints. In conclusion, customer experience (CX) in the context of service design encompasses the end-to-end experience a customer has with a company or brand. It involves understanding customer needs, designing meaningful interactions, and optimizing touchpoints to create a seamless and memorable experience that drives customer satisfaction, loyalty, and ultimately, business growth.

Customer Experience Mapping

Customer Experience Mapping is a service design tool used to visually represent and analyze the interactions and touchpoints between a customer and a service or product. It provides a comprehensive understanding of the customer journey, highlighting key moments of interaction, emotions, and pain points. Customer Experience Mapping typically involves the following steps: 1. Define the scope and objectives: Identify the specific service or product that will be mapped, as well as the objectives of the mapping exercise. This could be improving customer satisfaction, identifying areas of improvement, or enhancing the overall customer experience. 2. Gather customer insights: Conduct research and collect data to gain insights into customer behavior, needs, and expectations. This can be done through interviews, surveys, observations, or analyzing existing data. 3. Identify touchpoints: Identify all the touchpoints or points of interaction between the customer and the service or product. This could include physical locations, digital platforms, customer service interactions, or any other points of contact. 4. Map the customer journey: Create a visual representation of the customer journey, illustrating each touchpoint and the actions, emotions, and pain points experienced by the customer at each stage. This can be done using diagrams, flowcharts, or other visual tools. 5. Analyze and identify opportunities: Analyze the customer journey map to identify areas of improvement and opportunities to enhance the customer experience. This may involve identifying pain points, bottlenecks, or moments of delight. 6. Develop actionable insights: Based on the analysis, develop actionable insights and recommendations for improving the customer experience. This could include changes to processes, systems, or touchpoints, as well as opportunities for innovation or personalization. Overall, Customer Experience Mapping is a powerful tool that helps service designers and organizations gain a deeper understanding of their customers, enabling them to create more meaningful and tailored experiences that drive customer satisfaction and loyalty.

Customer Feedback Analysis Tools

A customer feedback analysis tool is a software or platform that helps businesses collect, organize, and analyze customer feedback data in order to gain insights that inform design and decision-making processes. It is an essential tool in the context of Design Thinking disciplines, as it enables organizations to understand the needs, preferences, and experiences of their customers effectively. By utilizing such tools, companies can collect feedback from various sources, such as surveys, social media, and customer service interactions, and analyze it to identify patterns, trends, and actionable insights.

These tools often offer features like sentiment analysis, text mining, and data visualization, allowing businesses to interpret and summarize large amounts of feedback data efficiently. They enable designers and decision-makers to distill critical information and identify pain points, opportunities, and areas for improvement. Customer feedback analysis tools also provide metrics and metrics tracking, allowing organizations to measure customer satisfaction and track the impact of design decisions over time.

Customer Feedback Analytics

Customer Feedback Analytics in the context of Design Thinking disciplines refers to the systematic analysis and interpretation of customer feedback data to gain valuable insights and inform the design process. It involves the collection, examination, and visualization of customer feedback data, such as surveys, reviews, and social media comments, to understand customer needs, preferences, and pain points.

By applying analytical techniques and tools, designers can identify patterns, trends, and correlations in customer feedback data. This allows them to uncover underlying customer needs and expectations, and make data-driven design decisions. Customer Feedback Analytics also helps in prioritizing design improvements based on the most critical customer issues or desires identified through the analysis.

The key aspect of Customer Feedback Analytics in Design Thinking is its human-centered approach. It focuses on empathizing with customers, understanding their experiences, and capturing their perspectives through their feedback. By analyzing this feedback, designers can gain a deep understanding of their target users and create solutions that truly meet their needs.

In summary, Customer Feedback Analytics in Design Thinking disciplines enables designers to make better informed decisions by turning raw customer feedback data into actionable insights. It enhances the design process by providing a foundation of customer knowledge, ultimately leading to the creation of innovative and successful products or services.

Customer Feedback Loops

A customer feedback loop is a process in service design that involves actively seeking and incorporating feedback from customers to continuously improve and enhance the overall customer experience. During the design and implementation of a service, a feedback loop allows organizations to gather insights and perspectives from their customers, enabling them to make informed decisions and optimize their service delivery. It helps organizations identify potential areas of improvement, address customer pain points, and align their services with customer preferences and expectations.

Customer Feedback Platforms

A customer feedback platform is a tool or software that allows businesses to collect, analyze, and manage feedback from their customers. It is an essential component in the context of Design Thinking disciplines as it enables businesses to understand and incorporate the needs, desires, and opinions of their customers in the design and development of products, services, and experiences.

Design Thinking is a human-centered approach to problem-solving that focuses on empathy, ideation, prototyping, and testing. It emphasizes the importance of understanding users' needs and preferences throughout the design process. A customer feedback platform plays a crucial role in this process by providing a systematic way to gather and analyze feedback directly from customers.

By utilizing a customer feedback platform, businesses can gather insights about the customer experience, identify pain points, and uncover areas for improvement. This feedback can be used to iterate and refine design concepts, ensuring that the final product or service meets the needs and expectations of the customers.

The platform enables businesses to collect feedback through various channels, such as surveys, online reviews, social media mentions, and customer support interactions. It organizes and analyzes the feedback, allowing businesses to identify patterns, trends, and key insights. These insights can then inform the decision-making process and guide the design and development of future iterations.

In summary, a customer feedback platform is an essential tool for businesses practicing Design

Thinking. It facilitates the incorporation of user feedback throughout the design process and supports the creation of user-centered solutions that meet customer needs and preferences.

Customer Feedback Surveys

Customer feedback surveys are a valuable tool within the context of Design Thinking disciplines. These surveys are structured questionnaires designed to gather feedback and insights from customers about their experiences with a product, service, or overall customer journey. The aim is to collect data and opinions directly from customers, allowing businesses to understand their needs, preferences, and pain points in order to improve and enhance their offerings.

Customer feedback surveys typically consist of a series of questions that cover various aspects of the customer experience, such as usability, satisfaction, perceived value, and areas of improvement. The questions are carefully crafted to elicit specific, actionable feedback that can guide decision-making and design iterations. They may include multiple-choice questions, open-ended questions, rating scales, or Likert scales to measure opinions and attitudes.

The data collected from these surveys is then quantitatively or qualitatively analyzed to identify trends, patterns, and common themes. This analysis helps businesses gain a deeper understanding of customer perceptions and priorities, enabling them to make informed design decisions based on real customer needs.

By engaging customers in the design process through feedback surveys, businesses can foster a user-centered approach, aligning their offerings to meet customer expectations and preferences. This iterative feedback loop is a fundamental aspect of Design Thinking, allowing businesses to continuously improve their products and services based on real user insights.

Customer Feedback Workshops

Customer Feedback Workshops are a collaborative and structured approach to gathering valuable insights and feedback from customers in order to inform the design and development of products, services, or experiences. These workshops typically follow the principles of Design Thinking, a human-centered problem-solving approach that emphasizes empathy, ideation, prototyping, and testing.

In a Customer Feedback Workshop, a diverse group of stakeholders, including designers, product managers, marketers, and customer service representatives, come together with the goal of gaining a deeper understanding of the customers' needs, desires, and pain points. The workshop facilitator guides participants through a series of activities and exercises designed to elicit feedback and generate insights.

During the workshop, participants may engage in activities such as empathy mapping, where they step into the shoes of the customer to gain a deeper understanding of their thoughts, feelings, and motivations. They may also conduct interviews or surveys to gather qualitative and quantitative data, respectively. Through interactive exercises such as brainstorming and idea generation, participants collaboratively explore potential solutions to address the identified customer needs.

The insights and feedback gathered from the Customer Feedback Workshop are then used to inform the design and development process. Designers and other stakeholders use this information to refine existing prototypes or develop new ones. The iterative nature of Design Thinking allows for continual testing and refinement, ensuring that the final product, service, or experience meets the customers' needs and expectations.

Customer Feedback

Customer feedback in the context of service design refers to the information, opinions, and suggestions provided by customers regarding their experiences and interactions with a service. It plays a crucial role in understanding and improving the overall quality, efficiency, and customer satisfaction of a service. By collecting and analyzing customer feedback, service designers can gain valuable insights into the strengths and weaknesses of their service. This feedback can be obtained through various channels such as surveys, interviews, online reviews, and social media platforms. One of the primary benefits of customer feedback is its ability to identify areas of improvement. By understanding the specific pain points and challenges faced by customers, service designers can make targeted adjustments to enhance the service experience. This can include refining processes, streamlining operations, or introducing new features that address customer needs and preferences. Additionally, customer feedback can also act as a driving force for innovation. By actively listening to customers, service designers can identify emerging trends, market demands, and potential opportunities for enhancement or expansion. This can enable them to stay ahead of the competition and continually adapt their services to meet changing customer expectations. Moreover, customer feedback serves as a valuable tool for measuring customer satisfaction and loyalty. By regularly collecting feedback and tracking customer sentiment over time, service designers can monitor the effectiveness of their service improvements and identify any areas that require further attention. Positive feedback can also serve as testimonials and marketing resources, generating trust and attracting new customers. In conclusion, customer feedback is a vital component of service design, as it provides valuable insights for improving the quality, efficiency, and customer satisfaction of the service. By actively seeking and utilizing customer feedback, service designers can make informed decisions and adjustments that drive continuous improvement and ensure the delivery of exceptional customer experiences.

Customer Insight Analytics

Customer Insight Analytics is a critical component of Design Thinking disciplines that involves the systematic collection and analysis of customer data to gain a deep understanding of their needs, preferences, and behaviors. It provides valuable insights that can inform and drive the design process, enabling designers to create products, services, and experiences that are tailored to meet the specific requirements and desires of their target customers.

By leveraging various analytical techniques and tools, such as data mining, predictive modeling, and statistical analysis, Customer Insight Analytics helps designers uncover meaningful patterns and trends in the data, allowing them to identify the key drivers of customer satisfaction and dissatisfaction. This knowledge enables designers to make informed design decisions, prioritize features and functionalities, and iterate on their designs based on real customer feedback and preferences.

Customer Insight Platforms

Customer Insight Platforms are strategic tools used in service design that help businesses gather, analyze, and interpret data to gain a deep understanding of their customers' needs, preferences, and behaviors. These platforms offer a comprehensive set of features and functionalities that enable businesses to collect customer data from various touchpoints, such as surveys, social media, website analytics, and customer feedback, and merge them into a single unified view. By utilizing customer insight platforms, businesses are able to track and measure customer interactions, identify patterns and trends, and make data-driven decisions to enhance the customer experience. These platforms provide businesses with the ability to segment their customers based on different criteria, such as demographics, purchasing behavior, and preferences, allowing businesses to tailor their services to specific customer segments.

Customer Insights Analysis

Customer insights analysis in the context of service design refers to the process of examining and interpreting data collected from customers to gain a deeper understanding of their behaviors, preferences, and needs. It involves the systematic analysis of qualitative and quantitative data to uncover actionable insights that can inform and improve the design of customer experiences and service offerings. In service design, customer insights analysis plays a crucial role in helping organizations make informed decisions about how to design and deliver services that meet the needs and expectations of their customers. By understanding customers at a deeper level, organizations can identify pain points, gaps in service delivery, and opportunities for innovation.

Customer Journey Mapping

Customer journey mapping is a service design tool that visually depicts the entire experience a customer has with a service or product. It seeks to understand and analyze the various touchpoints and interactions the customer goes through, from the initial awareness stage to the final post-purchase stage. The process of customer journey mapping involves researching and gathering data about customer interactions and emotions at each touchpoint, then organizing and structuring this information into a visual representation. The resulting map shows the entire customer journey, highlighting key moments, pain points, and opportunities for improvement.

Customer Journey

A customer journey is a term used in service design to describe the complete experience that a customer goes through when interacting with a specific service or product. It encompasses all the touchpoints and interactions between the customer and the service provider, from the initial awareness and consideration stages, through the purchase and usage stages, to the post-purchase stages of loyalty and advocacy. The customer journey is often visualized as a series of steps or stages, with each stage representing a different phase of the customer's experience. These stages may include awareness, research, evaluation, purchase, onboarding, support, and re-engagement. The specific stages and their order may vary depending on the nature of the service or product, as well as the target customer segment. Throughout the customer journey, the goal of service design is to create a seamless and positive experience for the customer, with the ultimate aim of meeting or exceeding their expectations. This involves understanding the customer's needs, motivations, and pain points at each stage of the journey, and designing the service in a way that addresses these effectively. By mapping out the customer journey, service designers can identify potential pain points, gaps in the service offering, and opportunities for improvement. This can lead to the implementation of strategies and initiatives that enhance the overall customer experience and drive customer satisfaction, retention, and loyalty. It is worth noting that the customer journey is not a linear or one-size-fits-all process. Different customers may have different paths and interactions with the service, influenced by factors such as their individual needs, preferences, and circumstances. Therefore, service designers need to take a customer-centric approach, understanding the various customer personas and designing for their specific journeys. In summary, a customer journey in the context of service design refers to the complete end-to-end experience that a customer has when interacting with a service or product. It involves understanding the customer's needs, designing the service to meet these needs, and continuously improving the customer experience based on feedback and insights.

Customer Pain Points

Customer Pain Points are specific issues or challenges that customers face when engaging with a product or service. These pain points can range from small inconveniences to significant obstacles that hinder the customer experience and satisfaction. They are usually identified through various research methods such as customer interviews, surveys, and feedback analysis. Pain points can be categorized into different types, including functional, emotional, and process-related. Functional pain points refer to difficulties or limitations in the product or service's performance, functionality, or features. Examples of functional pain points could be a slow website loading speed, a complicated user interface, or a lack of certain functionalities that customers desire. Emotional pain points, on the other hand, focus on the negative emotions or frustrations that customers may have during the customer journey. These may arise from poor customer service, unresponsive communication channels, or a lack of personalization in the experience. Emotional pain points are crucial because they can strongly influence customer loyalty and brand perception. Process-related pain points are related to inefficiencies or complications in the customer journey. This could include long waiting times, complicated onboarding processes, or complex return policies. These pain points can create disillusionment and dissatisfaction for customers, leading to a negative overall experience. In service design, identifying and addressing customer pain points is essential for creating a customer-centric and user-friendly experience. By understanding the specific challenges and frustrations customers face, businesses can tailor their products and services to better meet customer needs and expectations. This can be done through implementing improvements, redesigning processes, or adding new features that directly address the identified pain points. By effectively resolving these issues, businesses can enhance customer satisfaction, loyalty, and ultimately drive business growth.

Customer Persona

A customer persona in the context of service design refers to a fictional representation of a target customer segment. It is a detailed profile created based on research and analysis of customer data and insights. The purpose of developing customer personas is to gain a deep understanding of customers' characteristics, needs, goals, behaviors, and preferences. To create a customer persona, service designers collect and analyze various sources of information, such as demographic data, psychographic factors, customer feedback, observations, and interviews. These insights are used to define the persona's attributes, including age, gender, occupation, income level, education, interests, values, motivations, pain points, and communication habits. The customer persona is usually given a descriptive name and presented with a photo or illustration to make it more relatable. The persona profile often includes a brief biography, highlighting key aspects of the persona's lifestyle, background, and context. This helps designers to empathize with the customers and consider their unique perspectives throughout the service design process. Customer personas act as an important tool for service designers as they help align design decisions with users' needs and aspirations. Personas bring the customer segment to life, enabling designers to prioritize and tailor their solutions to cater to specific customer groups. They help the design team understand user journeys, uncover pain points, and identify opportunities for improvement. Service designers rely on customer personas to ensure that their solutions are user-centered and address the specific needs and expectations of the target customer segment. Personas also facilitate effective communication and collaboration among stakeholders by providing a shared understanding of the customer base.

Customer Profiling

The term "customer profiling" refers to the process of gathering and analyzing information about a target market or specific group of customers in order to understand their characteristics, needs, preferences, and behavior. It is an essential aspect of service design, as it provides valuable insights that can inform the development and improvement of products and services. Customer profiling involves collecting data through various methods, such as surveys, interviews, and observations, to create a comprehensive profile of the target customers. This profile typically includes demographic information (e.g., age, gender, location, income), psychographic information (e.g., values, interests, lifestyle), and behavioral information (e.g., buying habits, usage patterns, brand loyalty).

Customer Relationship Management (CRM)

CRM refers to Customer Relationship Management, which is a strategic approach that focuses on managing and nurturing relationships with customers. In the context of service design, CRM plays a crucial role in enhancing customer experiences, improving service quality, and increasing customer satisfaction. CRM involves the use of various technologies, tools, and processes to effectively manage customer interactions throughout their journey with a company or organization. It aims to create and maintain a positive and personalized relationship with customers by understanding their needs and expectations and delivering tailored services. One aspect of CRM is customer data management, which involves collecting, storing, and analyzing customer information. This data may include contact details, purchase history, preferences, and feedback. By having access to this data, businesses can gain insights into customer behavior, trends, and patterns, which can help in identifying opportunities for improving the service design and delivering a more personalized experience. CRM also includes customer engagement strategies. This involves developing and implementing communication channels that allow businesses to engage with customers on various platforms, such as social media, email, or online chat. By being present and available on these platforms, businesses can build trust and loyalty, provide timely assistance, and address customer concerns or inquiries promptly. Additionally, CRM encompasses customer service management. This involves streamlining and optimizing customer service processes to ensure prompt and efficient resolution of customer issues and complaints. By providing excellent customer service, organizations can not only address customer concerns but also enhance customer satisfaction and loyalty. Another important aspect of CRM is sales force automation. This involves automating and streamlining sales processes, such as lead generation, opportunity tracking, and order management. By using technology and automation tools, businesses can streamline their sales processes, improve sales forecasting accuracy, and enhance sales team productivity, leading to improved service design and customer satisfaction. Overall, CRM is an essential component of service design as it helps businesses understand their customers, meet their expectations, and deliver personalized services. By effectively managing customer relationships, organizations can create long-term customer loyalty, drive customer engagement, and ultimately achieve business success.

Customer Satisfaction (CSAT)

Customer Satisfaction (CSAT) refers to the measure of how well a product or service meets or exceeds customer expectations. It is an essential metric used in service design to evaluate the level of satisfaction that customers experience throughout their journey with a business. CSAT is typically measured through surveys or feedback forms that ask customers to rate their satisfaction on a scale, often ranging from "very unsatisfied" to "very satisfied." The data collected from these surveys is then used to calculate a CSAT score, which provides insights into the overall satisfaction of customers. The CSAT score plays a crucial role in service design as it helps businesses identify areas of improvement and make informed decisions to enhance the customer experience. By monitoring CSAT scores, organizations can determine whether their products or services meet customer needs and expectations, and identify areas where adjustments or enhancements are required. By continuously monitoring CSAT scores and acting upon feedback, companies can improve customer satisfaction, which, in turn, contributes to higher customer loyalty, repeat business, and positive word-of-mouth referrals. Conversely, low CSAT scores indicate areas of dissatisfaction that need to be addressed to prevent customer attrition and negative reviews. In service design, CSAT is often used alongside other metrics such as Net Promoter Score (NPS) and Customer Effort Score (CES) to gain a comprehensive understanding of the customer experience. While NPS measures customer loyalty and CES evaluates the amount of effort required to interact with a company, CSAT provides a direct measure of satisfaction, enabling businesses to assess the impact of their efforts to meet customer expectations. Ultimately, the goal of service design is to deliver exceptional experiences that fully satisfy customers. By utilizing CSAT as a key performance indicator, businesses can pinpoint areas for improvement, optimize their processes, and create experiences that leave customers delighted and loyal.

Customer Scenarios

A customer scenario, in the context of service design, refers to a detailed description of a specific situation or interaction between a customer and a service provider. It is used to gain a better understanding of the customer's needs, expectations, and experiences throughout their journey with the service. A customer scenario typically includes information about the customer's motivations, goals, and pain points, as well as the various touchpoints and channels they encounter during their interaction with the service. It helps service designers identify and address any potential issues or opportunities for improvement in order to create a more seamless and positive customer experience.

Customer Segmentation

Customer Segmentation is a method used in service design to divide a large customer base into smaller, distinct groups based on shared characteristics, needs, and preferences. This process helps businesses understand their customers better and tailor their products, services, and experiences to meet the specific requirements of each segment. Segmenting customers allows businesses to create targeted marketing strategies, improve customer satisfaction, and enhance the overall customer experience. By identifying distinct customer segments, businesses can identify the unique attributes and behaviors that define each group. This information enables them to develop personalized marketing messages, design customized products and services, and deliver personalized experiences that resonate with each segment's specific needs and desires.

Customer Surveys

Customer Surveys are an essential tool in service design that allows organizations to gather feedback and insights from their customers to improve and enhance their products or services.

These surveys consist of a series of predefined questions aimed at collecting specific information and opinions about the customer's experience. The primary purpose of customer surveys is to gather qualitative and quantitative data to understand customer perceptions, preferences, and satisfaction levels. By asking specific questions, organizations can gain valuable insights into various aspects of their products or services, including customer service, pricing, usability, and overall satisfaction. This information helps businesses identify areas of improvement and make data-driven decisions to enhance the overall customer experience.

Customer Touchpoint Optimization

Customer touchpoint optimization refers to the process of enhancing and refining all the interactions and touchpoints that a customer has with a business or service. It involves analyzing and improving each interaction point to create a seamless and positive customer experience. The goal of customer touchpoint optimization is to ensure that every interaction, whether it is online, offline, or through a customer service representative, is consistently excellent and aligns with the overall brand image and customer expectations. By optimizing touchpoints, businesses can create a cohesive and satisfying customer journey that ultimately leads to customer satisfaction, loyalty, and advocacy.

Customer Touchpoints

Customer touchpoints refer to the various points of interaction between a customer and a company throughout their customer journey. These touchpoints can occur through multiple channels, such as in-person interactions, phone calls, emails, social media, and website visits. In the context of service design, customer touchpoints play a crucial role in shaping the overall customer experience. They provide opportunities for companies to understand and meet their customers' needs, as well as leave a lasting impression on them.

Customer-Centered Design

Customer-centered design, also known as user-centered design, is a key principle within the discipline of Design Thinking. It is an iterative process that aims to create products, services, and experiences that meet the needs and desires of customers or end users. This approach places the customer or user at the center of the design process, focusing on empathy, collaboration, and continuous feedback.

The customer-centered design process typically involves several stages, including understanding the customer, ideation, prototyping, testing, and iteration. The first stage involves gaining a deep understanding of the customer through research, observation, and interviews. This helps designers to uncover insights into customers' needs, motivations, and pain points.

Based on these insights, the next stage involves generating a wide range of ideas and solutions through brainstorming and collaboration. These ideas are then refined and transformed into prototypes, which can be anything from physical models to digital mock-ups. Prototypes are used to gather feedback and insights from customers through testing and observation.

Finally, the design team iterates and refines the prototypes based on the feedback received, continuing to involve the customer throughout the process. This iterative nature ensures that the final design solution truly meets the needs of the customer and provides a seamless user experience.

Overall, customer-centered design is a human-centered approach that prioritizes the needs and wants of customers. By involving the customer in every step of the design process, designers can create solutions that truly resonate with their target audience and drive positive outcomes.

Customer-Centric Design

Customer-Centric Design is an approach in service design that places the needs, preferences, and experiences of customers at the forefront of the design process. It focuses on understanding and empathizing with customers to create personalized and meaningful solutions that meet their specific needs. Customer-Centric Design involves gathering insights about customers through various research methods such as interviews, observations, and surveys.

These insights help designers gain a deep understanding of customers' goals, motivations, behaviors, and pain points. By identifying and comprehending these factors, designers can develop services that address customers' needs effectively. The process of Customer-Centric Design involves multiple stages. Firstly, designers gather qualitative and quantitative data about customers, seeking to understand their desires and expectations. Next, this data is analyzed and synthesized to identify patterns, trends, and common pain points that customers face. This analysis forms the foundation for designing solutions that directly address these customer needs. Designers then work on ideating and prototyping potential service solutions, considering both the functional aspects of the service, as well as the emotional and experiential elements. The prototypes are tested and validated with customers, allowing them to provide feedback, insights, and suggestions for further improvement. This iterative process ensures that the final service design aligns with the customers' expectations and expectations. Customer-Centric Design recognizes that customers are not homogeneous—their needs, preferences, and experiences may vary. Therefore, it focuses on creating flexible and adaptable service designs that can be customized for different customer segments. It aims to create a seamless and positive experience for customers throughout their journey with the service, ensuring their satisfaction and loyalty. By adopting a Customer-Centric Design approach, organizations can differentiate themselves from competitors by providing exceptional and tailored services. It enhances customer engagement and brand perception, leading to increased customer satisfaction and loyalty. Ultimately, Customer-Centric Design enables organizations to deliver services that truly meet the needs and expectations of their customers, driving business growth and success.

Customer-Centric

A customer-centric approach in the context of Design Thinking disciplines refers to organizations focusing on meeting the needs and wants of their customers through the entire design process. It involves understanding the preferences, expectations, and challenges of customers before developing products or services. By putting the customer at the center of the design process, organizations can create solutions that resonate with their target market and deliver value.

This customer-centric approach involves a deep understanding of the customer's needs and desires. It requires organizations to engage in extensive research and observation to gain insights into their customers' context, behaviors, and motivations. Design thinkers actively seek to empathize with customers to uncover unmet needs and pain points that can be addressed through the design of their offerings.

Customer-Centricity

Customer-Centricity, in the context of service design, refers to the approach of placing the customer at the center of the design process and focusing on creating solutions that meet their specific needs and preferences. It involves understanding the customer's goals, motivations, and expectations, and using this knowledge to design services that are tailored to their unique requirements. Customer-centric service design aims to create an exceptional customer experience by considering every touchpoint and interaction the customer has with the service.

Cynefin Framework

The Cynefin Framework is a model used in service design to understand and categorize complex problems and situations. Developed by Dave Snowden, the framework helps in determining the most appropriate approach or solution based on the level of complexity and uncertainty present in a particular context. The framework consists of five domains or contexts, namely Simple, Complicated, Complex, Chaotic, and Disorder. Each domain represents a different level of complexity and requires a different management approach.

Data Visualization

Data visualization in the context of service design refers to the process of representing data and information in a visual format for the purpose of gaining insights, communicating, and making informed decisions. It involves transforming complex data sets into visual representations that are easy to understand and interpret. By using visual elements such as charts, graphs, and maps, data visualization allows service designers to analyze patterns, trends, and relationships within the data. It provides a means to explore and present information in a way that is visually appealing and accessible to a wide range of stakeholders.

Data-Driven Decision Making

Data-driven decision making in the context of service design refers to the practice of using data and information to inform and guide the design and implementation of services, with the goal of improving their effectiveness and efficiency. It involves the systematic collection, analysis, and interpretation of data from various sources to generate actionable insights and support informed decision making. By leveraging data, service designers can gain a deeper understanding of user needs, preferences, and behaviors. This helps them identify opportunities for improvement and make informed decisions about service concepts, features, and workflows. Data-driven decision making allows service designers to validate assumptions, test hypotheses, and measure the impact of design changes on key performance indicators.

Data-Driven Design Thinking

Data-Driven Design Thinking is a discipline within the field of Design Thinking that emphasizes the use of data and analytics to inform the design process. It involves incorporating quantitative and qualitative data into the various stages of the design thinking process, including empathizing, defining, ideating, prototyping, and testing.

This approach recognizes that data can provide valuable insights and guide decision-making in design. By leveraging data, designers can better understand user needs, preferences, and behaviors, and make more informed design decisions. This, in turn, can lead to the creation of more effective and impactful solutions that address real user problems.

Data-Driven Design

Data-Driven Design is a methodology within the context of Design Thinking disciplines that emphasizes the use of data to inform and drive the design process. It is a systematic and iterative approach that integrates user insights and feedback, market research, and other relevant data sources to guide decision-making and design solutions that meet the needs and preferences of the target audience.

By collecting and analyzing data throughout the design process, practitioners of Data-Driven Design are able to gain valuable insights into user behavior, preferences, and pain points. This information is used to inform every step of the design process, from problem definition and ideation to prototyping and testing. By using data as a foundation for decision-making, designers are able to minimize bias and subjective opinions, leading to more effective and efficient design solutions.

Data-Driven Insights

Data-Driven Insights, within the context of Design Thinking disciplines, refer to the collection, analysis, and interpretation of data to inform the decision-making process during the design phase. It involves using various data sources and techniques to gain a deeper understanding of user needs, preferences, and behaviors, ultimately leading to more effective design solutions.

Design Thinking emphasizes a human-centered approach, where the needs and experiences of users are central to the design process. Data-Driven Insights provide designers with valuable information and perspectives that can guide their decision-making and help them create meaningful and impactful solutions.

Design Activism

Design Activism is a discipline within the realm of Design Thinking that aims to bring about social and environmental change through the creative and intentional application of design principles and strategies. It involves using the power of design to address pressing societal issues, challenge systemic inequalities, and promote sustainable and inclusive solutions.

Design activists employ a range of design methods and tools to effectively communicate and engage with stakeholders, challenge norms and assumptions, and develop innovative approaches to complex problems. This may include designing visual campaigns, organizing participatory design workshops, creating prototypes or interventions, collaborating with communities and organizations, and advocating for policy changes.

Design Activism is rooted in the belief that design has the potential to go beyond aesthetics and functionality, and can be a powerful catalyst for positive change. It recognizes that design decisions have the ability to shape behaviors, influence perceptions, and transform systems. By applying a critical and human-centered approach, design activists seek to empower marginalized communities, raise awareness about important issues, and foster a more equitable and sustainable society.

In summary, Design Activism is a proactive and socially conscious practice that uses design as a tool for creating positive impact. It combines the principles of design thinking with a commitment to social justice, environmental stewardship, and community empowerment. Through thoughtful and purposeful design interventions, design activists strive to address wicked problems and contribute to a more just and sustainable world.

Design Advocacy

The phrase "Design Advocacy" refers to the act of promoting and defending the value and importance of design thinking disciplines. It involves advocating for the integration of design thinking into various areas such as business, government, education, and social sectors. Design advocacy recognizes that design thinking disciplines contribute to problem-solving, innovation, and the creation of meaningful experiences. It emphasizes that design is not just about aesthetics, but also about understanding user needs, challenging assumptions, and exploring different possibilities. Design advocates aim to raise awareness and educate others about the benefits and potential of design thinking. They actively engage in conversations, events, and initiatives to share their knowledge and experiences. They highlight examples of successful design-driven projects and demonstrate how design thinking can lead to more effective solutions. Advocates also work towards breaking down barriers and misconceptions surrounding design thinking. They strive to overcome resistance to change and establish a culture that values and embraces design as a strategic asset. By doing so, they help organizations and individuals embrace a human-centered approach that can lead to improved outcomes and enhanced user experiences. In summary, design advocacy is the proactive effort to promote the value and significance of design thinking disciplines in various domains. It involves educating others, highlighting successful design-driven projects, and breaking down barriers to create a more design-conscious society. ---

The phrase "Design Advocacy" refers to the act of promoting and defending the value and importance of design thinking disciplines. It involves advocating for the integration of design thinking into various areas such as business, government, education, and social sectors.

Design advocacy recognizes that design thinking disciplines contribute to problem-solving, innovation, and the creation of meaningful experiences. It emphasizes that design is not just about aesthetics, but also about understanding user needs, challenging assumptions, and exploring different possibilities.

Design Analysis

Design analysis is a systematic process that involves the evaluation and examination of a design solution in order to identify its strengths, weaknesses, and potential for improvement. It is an essential component of the Design Thinking discipline, which aims to create innovative and effective design solutions by focusing on user needs and experiences.

During design analysis, designers carefully assess various aspects of a design, including its functionality, aesthetics, usability, and overall effectiveness in meeting the intended objectives. This examination is carried out through a combination of qualitative and quantitative methods, such as user testing, expert evaluations, surveys, and data analysis.

The main goal of design analysis is to gain valuable insights that can inform the iterative design process. By identifying areas of improvement and understanding how users interact with the design solution, designers can make informed decisions and refine their designs to better meet user needs and expectations.

In addition, design analysis involves considering the broader context within which the design exists, including social, cultural, and environmental factors. This holistic approach allows designers to create designs that are not only visually appealing, but also sustainable, inclusive, and meaningful to the target audience.

Design Brief

A design brief in the context of service design is a formal document that outlines the goals, objectives, and requirements for a service design project. It serves as a guide that helps service designers and stakeholders to understand and align on the scope and expectations of the project. The design brief typically includes information about the target audience or users of the service, their needs and pain points, as well as any existing challenges or opportunities. It also includes the desired outcomes or goals that the service design project aims to achieve. Additionally, the design brief outlines any specific requirements or constraints that need to be considered during the design process. This can include technical limitations, budget constraints, regulatory requirements, or any other factors that may impact the design decisions. Furthermore, the design brief may include information about the timeline and milestones for the project, as well as any key stakeholders or decision-makers who need to be involved throughout the process. The design brief plays a crucial role in guiding the service design process from start to finish. It helps to ensure that all parties involved have a clear understanding of the project's objectives and requirements, and provides a framework for making design decisions and evaluating the success of the project. In conclusion, a design brief in the context of service design is a formal document that outlines the goals, objectives, requirements, and constraints for a service design project. It provides a clear direction for the design process and serves as a reference point for stakeholders involved.

Design Challenge

Design Thinking is a problem-solving approach that incorporates empathy, collaboration, and experimentation to create innovative solutions. It is a discipline that combines the analytical and creative processes to understand user needs, redefine problems, and generate ideas.

The first step in the Design Thinking process is empathizing with the end users to gain an understanding of their perspectives and needs. This involves conducting research, interviews, and observations to gather insights. The next step is defining the problem, which requires synthesizing the information gathered and identifying the root causes of the issues faced by the users.

Once the problem is defined, the Design Thinking process moves into the ideation phase. This involves brainstorming and generating a broad range of ideas to address the defined problem. The focus is on quantity rather than quality, as all ideas are considered valuable and potential sources of innovation.

The next stage is prototyping, where selected ideas are transformed into tangible representations. These prototypes can be physical models, mock-ups, or digital simulations that allow for testing and iteration. The goal is to gather feedback and refine the designs based on user insights.

The final stage of the Design Thinking process is testing. This involves evaluating the prototypes with users to determine their effectiveness and desirability. The feedback received is used to make further refinements and improvements to the designs.

Throughout the Design Thinking process, collaboration and interdisciplinary teamwork are essential. It encourages a diverse range of perspectives and expertise to be brought together to solve complex problems. The iterative nature of Design Thinking allows for continuous learning and improvement, ensuring that the final solutions meet the needs of the end users.

Design Charette

A design charette in the context of service design refers to a collaborative workshop or meeting where participants come together to generate innovative ideas and solutions for a specific problem or challenge related to a service. It is a process that encourages creativity, teamwork, and collective thinking, with the aim of developing and refining concepts that can improve the overall service experience. During a design charette, a diverse group of individuals with different backgrounds, skills, and perspectives are brought together, including service designers, stakeholders, subject matter experts, and end users. The participants engage in structured activities and exercises facilitated by a trained professional to explore, discuss, and ideate potential solutions. The goal is to enable a comprehensive exploration of possible ideas and generate a wide range of perspectives before converging on the most promising concepts. The charette typically follows a structured timeline, starting with a clear problem statement or design challenge. Participants then engage in activities such as brainstorming, sketching, role-playing, and prototyping, depending on the nature of the problem at hand. The ideas generated during the charette are not bound by traditional constraints or limitations, allowing participants to think outside the box and explore unconventional approaches. Throughout the process, an emphasis is placed on collaboration and open communication. Participants are encouraged to build upon each other's ideas, challenge assumptions, and provide constructive feedback. By leveraging the collective knowledge and expertise of the group, the design charette aims to foster a holistic and inclusive approach to problem-solving. The outcome of a design charette is a set of refined and validated concepts that address the specific service design challenge. These concepts may include new service features, process improvements, organizational changes, or technological enhancements. The ideas generated are often further developed into prototypes or design concepts that can be tested and evaluated before implementation. Overall, the design charette is a valuable tool in service design, enabling cross-disciplinary collaboration, creative thinking, and the generation of innovative solutions. It fosters a participatory and inclusive approach that empowers stakeholders and end users to contribute to the design process, ultimately leading to improved service experiences.

Design Collaboration

Design Collaboration refers to the process of working together, in a structured and collaborative manner, to generate and develop ideas, concepts, and solutions in the field of design. It involves the active participation and contribution of multiple individuals with diverse backgrounds, skills, and perspectives.

Design Collaboration plays a crucial role in Design Thinking disciplines as it enables teams to leverage the collective intelligence and creativity of its members. Through collaborative efforts, different viewpoints and expertise are brought together to solve complex problems, explore new possibilities, and create innovative designs.

Design Criteria

Design criteria refers to the specific guidelines or requirements that designers must consider and adhere to when creating a product, system, or experience. It serves as a framework to guide the design process and ensure that the resulting solution meets the needs and expectations of its users.

In the context of Design Thinking disciplines, design criteria play a critical role in defining the problem statement and facilitating the ideation and prototyping stages. They help designers focus on the desired outcome and provide constraints within which they can explore innovative solutions.

The design criteria should be well-defined, measurable, and actionable. They should be based on thorough research and understanding of the target audience, their pain points, and the context in which the design will be used. Designers can gather information through user interviews, observations, and surveys to identify key requirements and preferences.

For example, if designing a website, some potential design criteria may include usability, accessibility, visual appeal, and responsiveness. These criteria can guide decisions related to navigation, layout, color scheme, and interactions.

Design criteria should also ensure that the solution aligns with the goals and objectives of the project. They should be realistic and feasible within the given time, budget, and resource constraints. Designers should regularly evaluate the design against the criteria, seeking feedback from users and stakeholders to refine and improve the solution.

In summary, design criteria are essential for designing successful and user-centered solutions. They provide a clear direction, prevent scope creep, and help designers make informed decisions throughout the design process.

Design Criticism

Design Criticism, in the context of Design Thinking disciplines, refers to the evaluation and analysis of design solutions or ideas with the intention of providing constructive feedback and improving the overall quality of the design. It involves a systematic approach to assessing the effectiveness, creativity, usability, and aesthetics of a design, with the goal of identifying strengths, weaknesses, and areas for potential enhancement.

By critically examining a design, Design Criticism helps designers and teams refine their concepts, iterate on their solutions, and make informed decisions throughout the design process. It encourages designers to consider multiple perspectives, challenge assumptions, and explore alternative approaches, ultimately leading to more innovative and user-centered designs.

Design Critique Platforms

A Design Critique Platform is a digital tool or application that enables designers and teams to give and receive feedback on design projects in order to improve their quality and enhance the creative process. It is used within the context of Design Thinking disciplines to facilitate collaboration, iterative design, and continuous improvement.

Design Critique Platforms provide a central hub or virtual space where designers, stakeholders, and other relevant parties can come together to discuss, evaluate, and make suggestions on design concepts, prototypes, or completed works. These platforms often include features such as comment threads, annotation tools, versioning capabilities, and project management functionalities to support the exchange of feedback and allow for efficient communication and documentation.

Design Critique

Service design is a multidisciplinary approach that focuses on creating and improving services to better meet the needs and expectations of both customers and service providers. It involves the strategic and systematic design, development, and implementation of service processes, interactions, and experiences. Service design takes into consideration the entire service journey, from the initial contact with a customer to the final delivery of the service. It looks at all the touchpoints and interactions that occur throughout this journey, including physical, digital, and human interactions. The main goal of service design is to create services that are user-centered and provide value to both customers and service providers. It aims to understand the needs and desires of customers and design services that address these needs in the most efficient and effective way possible. This requires a deep understanding of customer behavior, motivations, and preferences. Service design also considers the business goals and objectives of the service provider. It looks at how the service can be optimized to meet these goals while also delivering value to customers. This involves identifying opportunities for innovation and differentiation in the market, as well as finding ways to improve operational efficiency and reduce costs. In order to achieve these goals, service design utilizes a variety of tools and methods. These can include customer journey mapping, service blueprinting, stakeholder analysis, persona development, prototyping, and testing. These tools and methods help service designers gain insights into customer needs, pain points, and expectations, and guide the design and development of services that meet these requirements. Overall, service design is a holistic and collaborative approach that brings together different disciplines and perspectives to create and improve services. It acknowledges that services are complex systems that involve multiple stakeholders and touchpoints, and seeks to optimize these systems for the benefit of both customers and service providers.

Design Ecosystem

A design ecosystem is a complex network of interconnected elements and processes that work together to support and enhance the practice of design thinking. It encompasses all the components and factors that contribute to the creation of innovative and user-centered design solutions.

At the core of a design ecosystem lies the concept of empathy, which involves understanding and appreciating the needs, desires, and challenges of the users or stakeholders. This empathy-driven approach allows designers to gain deep insights into the users' perspectives, enabling them to identify and address unmet needs effectively.

Within a design ecosystem, collaboration and interdisciplinary teamwork play a crucial role. Designers often work alongside professionals from various fields, such as marketing, engineering, psychology, and business, to leverage diverse expertise and perspectives. This collaborative approach encourages the exchange of ideas and enables the creation of holistic and comprehensive design solutions.

Additionally, a design ecosystem fosters creativity and innovation by providing designers with access to a range of tools, resources, and methodologies. This includes research techniques, prototyping tools, user testing facilities, and design thinking frameworks. By utilizing these resources, designers can iterate, refine, and validate their ideas, ensuring that their solutions are not only aesthetically pleasing but also functional and user-friendly.

Design Empowerment

Design Empowerment is a concept within the realm of Design Thinking that focuses on fostering the ability of individuals or communities to actively participate in the design process and make informed decisions that positively impact their lives.

Design Empowerment recognizes that design is not limited to professionals or experts, but is a collaborative and inclusive process that involves the end users or stakeholders who will ultimately be affected by the design outcome. It aims to democratize design by giving people the tools, knowledge, and agency to actively engage in the design process, rather than being passive recipients of designs created by others.

Design Ethics

Design Ethics refers to the set of moral principles and values that guide the actions and decisions of designers in the context of design thinking disciplines. It involves considering the societal impact, fairness, and responsibility of design solutions.

Designers are often faced with challenges that require them to balance various interests, including those of their clients, users, and the wider community. Design Ethics helps designers navigate these complexities by providing a framework for thoughtful and ethical decision-making.

Design Ethnography

Design Ethnography is a research approach used in the field of service design that aims to understand and gain insights into the lived experiences, behaviors, and needs of users and stakeholders. It involves immersing oneself in the context of the service, observing and interacting with individuals and communities, and conducting in-depth interviews to uncover deep-seated needs, desires, and motivations. This research method is based on the principles of ethnography, a field that traditionally focuses on the study of cultural practices and social interactions. However, in the context of service design, Design Ethnography expands its scope to examine not only cultural and social aspects, but also the specific dynamics and touchpoints within a service environment. Design Ethnography is characterized by its participatory nature.

Researchers actively engage with users and stakeholders, often adopting a 'fly on the wall' approach, observing and documenting activities and interactions without disrupting the natural flow. This allows them to gain a deeper understanding of the context and identify potential pain points and opportunities for improvement. Through Design Ethnography, service designers can gain valuable insights that inform the design process. By empathizing with users and stakeholders and understanding their perspectives, designers can uncover unmet needs, identify gaps in the service ecosystem, and generate innovative solutions that address these challenges. Designers often employ a variety of tools and techniques during the ethnographic research process. These may include visual documentation such as photography or video, creating journey maps or personas to represent user experiences, and using cultural probes or artifacts to elicit responses and reflections from participants. In conclusion, Design Ethnography is a research approach in service design that employs ethnographic principles to gain a deep understanding of user experiences, behaviors, and needs. By immersing themselves in the service context and actively engaging with users and stakeholders, designers can generate valuable insights that inform the design process and lead to more user-centered and impactful service solutions.

Design Feedback Platforms

Design Feedback Platforms are digital tools or systems that facilitate the collection, analysis, and management of feedback related to design projects within the context of Design Thinking disciplines.

These platforms provide a structured and efficient way for designers and design teams to gather insights and opinions from various stakeholders, including clients, users, and internal team members. The feedback can be related to different aspects of the design, such as user experience, aesthetics, functionality, and overall satisfaction.

Design Fiction

Design Fiction is a concept used in service design to create imaginary scenarios that explore possible futures and inform the design process. It involves the use of storytelling and speculative design techniques to envision how a service could be in the future. Design Fiction is not about predicting the future, but rather about engaging with the possibilities and implications of different futures. It allows designers to challenge assumptions, question the status quo, and imagine alternative realities.

Design Hacking

Design hacking is a concept rooted in the principles of design thinking, which involves the exploration and application of innovative strategies to solve complex problems and deliver meaningful solutions. It encompasses a multidisciplinary approach that combines elements of creativity, empathy, analysis, and experimentation.

At its core, design hacking challenges traditional thinking and breaks away from established norms and conventions. It involves questioning existing assumptions, reframing problems, and seeking alternative perspectives to uncover new opportunities for improvement. Design hackers utilize a diverse range of tools, methods, and mindsets to deconstruct and reconstruct ideas, systems, and processes.

Design Heuristics

Design heuristics in the context of service design refer to a set of guiding principles or rules that help designers make informed decisions about the design of services. These heuristics are based on experience, empirical evidence, and best practices, and can be used as a framework to evaluate and improve the quality of service design. Design heuristics provide a structured approach to problem-solving and decision-making in service design. They help designers prioritize and allocate resources effectively, make informed design choices, and ensure that the resulting service meets the needs and expectations of its users. These heuristics can be applied at various stages of the design process, from user research and ideation to prototyping and testing.

Design Impact

Design impact refers to the positive change or influence that a design solution has on its intended users or the broader community. It is a key measure of the effectiveness and success of a design thinking initiative. Design impact goes beyond the aesthetics or functionality of a product or service and focuses on the overall benefits and improvements it brings to individuals and society.

The goal of design impact is to create meaningful solutions that address real-world problems and meet the needs and aspirations of users. It involves understanding the context and challenges faced by the target audience, empathizing with their experiences, and designing solutions that have a positive and lasting impact. Design impact is not limited to tangible outcomes but can also encompass intangible aspects such as emotional well-being, empowerment, and social change.

In the design thinking disciplines, design impact is a fundamental driver that guides the entire design process. It encourages designers to adopt a human-centered approach, where the needs and desires of users are at the forefront of decision-making. By prioritizing design impact, designers can create solutions that not only fulfill functional requirements but also resonate with users on a deeper level.

Furthermore, design impact is not a one-time achievement but an ongoing process. It involves continuous evaluation and iteration to ensure that the design solution remains relevant and effective in its intended context. By measuring and analyzing the impact of their designs, designers can gain valuable insights and make informed decisions for future iterations or new design projects.

Design Innovation

Design Innovation is a process of creating new and improved products, services, or systems that address specific user needs and challenges. It involves applying a systematic and human-centered approach to generate innovative ideas and solutions.

In the context of Design Thinking disciplines, Design Innovation refers to the mindset and methods used to foster creativity and solve complex problems. It emphasizes empathy, collaboration, and experimentation to unlock new possibilities and enhance user experiences.

Design Language

Design language is a fundamental element in the discipline of Design Thinking. It refers to a set of visual, verbal, and interactive design principles and guidelines that are used to establish consistency and coherence across different design artifacts and experiences.

In Design Thinking, a design language serves as a common language or visual vocabulary that allows designers to communicate and align with each other, as well as with stakeholders and users. It helps to convey the intended message, evoke emotional responses, and facilitate understanding and usability in design solutions.

Design Leadership

Design leadership in the context of service design refers to the ability to guide and inspire multidisciplinary teams in creating and delivering exceptional service experiences. It is the practice of leading the design process and ensuring that design thinking principles are integrated into every stage of service development and delivery.A design leader is not only responsible for the overall direction of the design team but also plays a crucial role in fostering a culture of creativity, collaboration, and continuous improvement. They are not just managers or administrators but also facilitators and catalysts for innovation and change.

Design Mindset

A design mindset refers to the ways of thinking and approaching problems that are characteristic of design thinking disciplines. It is a mindset that is characterized by a focus on empathy, curiosity, and the ability to think divergently and iteratively.

Design thinking is an approach to problem-solving that puts the needs and experiences of users at the center. It involves understanding and empathizing with users, defining the problem, generating and iterating on ideas, and testing and implementing solutions. A design mindset is necessary for effectively engaging in this process.

Design Opportunity Workshops

Design Opportunity Workshops are collaborative sessions conducted in the context of service design to identify opportunities for improvement or innovation in a specific service or experience. These workshops bring together diverse stakeholders including designers, customers, employees, and other relevant individuals to explore and ideate potential solutions. The primary goal of Design Opportunity Workshops is to uncover pain points, challenges, and gaps in existing services, which can be transformed into opportunities for meaningful improvements. By engaging participants in an interactive and inclusive environment, these workshops facilitate a deeper understanding of user needs, expectations, and aspirations. During the workshop, participants are encouraged to share their insights, experiences, and ideas through various activities and exercises. This can include brainstorming, group discussions, role-playing, and creative problem-solving techniques. The facilitator guides the process, ensuring that all voices are heard and that the session remains focused and productive. Through Design Opportunity Workshops, service designers aim to foster a collaborative mindset and help stakeholders think creatively about how to address complex challenges. The workshops provide a platform for participants to empathize with users, uncover hidden opportunities, and co-create innovative solutions. By the end of a Design Opportunity Workshop, participants typically have a clearer understanding of the service's pain points, as well as potential opportunities to create value for users. This collective insight and ideation process inform the subsequent stages of service design, such as prototyping and implementation. In summary, Design Opportunity Workshops are collaborative sessions that leverage the expertise and perspectives of diverse stakeholders to identify opportunities for improvement and innovation in a given service or experience. By encouraging active participation and creative thinking, these workshops enable service designers to uncover insights, generate ideas, and co-create impactful solutions.

Design Opportunity

A design opportunity in the context of service design refers to a specific area or aspect of a service that could be improved or optimized through design interventions. It is an identified gap or challenge that presents an opportunity for designers to make positive changes and enhance the overall user experience. Design opportunities typically arise after conducting in-depth research and analysis of the service in question. This may include interviews with stakeholders, user observations, data analysis, and other research methods. By thoroughly understanding the service and its current state, designers can identify pain points, inefficiencies, or areas where the service falls short of meeting user needs and expectations. Once a design opportunity is identified, designers can begin the process of developing innovative solutions to address the specific challenge. This involves ideation, prototyping, and testing different concepts and ideas to find the most effective and feasible solution. The goal is to create a design that not only addresses the identified opportunity but also aligns with the overall service strategy and objectives. Design opportunities in service design can range from small, incremental improvements to more transformative changes. They can involve various dimensions of the service, including its physical, digital, and social aspects. For example, a design opportunity could be to streamline the user journey by eliminating unnecessary steps and simplifying processes. Another opportunity could be to enhance the service's digital interface to make it more user-friendly and intuitive. Design opportunities are valuable in service design as they provide designers with a clear focus and direction for their efforts. They enable designers to prioritize their design interventions and ensure that they are addressing the most critical challenges. By taking advantage of design opportunities, organizations can improve their services, create better user experiences, and ultimately differentiate themselves in the market. In conclusion, design opportunities in service design refer to specific areas or aspects of a service that present potential for improvement through design. They are identified through research and analysis and serve as a starting point for developing innovative solutions. Design opportunities help designers focus their efforts and enhance the overall user experience of a service.

Design Ops Platforms

A Design Ops Platform refers to a specialized tool or software that facilitates and enhances the application of Design Thinking disciplines within an organization. It is designed to streamline and optimize the design process, promoting collaboration, communication, and efficiency among designers, stakeholders, and other team members involved in the product development life cycle.

The primary aim of a Design Ops Platform is to provide a centralized and integrated system that empowers designers to manage, coordinate, and execute design projects effectively. It offers a range of features and functionalities that enable designers to visualize, iterate, and refine their design concepts, while also fostering collaboration and communication within design teams and cross-functional stakeholders.

Through the integration of various design tools, resources, and workflows, a Design Ops Platform enables designers to access and share design assets, guidelines, and best practices easily. It also facilitates the creation and maintenance of design systems, style guides, and libraries, ensuring consistency and coherence across different design projects and teams.

The implementation of a Design Ops Platform allows organizations to effectively manage their design operations, scale design capabilities, and align design efforts with business objectives. It helps to minimize inefficiencies, reduce duplicated efforts, and improve overall design quality and productivity, ultimately leading to better user experiences and increased customer satisfaction.

Design Ops

Design Ops, short for Design Operations, is a discipline that focuses on streamlining and optimizing the design process within an organization. It involves establishing efficient workflows, tools, and systems to enable designers to work more effectively and efficiently.

The main goal of Design Ops is to create an environment that supports collaboration, innovation, and creativity while ensuring consistency and alignment across different design teams and projects. By implementing consistent practices and standards, Design Ops helps foster a culture of design excellence and improves the overall quality of designs.

Design Ops teams are responsible for managing design resources, such as design libraries, style guides, and templates, to facilitate reusability and consistency. They also play a crucial role in facilitating communication and coordination between designers, developers, and other stakeholders throughout the design process.

In addition, Design Ops often involves conducting research and collecting feedback from designers and other team members to identify pain points and opportunities for improvement. This data-driven approach enables Design Ops teams to make informed decisions and implement strategies that enhance productivity and optimize design outcomes.

Overall, Design Ops is a strategic discipline that aims to enhance the efficiency, collaboration, and quality of design processes within an organization. By implementing Design Ops practices, companies can benefit from improved productivity, enhanced design outcomes, and a more cohesive and aligned design culture.

Design Patterns

Design Patterns, in the context of service design, refer to established solutions or templates that can be applied to common design problems in order to create more effective and efficient services. These patterns serve as a guide or framework, providing a proven approach to solving recurring design challenges. A design pattern typically consists of a set of best practices, principles, and guidelines that can be used to address specific design problems. It is a reusable solution that has been developed and refined over time, based on the collective experience and expertise of designers and practitioners in the field.

Design Philosophy

Design Philosophy refers to a set of guiding principles and beliefs that shape the approach and mindset of designers in the context of Design Thinking disciplines. It encompasses the fundamental values and considerations that inform the design process and guide decision-making throughout the creation of a design solution.

A Design Philosophy can include various elements, such as prioritizing user-centric design, embracing collaboration and iteration, valuing empathy and understanding, and fostering a focus on sustainability and ethical practices. It encapsulates the designer's perspective on the purpose and impact of their work, as well as the desired outcomes and values they aim to achieve through their designs.

Design Principles

Design principles are fundamental guidelines that inform the decision-making process in design thinking disciplines. These principles serve as a framework for designers to create impactful and user-centered solutions to complex problems.

Design thinking emphasizes a holistic approach that balances visual aesthetics with functionality and usability. Design principles provide a set of best practices and standards that guide designers in achieving these goals.

One key design principle is "simplicity." Designers strive to simplify the user experience by removing unnecessary complexity and reducing cognitive load. This involves streamlining interfaces, eliminating clutter, and prioritizing the most important elements. Simplicity enhances usability and ensures that users can easily understand and interact with the design.

Another important principle is "consistency." Consistency refers to maintaining uniformity and coherence in design elements and patterns throughout the entire project. By using consistent typography, colors, and layout, designers create visual harmony and facilitate intuitive navigation for users. Consistency also helps establish a brand identity and reinforces the product or service's credibility.

Moreover, "accessibility" is a critical design principle. Designers ensure that their solutions are accessible to people of all abilities, including those with disabilities. This involves following guidelines for color contrast, providing alternative text for images, and designing for various assistive technologies. By incorporating accessibility, designers can create inclusive experiences that reach a wider audience and promote equality.

In conclusion, design principles are foundational concepts that guide designers' decision-making processes in design thinking. Simplicity, consistency, and accessibility are just a few examples of these principles that help designers create user-centered and impactful solutions. By adhering to these principles, designers can ensure their designs are intuitive, aesthetically pleasing, and accessible to all.

Design Protocols

Design Protocols refer to the established set of guidelines and procedures that facilitate the effective implementation of Design Thinking disciplines. These protocols serve as a framework for conducting design activities and ensure consistency, collaboration, and efficiency throughout the design process.

In the context of Design Thinking disciplines, design protocols encompass various stages of the design process, including problem definition, ideation, prototyping, and testing. These protocols outline specific steps and methodologies to be followed, providing a structured approach to design challenges.

Design protocols typically begin with a thorough understanding of the problem or opportunity at hand. This involves conducting user research, collecting data, and analyzing insights to gain empathy and define the problem statement. The protocols then guide designers through the ideation phase, encouraging the generation of a wide range of ideas and facilitating divergent thinking.

Once ideas are generated, design protocols help in selecting and refining potential solutions. This involves evaluating the feasibility and desirability of each idea, considering technical constraints, user needs, and business objectives. Prototyping is another crucial aspect of design protocols, allowing designers to create tangible representations of their ideas for testing and validation.

Throughout the design process, protocols emphasize the importance of feedback and iteration. This involves testing prototypes with users, gathering feedback, and refining the design based on insights gained. Design protocols also encourage collaboration and cross-functional teamwork, as design activities often require input from various disciplines and perspectives.

In summary, design protocols provide a structured framework for Design Thinking disciplines, guiding designers through the various stages of the design process. By following these protocols, designers can effectively tackle complex challenges, enhance collaboration, and create solutions that address user needs and business objectives.

Design Psychology

Design Psychology, within the context of Design Thinking disciplines, refers to the application of psychological principles and theories to inform the design process. It involves understanding and incorporating human behavior, emotions, and cognitive processes into the design of products, services, or systems in order to enhance user experiences and achieve desired outcomes.

The main objective of Design Psychology is to create designs that are user-centered, intuitive, and visually appealing, while also ensuring they meet the needs, desires, and values of the target audience. By integrating psychological knowledge, designers can effectively address user preferences, motivations, and limitations, enabling them to create designs that are more engaging, satisfying, and meaningful.

Design Research Tools

Design research tools are techniques, methods, and instruments used by designers and design thinkers to gather information, generate insights, and gain a deeper understanding of the needs, desires, and behaviors of the users or customers they are designing for.

These tools can range from traditional qualitative research methods such as interviews, observations, and surveys, to more innovative approaches like co-creation workshops, journey mapping, and prototyping. The purpose of using design research tools is to uncover meaningful and actionable insights that can inform the design process and lead to the creation of more effective, user-centered solutions.

Design Research

Design research in the context of service design refers to the systematic process of gathering, interpreting, and applying insights and knowledge to inform the design of services that meet the needs and expectations of users. This process involves conducting qualitative and/or quantitative research methods to gain an understanding of users' behaviors, motivations, and preferences in relation to a specific service or set of services. Design researchers employ various techniques such as interviews, observations, surveys, and co-creation sessions to collect data and generate actionable insights.

Design Researcher

A Design Researcher is an individual who conducts research to gain insights and understanding into the needs, desires, and behaviors of users or customers. They employ various research methods and techniques to gather data and analyze it in order to inform the design process and decision making.

Design Researchers apply their knowledge and skills to identify opportunities and challenges, and to develop innovative solutions that address user needs. They collaborate closely with multidisciplinary teams, including designers, engineers, and business professionals, to develop a deep understanding of user needs and to ensure that the design process is informed by user insights.

Design Sprint Facilitation Kits

A Design Sprint Facilitation Kit is a collection of tools, materials, and resources used in the facilitation of Design Sprints, which are a core component of the Design Thinking process.

The Design Thinking discipline is a human-centered approach to problem-solving that emphasizes empathy, collaboration, and iteration. A Design Sprint, a specific method within Design Thinking, is a time-constrained, intensive process that allows cross-functional teams to quickly explore, prototype, and validate ideas for solving complex problems.

The Facilitation Kit is designed to support the facilitator in guiding the Design Sprint process effectively. It typically includes physical materials such as sticky notes, whiteboards, markers, and templates, as well as digital tools for collaboration and communication.

The Kit enables the facilitator to create a structured and engaging environment that promotes creativity, collaboration, and focused problem-solving. It helps the team to visualize and organize their ideas, make decisions, and iterate rapidly. The use of the Kit fosters a user-centered mindset, ensuring that the team remains focused on the needs and desires of the end-users throughout the Sprint.

By providing a set of standardized tools and materials, the Facilitation Kit not only streamlines the facilitator's role but also enables consistency and repeatability in the Design Sprint process. It ensures that teams can follow a proven methodology, regardless of their level of experience or expertise in Design Thinking.

Design Sprint Playbooks

Design Sprint Playbooks are a set of guidelines that outline the activities, tasks, and timeframes involved in conducting a Design Sprint, which is a structured brainstorming and problem-solving process in the field of Design Thinking. It provides a step-by-step approach for teams to collaboratively tackle complex problems and generate innovative solutions. The playbook serves as a roadmap, ensuring that the Design Sprint follows a predefined structure and allows for efficient and effective collaboration among participants.

Design Sprint Playbooks typically include detailed instructions for each phase of the Design Sprint, such as the Understand, Define, Ideate, Prototype, and Test stages. These instructions may include specific methods, tools, and techniques that teams can utilize during each phase to facilitate the generation of ideas, prototype development, and user testing. Additionally, the playbooks may provide tips, templates, and examples to help teams complete each phase successfully. By following the playbook, teams can ensure that they are following a tested and proven process, leading to the creation of user-centered and validated solutions.

Design Sprint

A Design Sprint is a highly structured and time-constrained process that follows the principles of Design Thinking, aimed at solving complex problems and rapidly prototyping innovative solutions. It involves a diverse group of stakeholders working collaboratively over a set period of time, typically five days, to explore, ideate, and validate ideas.

The Design Sprint begins with a "problem framing" phase, where the team identifies and clarifies the challenge they are trying to address. This phase includes activities such as creating a shared understanding of the problem, conducting research, and defining clear goals and success metrics.

Next, the team engages in a series of ideation and sketching exercises to generate a wide range of possible solutions. These exercises often involve activities like brainstorming, mind mapping, and sketching interfaces or storyboards.

After ideation, the team goes through a process of converging and selecting the most promising ideas. This phase includes techniques like dot voting, where each team member selects their favorite ideas, and a "heat map" exercise to visually represent the consensus of the group.

Once a set of ideas have been selected, the team creates low-fidelity prototypes, often using tools like pen and paper or digital prototyping software. These prototypes aim to quickly test and validate assumptions about the proposed solutions.

Finally, the team conducts user testing, where real users interact with the prototypes and provide feedback. This feedback is used to refine and iterate on the designs, allowing the team to make informed decisions about which solutions to pursue further.

Design Sprints

A design sprint is a structured and time-bound process used in service design to quickly and collaboratively develop and test ideas and prototypes. It is a proven method to accelerate innovation and problem-solution identification, enabling teams to efficiently solve complex challenges and drive customer-centered solutions. During a design sprint, cross-functional teams, including designers, researchers, product managers, and subject matter experts, come together to address a specific design challenge. The process typically spans five days, allowing participants to move from problem definition to solution validation within a compressed timeframe. The first day of the design sprint is dedicated to understanding the problem and defining the goals. Key stakeholders and domain experts share their insights and knowledge, which helps the team gain a holistic understanding of the challenge at hand. By the end of day one, the team develops a shared understanding of the problem and identifies a specific target for the sprint. On the second day, participants engage in collaborative ideation sessions. They generate as many ideas as possible to solve the defined problem. Techniques like brainstorming, mind mapping, and sketching are used to spark creativity and explore diverse perspectives. By the end of this day, the team converges on a select few ideas that have the potential to address the problem effectively. Day three is dedicated to building prototypes based on the chosen ideas. The team develops low-fidelity prototypes that represent the envisioned solution. These prototypes can be simple sketches, wireframes, or even interactive mockups, depending on the complexity of the solution. The focus is on creating tangible artifacts that can be used for testing and validation. Prototypes created on day three are put to the test on day four. The team conducts user testing and gathers valuable feedback to refine and iterate on their ideas. This feedback-driven approach ensures that the prototypes are aligned with users' needs and expectations. It also helps identify potential usability issues and areas for improvement. The final day of the design sprint is dedicated to making decisions based on the testing outcomes. The team reviews the feedback, evaluates the prototypes, and decides on the next steps. This can involve further iterations, refining the solution, or even pivoting based on the insights gained during the sprint. At the end of the design sprint, the team has a concrete plan for implementing the solution and a shared vision of the path forward.

Design Strategy

A design strategy in the context of service design refers to a comprehensive plan or approach that guides the design process for creating a service. It involves defining the goals, objectives, and values of the service, as well as identifying the target audience and understanding their needs and expectations.The design strategy serves as a roadmap for designers, enabling them to make informed decisions throughout the design process. It outlines the key principles and guidelines that should be followed to ensure that the service meets the desired objectives and delivers value to the target audience.

Design Studio Method

The Design Studio Method is a collaborative approach used in the field of service design to generate ideas, explore different perspectives, and create innovative solutions for a specific service or problem. It is typically conducted in a dedicated physical space known as a design studio, where cross-functional teams come together to engage in creative and iterative design activities. The method follows a structured process that encourages active participation, open communication, and a focus on the end-users. It involves a series of workshops or design sprints, usually lasting a few days, during which the team members collectively brainstorm, sketch, prototype, and evaluate concepts and ideas.

Design Studio

A design studio is a dedicated space where design thinking disciplines are applied to solve problems and create innovative solutions. It is a collaborative environment that brings together designers, engineers, and other creative professionals to work on projects and explore new ideas.

Design studios follow the principles of design thinking, which is a human-centered approach to problem-solving. This approach involves understanding the needs and desires of the end-users, challenging assumptions, and generating a wide range of ideas through brainstorming and prototyping. The design thinking process typically consists of five stages: empathize, define, ideate, prototype, and test.

In a design studio, teams apply these stages to tackle complex challenges in various fields such as product design, graphic design, architecture, and user experience design. The space is equipped with tools and resources that facilitate the design process, including drawing boards, computer workstations, 3D printers, and prototyping materials.

Design studios foster collaboration and cross-disciplinary communication. They encourage a culture of experimentation, where failure is seen as an opportunity for learning and improvement. The physical layout of the studio is often open and flexible, allowing for easy collaboration and exchange of ideas.

Overall, a design studio is a creative and dynamic environment where design thinking disciplines are practiced. It serves as a hub for innovation, enabling designers and other professionals to come together, collaborate, and generate impactful solutions to complex problems.

Design Studios

A design studio is a service-based business that provides specialized design solutions to clients. It is a creative agency that focuses on delivering design-related services, such as graphic design, web design, industrial design, and interior design. Design studios often have a team of skilled designers who possess the necessary expertise and experience in their respective design fields. These designers collaborate with clients to understand their requirements and objectives, and then create innovative and visually appealing design solutions to meet those needs. The primary goal of a design studio is to create designs that are not only aesthetically pleasing but also functional and effective. They aim to solve problems and enhance the overall user experience through their designs. Design studios may also offer additional services such as branding, marketing strategy, and user research to provide comprehensive design solutions. Design studios follow a systematic approach to their design process, which typically includes the following steps: Analyzing the client's needs and objectives: Design studios begin by thoroughly understanding the client's requirements, brand identity, and target audience. They conduct research and gather relevant information to guide the design process. Concept development: Once the requirements are understood, the design studio generates multiple design concepts and ideas. These concepts are presented to the client for feedback and further refinement. Design creation and refinement: The chosen concept is developed further to create detailed designs. The design studio iterates and refines the designs based on client feedback, ensuring that the final design meets all the necessary criteria. Delivery and implementation: Once the final design is approved, the design studio delivers the necessary files and assets to the client for implementation in their desired medium. They may also provide support during the implementation process to ensure a smooth transition. In conclusion, a design studio is a specialized service provider that creates innovative and visually appealing design solutions to meet client requirements. With their expertise and systematic approach, design studios play a crucial role in shaping the visual identity and user experience of brands and products.

Design System

A Design System is a set of guidelines, principles, and resources that provide a consistent and cohesive foundation for creating and designing digital products or services. It encompasses various elements such as typography, color palette, iconography, grid systems, and component libraries, among others.

The purpose of a Design System is to establish a shared language and unified visual identity, enabling design teams to work efficiently and effectively by promoting collaboration and reducing redundancy. By following the guidelines and utilizing the provided resources, designers can ensure a cohesive and seamless user experience across different platforms and devices.

Design Thinking Approach

Design Thinking is a human-centered, iterative problem-solving approach that emphasizes empathy, collaboration, and experimentation to generate innovative solutions. It involves a deep understanding of users' needs and desires, as well as a willingness to challenge assumptions and think outside the box.

At its core, Design Thinking is a mindset that encourages continuous learning and adaptation throughout the design process. It starts with empathizing with the target audience, seeking to gain insight into their experiences, challenges, and goals. By truly understanding their needs, Design Thinkers can identify pain points and opportunities for improvement.

With a clear understanding of the problem, Design Thinkers move on to the Define phase, where they synthesize their research findings and define a specific problem statement. This step helps to frame the challenge and set goals for the design process, ensuring that the solutions remain focused and purposeful.

The Ideate phase is where creativity and brainstorming come into play. Design Thinkers generate a wide range of ideas and possibilities, allowing themselves and their team to think freely and without judgment. This phase encourages wild ideas and encourages collaboration to find the most promising concepts.

Once ideas have been generated, the Design Thinkers move on to the Prototype phase. Here, low-fidelity prototypes are created to quickly test and iterate on potential solutions. These prototypes can range from physical models to digital mock-ups, allowing for rapid feedback and refinement.

The final phase, Test, involves obtaining feedback from users and stakeholders to evaluate the effectiveness of the prototype. Based on the feedback received, the Design Thinkers refine and iterate on their designs until a suitable solution is found.

Throughout the entire process, Design Thinking emphasizes a bias towards action and learning by doing. It encourages a holistic and interdisciplinary approach, combining analytical thinking with creative problem-solving to tackle complex challenges and create meaningful experiences for users.

Design Thinking Card Decks

Design Thinking Card Decks are tools used in the practice of Design Thinking, a human-centered approach to problem-solving and innovation. These card decks consist of a set of cards that help facilitate the various stages and activities involved in the Design Thinking process.

The cards in a Design Thinking Card Deck are designed to stimulate creativity, encourage collaboration, and foster empathy. Each card represents a different aspect or element of the Design Thinking methodology, such as user personas, problem statements, brainstorming prompts, ideation techniques, and prototyping methods. These cards can be used individually or in combination to guide Design Thinking practitioners through the different stages of the process.

Design Thinking Card Decks are typically used in workshops, brainstorming sessions, or collaborative design activities. They provide a structured and visual way for teams to explore and generate ideas, prototype solutions, and iterate on concepts. By using the cards, practitioners can break away from traditional thinking patterns and approach problems from a more creative and user-centered perspective.

The use of Design Thinking Card Decks can enhance the effectiveness of Design Thinking exercises by providing prompts, constraints, and inspiration to participants. They serve as a tangible and portable resource that helps teams stay focused, engaged, and aligned throughout the design process. The cards can be shuffled, rearranged, and combined in various ways to encourage interdisciplinary collaboration and trigger new insights.

Design Thinking Facilitation

Design Thinking Facilitation refers to the process of guiding and supporting a group or team through the various stages of the Design Thinking methodology. It involves creating an environment where participants feel comfortable and empowered to collaborate, ideate, and iterate on solutions to complex problems.

The facilitator plays a crucial role in Design Thinking by ensuring that the process is structured, inclusive, and productive. They help to define the problem statement, clarify goals, and establish a shared understanding among the team. They also encourage open and honest communication, active listening, and empathy for end-users or customers.

During the ideation phase, the facilitator facilitates brainstorming sessions, encourages wild and creative ideas, and promotes divergent thinking. They ensure that all ideas are captured and documented, and help the team generate a wide range of potential solutions. The facilitator also guides the team through the process of converging on the most promising ideas and concepts.

Throughout the prototyping and testing phases, the facilitator organizes and oversees the creation of prototypes, facilitates user testing sessions, and helps the team gather feedback. They encourage a fail-fast mentality and foster a culture of experimentation and learning from mistakes.

Overall, Design Thinking Facilitation is about empowering teams to think critically and creatively, collaborate effectively, and approach problem-solving in a human-centered way. The facilitator creates a positive and supportive environment where everyone's contributions are valued, and guides the team through the iterative process of Design Thinking to ultimately deliver innovative and user-centric solutions.

Design Thinking Framework

Design Thinking is a human-centered approach to problem-solving and innovation that puts the needs and desires of users at the forefront of the design process. It is a framework that guides designers in creating solutions that are not only functional but also intuitive and meaningful to users. The core principles of Design Thinking revolve around empathy, collaboration, iteration, and experimentation.

Empathy is a crucial aspect of Design Thinking, as it requires designers to understand the needs, motivations, and challenges of users through observation, interviews, and other forms of research. By gaining deep insights into user experiences, designers can develop a deep understanding of the problem they are trying to solve.

Collaboration is another essential element of Design Thinking. It encourages multidisciplinary teams to work together, bringing diverse perspectives and expertise to the table. This collaborative approach ensures that a wide range of ideas and solutions are explored and considered.

The iterative nature of Design Thinking involves continuously refining and improving solutions based on feedback and testing. By prototyping and testing early and often, designers can validate ideas, uncover potential flaws, and make necessary adjustments. This iterative process allows for continuous learning and refinement of the design solution.

Lastly, experimentation plays a crucial role in Design Thinking. It encourages designers to take risks, think outside the box, and explore alternative possibilities. By embracing failure as a valuable learning opportunity, designers can push the boundaries of creativity and innovation.

In conclusion, Design Thinking is a disciplined and flexible framework that promotes user-centric problem-solving through empathy, collaboration, iteration, and experimentation.

Design Thinking Mindset

The design thinking mindset refers to the set of attitudes, beliefs, and values that guide the approach to problem-solving and innovation in the context of design thinking disciplines. It emphasizes a human-centered and empathetic approach, seeking to understand the needs and desires of the end-users or customers. Design thinkers approach problems with a mindset of curiosity, experimentation, and iteration, consistently questioning assumptions and challenging the status quo.

The design thinking mindset is characterized by a collaborative and interdisciplinary approach, recognizing that diverse perspectives and expertise contribute to more holistic and innovative solutions. It encourages open-mindedness, creativity, and a willingness to embrace ambiguity and uncertainty throughout the design process.

Design Thinking Playbooks

Design Thinking Playbooks are guides or frameworks that provide step-by-step instructions and strategies for applying Design Thinking principles and techniques to solve complex problems. They are designed to help individuals or teams navigate the design process and generate innovative solutions.

The main purpose of a Design Thinking Playbook is to provide a structured approach to problem-solving by promoting empathy, collaboration, and creativity. It typically consists of a series of activities and exercises that guide users through the different stages of the design process, from understanding user needs to prototyping and testing ideas.

Design Thinking Principles

Design Thinking principles are a set of guiding beliefs and ideas that shape the practice of Design Thinking. These principles guide designers and innovators in their approach to problem-solving and help in creating user-centered solutions. The following are four key design thinking principles:

1. Human-Centered: Design Thinking is grounded in the understanding and empathy for the needs and experiences of the end-users. It emphasizes the importance of putting people at the center of the design process and involving them in co-creating solutions. By deeply understanding the target users' thoughts, emotions, and behaviors, designers can develop solutions that truly meet their needs.

2. Iterative: Design Thinking is an iterative process that involves rapid prototyping, testing, and refining of ideas. It encourages designers to embrace failures and learn from them. Through repeated cycles of ideation, prototyping, and testing, designers can continuously improve their solutions, leading to more innovative and effective outcomes.

3. Collaborative: Design Thinking encourages collaboration and teamwork. It recognizes the value of diverse perspectives and expertise in the design process. By involving stakeholders from different backgrounds and disciplines, designers can generate a wide range of ideas and ensure the relevance and feasibility of their solutions.

4. Experimental: Design Thinking is characterized by the willingness to take risks and explore new possibilities. It encourages designers to think outside the box and challenge assumptions. By embracing experimentation and adopting a mindset of continuous learning, designers can uncover innovative solutions that may not have been considered initially.

Design Thinking Process

Design Thinking is a human-centered approach to problem-solving that emphasizes empathy, collaboration, and experimentation. It involves a structured process of understanding the needs and desires of users, generating ideas, prototyping and testing solutions, and iterating on designs based on feedback.

The Design Thinking process consists of five stages: Empathize, Define, Ideate, Prototype, and Test. In the Empathize stage, designers immerse themselves in the user's experiences, observing and empathizing with their needs and frustrations. The Define stage involves synthesizing the insights gathered from the empathy stage to identify the core problem to be solved. In the Ideate stage, designers generate a wide range of ideas to address the identified problem. These ideas are then narrowed down and developed into concepts during the next stage, Prototype. Prototyping involves creating low-fidelity representations of design solutions to gather feedback and refine the concepts. The final stage, Test, involves testing the prototypes with users to validate assumptions, gather feedback, and make further improvements to the design.

Design Thinking Toolkits

Design Thinking Toolkits are resources or sets of tools and techniques that are specifically designed to support and facilitate the practice of Design Thinking. In the context of various Design Thinking disciplines, these toolkits provide a structured approach and a collection of methods to navigate and solve complex problems.

Design Thinking Toolkits typically include tools such as personas, journey maps, empathy maps, brainstorming techniques, prototyping methods, and user testing frameworks. These tools are used to enhance the understanding of users' needs and experiences, generate innovative ideas, visualize concepts, and validate solutions. By employing these tools, teams can collaborate more effectively, generate a wider range of ideas, and make more informed decisions during the problem-solving process.

Design Thinking Training Kits

Design Thinking Training Kits are comprehensive resources that provide instruction and guidance in the principles, processes, and tools of Design Thinking. These kits are designed to enable individuals or teams to learn and apply Design Thinking methodologies in order to solve complex problems and drive innovation.

The training kits typically consist of a combination of instructional materials, exercises, and case studies that guide participants through a step-by-step process of engaging in Design Thinking activities. They are typically used in workshop or training settings, where facilitators can guide participants through the materials and encourage active participation and collaboration.

Through the use of Design Thinking Training Kits, individuals and teams are able to develop a deep understanding of user needs and experiences, generate and test innovative ideas, and iterate on solutions to create meaningful and impactful outcomes. These kits provide a structured and practical approach to problem-solving, emphasizing empathy, creativity, and collaboration.

In addition to the instructional materials, exercises, and case studies, Design Thinking Training Kits may also include physical or digital tools and templates to support the various stages of the Design Thinking process. These tools can help participants to visualize and communicate ideas, gather and analyze data, and prototype and test concepts.

Design Thinking Workshop

Design Thinking is a collaborative, human-centered approach to problem-solving that is focused on creating innovative solutions. It is a multidisciplinary approach that combines empathy, creativity, and rationality to tackle complex problems and generate ideas that meet the needs of the end-users.

In the context of Design Thinking disciplines, the process can be divided into five main stages: Empathize, Define, Ideate, Prototype, and Test.

Design Thinking Workshops

Design thinking workshops are collaborative problem-solving sessions in the context of service design. These workshops aim to engage a diverse group of stakeholders in generating innovative solutions for improving the design and delivery of services. In a design thinking workshop, participants from various backgrounds, such as designers, clients, customers, and subject matter experts, come together to explore user needs, understand problems, and ideate potential solutions. The workshop follows a structured process that encourages empathy, experimentation, and iteration. The first phase of a design thinking workshop is the empathize phase, where participants immerse themselves in the users' experiences and gain a deep understanding of their needs, challenges, and aspirations. This phase involves various research techniques, including interviews, observations, and data analysis, to build empathy and uncover insights that inform the subsequent steps. Next comes the define phase, where the workshop participants synthesize the information gathered in the empathize phase to redefine the problem statement. Through collaborative activities such as affinity mapping and problem framing, the group refines and narrows down the focus to a specific challenge or opportunity that they want to address. Following the define phase, the ideate phase kicks in, during which participants engage in open-ended brainstorming sessions to generate a wide range of ideas. The workshop facilitator encourages a non-judgmental environment to encourage creativity and foster a safe space for participants to freely share their thoughts and perspectives. As a result, diverse and innovative ideas emerge, providing a rich pool of possibilities for solving the defined problem. Once the ideation phase is complete, the participants move on to the prototype phase, where they transform the selected ideas into tangible representations. This can involve sketching, storyboarding, or even creating low-fidelity prototypes. The prototypes serve as tools for visualizing and communicating the proposed solutions, allowing the participants to gather feedback and iterate on their ideas. The final phase of a design thinking workshop is the test phase, where participants gather feedback on their prototypes from users, clients, or other stakeholders. This feedback informs further iterations and refinements, ensuring that the proposed solutions address the user needs effectively and align with the desired outcomes.

Design Thinking

Design Thinking, in the context of service design, refers to a creative problem-solving approach that focuses on the needs and desires of users or customers. It involves a systematic and iterative process that emphasizes empathy, experimentation, and collaboration to address complex service-related challenges. At its core, Design Thinking aims to understand the needs and motivations of users to develop innovative solutions that meet those needs effectively. It goes beyond simply addressing the functional aspects of a service by considering the emotional and experiential elements that impact user satisfaction.

Design Validation

Design validation is a process used in service design to assess and ensure the effectiveness, efficiency, and feasibility of a service design solution. It involves evaluating whether the design solution meets the intended purpose, objectives, and user needs, while also taking into consideration the technical constraints and implementation requirements. During design validation, various methods and techniques are employed to test and verify the design solution, identify potential issues or limitations, and gather feedback from stakeholders and end users. These methods may include usability testing, prototype evaluation, user interviews, surveys, and data analysis.

Design Workshop

Service design is a collaborative and user-centric approach to designing and improving services. It involves understanding the needs and expectations of users, and then designing and implementing a service that meets those needs effectively and efficiently. Service design takes a holistic approach, considering not only the service itself but also the entire user journey and the various touchpoints along the way. This includes everything from the initial contact with the service, through the delivery of the service, to the post-service experience. It takes into account the physical, digital, and emotional aspects of the service, as well as the people, processes, and technology involved.

Design Workshops

A design workshop is a collaborative process that brings together individuals from various disciplines to generate and explore ideas, solve problems, and develop innovative solutions. It is a core component of design thinking, a human-centered approach to problem-solving that emphasizes empathy, experimentation, and iteration.

During a design workshop, participants engage in activities such as brainstorming, ideation, prototyping, and testing. These activities are designed to foster creativity, encourage out-of-the-box thinking, and facilitate the co-creation of ideas and concepts. The workshop is typically facilitated by a trained design thinking practitioner who guides the participants through the various stages of the design process.

Design For All

Design for All is a concept within the discipline of Design Thinking that aims to create products, services, and environments that are accessible, inclusive, and usable by all individuals, regardless of their abilities or disabilities. It takes into consideration the diverse needs, preferences, and limitations of users, with the goal of promoting equal opportunities and eliminating barriers to participation.

This approach recognizes that design should not be limited to a specific demographic or target audience, but should instead cater to a broad range of users. It advocates for the adoption of universal design principles, which involve considering the needs of individuals with varying physical, sensory, cognitive, and emotional capabilities from the outset of the design process. By prioritizing inclusivity, Design for All seeks to enhance the user experience for everyone, rather than creating separate solutions for specific groups.

Design For Behavior Change

Design for Behavior Change is a discipline within Design Thinking that focuses on creating intentional and purposeful design solutions to influence and shape human behavior. It is a systematic approach that considers the psychological, social, and environmental factors that influence behavior and seeks to leverage design principles to encourage positive behavioral changes.

Design for Behavior Change involves understanding the target audience and their motivations, desires, and barriers to behavior change. By empathizing with users and gaining insights into their needs, designers can create interventions that effectively promote behavior change. This discipline recognizes that behavior is not solely determined by individual choice but is influenced by a complex interplay of external factors, such as social norms, cultural values, and physical environments.

Design For Delight

Design for Delight is a key principle in the field of Design Thinking. It is a mindset and approach that focuses on creating products, services, and experiences that delight users and customers. This approach goes beyond just meeting basic functional needs and aims to create memorable, enjoyable, and meaningful interactions.

Design for Delight involves understanding the emotions, aspirations, and desires of users and crafting solutions that not only fulfill their needs but also exceed their expectations. It is based on the belief that delighting users leads to increased engagement, loyalty, and advocacy.

Design For Emotion

Design for Emotion is a discipline within Design Thinking that focuses on creating products, services, or experiences that elicit emotional responses from users. It recognizes that emotions play a significant role in human behavior and decision-making, and aims to design with these emotions in mind.

Emotional design seeks to go beyond mere functionality and usability, striving to create meaningful and engaging experiences that connect with users on an emotional level. It involves understanding the target audience's emotional needs, desires, and aspirations, and incorporating these insights into the design process.

This discipline emphasizes the use of visual aesthetics, storytelling, and sensory elements to evoke specific emotional responses. It recognizes that visuals, colors, typography, and other design elements can have a profound impact on how users feel about a product or service. By strategically leveraging these elements, designers can create experiences that elicit positive emotions such as joy, excitement, or trust.

Design for Emotion also considers the context in which the product or service will be used, as different situations and environments can elicit different emotional responses. For example, a design for a mobile app used during a stressful situation may prioritize calming and reassuring elements to help users feel more at ease.

The goal of Design for Emotion is to create products that not only meet functional and usability requirements but also resonate with users on an emotional level. By designing for emotion, designers can create more meaningful and memorable experiences that foster stronger connections between users and the products or services they interact with.

Design For Good

Design for Good refers to the application of design thinking principles and methodologies to solve social, environmental, and humanitarian challenges. It involves using the power of design to address complex problems, improve lives, and create positive social impact.

Design for Good takes a human-centered approach, placing the needs, experiences, and values of the people impacted by the problem at the forefront of the design process. It requires understanding the context and perspectives of the individuals and communities affected, and designing solutions that are inclusive, equitable, and sustainable.

Design For Manufacturability

Design for Manufacturability is a concept within the field of Design Thinking that focuses on optimizing the design of a product or system for easy and efficient manufacturing. It involves considering various factors related to the manufacturing process early in the design stage, in order to minimize production costs, maximize quality, and reduce time to market.

The goal of Design for Manufacturability is to ensure that the design of a product or system is aligned with the capabilities and constraints of the manufacturing process. This includes considering issues such as material selection, component design, assembly methods, and production equipment. By addressing these aspects during the design phase, potential manufacturing problems can be identified and resolved early on, resulting in a smoother production process and ultimately a better-quality product.

Design-Driven Innovation

Design-Driven Innovation, within the context of Design Thinking disciplines, can be defined as an approach that puts emphasis on the role of design in driving innovation and creating value for businesses and customers alike. It is an iterative and human-centric process that involves deeply understanding user needs, discovering insights, and creating solutions that are desirable, feasible, and viable.

In Design-Driven Innovation, design serves as a powerful tool to uncover hidden opportunities and generate breakthrough ideas. It goes beyond mere aesthetics and extends into problem-solving, strategy, and business model innovation. By integrating design principles and practices into the innovation process, companies can gain a competitive edge by creating products, services, and experiences that truly resonate with their target audience.

Design-Driven Innovation encourages cross-functional collaboration and multidisciplinary thinking, bringing together designers, engineers, marketers, and other stakeholders to work collaboratively towards a common goal. It emphasizes empathy, allowing designers to deeply understand and empathize with users to uncover their latent needs and design solutions that address those needs effectively.

By adopting a Design-Driven Innovation approach, organizations can foster a culture of innovation, where experimentation, prototyping, and iteration are embraced as essential components of the design process. It helps businesses to differentiate themselves in the market by creating products and services that are not only functional but also emotionally resonant, delightful, and meaningful to the end-users.

Design-Led Innovation

Design-Led Innovation refers to an approach that places design at the core of the innovation process. It is rooted in the principles of Design Thinking, which emphasizes user-centricity, empathy, collaboration, and iterative problem-solving.

Design-Led Innovation integrates the expertise and perspective of designers with those of cross-functional teams, encouraging a collaborative effort to identify and solve complex problems. It goes beyond merely considering aesthetics and visual appeal, instead focusing on understanding user needs, desires, and behaviors to create meaningful and desirable solutions.

Desirability Testing

Desirability testing is a method used in service design to assess the appeal and attractiveness of a service or product to its intended users. It involves gathering feedback and insights from users to understand their preferences, emotions, and overall subjective opinions about the service. The goal of desirability testing is to evaluate the desirability and user experience of a service, and to identify any areas for improvement or potential enhancements. In desirability testing, participants are typically shown prototypes or mock-ups of a service and are asked to provide their thoughts, feelings, and reactions to it. This can be done through various qualitative research methods, such as interviews, surveys, or observational studies. By collecting feedback from users, designers can gain valuable insights into how users perceive and interact with the service, and whether it meets their expectations and needs. This type of testing is crucial in the early stages of service design, as it allows designers to gauge whether their ideas align with the desires and preferences of their target audience. It helps to ensure that the service meets the needs and expectations of users, and that it is appealing and engaging to them. Desirability testing also helps designers to identify any usability issues or areas of confusion that may hinder the overall user experience. The insights gathered from desirability testing can inform design decisions and help prioritize improvements or modifications to the service. By understanding the desirability factors that affect user perceptions and emotions, designers can make informed decisions about how to create a more desirable and engaging service. Overall, desirability testing is an essential step in the service design process, as it enables designers to evaluate the appeal and attractiveness of their service to users. By collecting feedback on users' preferences, emotions, and subjective opinions, designers can make informed decisions about how to improve the service and create a more desirable user experience.

Diary Studies

A diary study is a research method commonly used in service design to gain in-depth insights into the everyday experiences and interactions of users with a service over an extended period of time. During a diary study, participants are asked to keep a detailed record or diary of their activities, thoughts, and emotions related to their use of a particular service. These diaries can take various forms, such as physical notebooks, online journals, or even voice or video recordings. Participants are typically provided with guidelines or prompts to help them structure their entries and focus on specific aspects of their interactions with the service. The main objective of a diary study is to capture rich and detailed qualitative data that reflects the real-life context in which users engage with a service. By collecting data over an extended period, researchers can gain a comprehensive understanding of users' behaviors, needs, pain points, and aspirations throughout their entire service journey. Diary studies offer several advantages in the context of service design. Firstly, they provide firsthand, unfiltered insights into users' experiences, allowing researchers to uncover subtle nuances and nuances that may be missed in other research methods. Additionally, diary studies offer a longitudinal perspective, enabling researchers to observe patterns and changes in users' behaviors and perceptions over time. However, diary studies also present some limitations. Participants may experience compliance issues, forgetting to make entries or not recording details accurately, which can affect the reliability of the data. Additionally, self-reporting may introduce biases, as participants may not always accurately recall or report their experiences. Researchers must carefully consider these limitations and employ strategies to mitigate them, such as providing clear instructions, reminders, and incentives for participation.

Digital Ecosystem

A digital ecosystem, in the context of service design, refers to the interconnected network of digital platforms, technologies, and actors that collaborate and interact with one another to deliver seamless and integrated services to users. It encompasses a wide range of digital components, including websites, mobile applications, social media channels, cloud computing infrastructure, databases, APIs, and more. In a digital ecosystem, various actors, such as organizations, customers, third-party service providers, and developers, work together to create, manage, and consume digital services. These actors can be both human and non-human, and they all play a crucial role in shaping the ecosystem and influencing the experiences of users. The foundation of a digital ecosystem lies in the concept of interoperability, which refers to the ability of different digital components to exchange and utilize data seamlessly. Interoperability enables the integration of diverse services, systems, and applications, allowing for a holistic and cohesive user experience. It eliminates the silos and fragmentation that often exist in traditional service delivery models and fosters collaboration and innovation among different stakeholders. A key aspect of a digital ecosystem is the availability of APIs (Application Programming Interfaces) that enable the interaction and integration of different digital services. APIs act as bridges between various components within the ecosystem, allowing them to communicate and share data effectively. They facilitate the development of scalable and modular services, enabling organizations to easily extend and adapt their offerings based on evolving user needs and market trends. Moreover, a digital ecosystem is characterized by continuous evolution and adaptation. It is not a static entity but rather a dynamic and responsive system that evolves in response to changing user expectations, technological advancements, and market dynamics. Organizations operating within a digital ecosystem need to embrace agility, innovation, and user-centricity to thrive in this rapidly changing landscape.

Digital Ethnography

Digital ethnography is a research methodology used in the context of service design to understand and analyze digital experiences and behavior. It involves the application of ethnographic principles and techniques to the online environment to gain insights into how people interact with digital services, platforms, and interfaces. By immersing themselves in online communities, social media platforms, and digital interactions, researchers can observe and document users' behaviors, attitudes, and motivations. Digital ethnography allows for a deep understanding of the cultural, social, and contextual factors that shape people's experiences and interactions with digital services.

Digital Innovation

Digital innovation, in the context of service design, refers to the development and implementation of new digital solutions or technologies that enhance the delivery and experience of services. It encompasses the use of digital tools, platforms, and strategies to improve efficiency, effectiveness, and customer satisfaction in service interactions. By leveraging digital innovation, service designers can transform traditional service offerings into more user-centric and streamlined experiences. This can involve the integration of digital technologies such as artificial intelligence, machine learning, Internet of Things, or virtual reality, among others, to create innovative and personalized solutions.

Digital Prototyping Tools

Digital prototyping tools are software applications that enable designers and design teams to create interactive and realistic representations of their design concepts. These tools are an integral part of the design thinking discipline, which emphasizes a user-centered approach to problem-solving and innovation.

In the context of design thinking, digital prototyping tools serve multiple purposes. First and foremost, they allow designers to quickly and efficiently test and validate their ideas in a digital environment. By creating interactive prototypes, designers can simulate real-world user interactions and gather valuable feedback from stakeholders and potential users. This feedback loop is essential to the design thinking process, as it helps designers iterate and refine their concepts based on real user needs and preferences.

Additionally, digital prototyping tools enable designers to communicate and collaborate effectively with their team members and stakeholders. These tools often provide features that facilitate the sharing and presentation of design ideas, making it easier for all parties involved to understand and contribute to the design process.

Digital Prototyping

Digital Prototyping is a key component of the Design Thinking discipline, essential for transforming ideas and concepts into tangible and interactive digital products.

It involves the creation of digital representations, often in the form of interactive mockups or wireframes, that simulate the functionality and user experience of a product. These prototypes are developed using specialized software tools, enabling designers and stakeholders to visualize and test the product's features, interactions, and user interfaces.

By bringing ideas to life in a digital format, digital prototyping provides several benefits within the Design Thinking process. Firstly, it allows designers to rapidly iterate and refine their concepts in response to feedback and evolving requirements. It bridges the gap between abstract ideas and concrete designs, facilitating collaboration and communication among cross-functional teams and stakeholders.

Furthermore, digital prototypes offer a cost-effective and time-efficient way to evaluate the feasibility and viability of a product early in the design phase, before investing significant resources in its development. By testing the prototype with potential users, designers can gather valuable insights and user feedback, helping them make informed decisions and identify areas for improvement.

In conclusion, digital prototyping is a vital tool in the arsenal of Design Thinking practitioners. It enables the visualization, exploration, and validation of ideas in a digital format, fostering iterative design and facilitating user-centered decision-making throughout the product development lifecycle.

Digital Storytelling

Digital storytelling is a powerful method within the realm of Design Thinking disciplines that combines the art of storytelling with modern technology to convey meaningful narratives and messages. It involves the strategic use of digital media, such as images, videos, audio, and interactive elements, to create immersive and engaging experiences for the intended audience.

Through digital storytelling, designers can communicate complex ideas, emotions, and insights in a visually compelling and easily digestible format. By incorporating multimedia elements, such as visuals, sounds, and interactive features, designers can captivate the audience's attention and evoke emotions, leading to a deeper understanding and connection with the story being told.

Digital Transformation

Digital Transformation in the context of service design refers to the process of utilizing digital technologies and strategies to fundamentally change and improve the way services are created, delivered, and experienced. It involves the integration of digital solutions into all aspects of service design, with the aim of enhancing customer experiences, optimizing operational efficiency, and achieving business objectives. In the traditional service design approach, services are mostly delivered through physical channels with limited digital involvement.

However, with the advancements in technology and changing customer expectations, organizations are now required to adapt and transform their services to meet the growing demand for digital interactions. Digital Transformation involves a holistic approach that encompasses the entire service ecosystem. This includes understanding customer needs and pain points, mapping the customer journey, redefining processes and workflows, and implementing digital solutions to streamline and enhance service delivery. The core principles of Digital Transformation in service design include: 1. Customer-centricity: Placing the customer at the center of the service design process and prioritizing their needs and preferences. This involves leveraging digital tools to gather customer feedback, analyze data, and personalize experiences. 2. Process optimization: Redesigning existing processes to eliminate inefficiencies and bottlenecks. This can involve automating manual tasks, implementing workflow management systems, and using analytics to gain insights for continuous improvement. 3. Collaboration and co-creation: Engaging stakeholders from different departments and disciplines to foster innovation and create seamless experiences. Digital Transformation encourages cross-functional collaboration and encourages the co-creation of solutions through iterative design processes. 4. Scalability and agility: Leveraging digital technologies that allow services to scale and adapt to changing market conditions quickly. This includes utilizing cloud-based solutions, agile project management methodologies, and scalable infrastructure to enable flexibility and responsiveness. Overall, Digital Transformation in service design seeks to leverage digital technologies to enhance the value and impact of services. It requires organizations to embrace change, adopt a customer-centric mindset, and continuously innovate in order to stay competitive in a rapidly evolving digital landscape.

Divergent Thinking

Divergent thinking is a crucial aspect of the design thinking process, which involves generating a wide range of ideas and exploring various possibilities without judgment or constraint. It is a cognitive process that encourages creativity, innovation, and open-mindedness.

During divergent thinking, designers aim to break away from conventional or linear thinking patterns and instead focus on generating multiple potential solutions or perspectives. This process encourages exploration and ideation, allowing designers to consider diverse viewpoints, challenge assumptions, and explore unconventional approaches.

Divergent And Convergent Thinking

Divergent thinking is a cognitive process within the context of Design Thinking that involves generating a wide range of ideas, possibilities, and solutions. It encourages the exploration of different perspectives, options, and approaches, aiming to uncover new insights and possibilities.

Convergent thinking, on the other hand, is a cognitive process within the context of Design Thinking that involves narrowing down and selecting the most promising ideas, possibilities, and solutions. It focuses on evaluating and refining the options generated through divergent thinking, leading to a feasible and effective solution based on the given criteria and constraints.

Eco-Centric Design

Eco-Centric Design refers to a design approach that prioritizes the ecological aspects and sustainability in the design process. It emphasizes the integration of environmentally friendly practices, materials, and strategies throughout the entire design lifecycle.

In the context of Design Thinking, Eco-Centric Design requires designers to consider the environmental impact of their designs. They need to analyze and understand the environmental factors, such as resource consumption, pollution, and carbon footprint, associated with their design decisions.

Ecological Design Thinking

Ecological Design Thinking is a discipline within the broader field of Design Thinking that focuses on creating sustainable solutions for the built environment and natural ecosystems. It considers the interactions between humans, nature, and technology to develop innovative designs that minimize negative environmental impacts and enhance ecological health.

Ecological Design Thinking involves a holistic approach to problem-solving, seeking to understand the complex and interconnected systems that shape our world. It embraces principles such as biomimicry, regenerative design, and systems thinking to inform the design process. By studying and imitating nature's strategies, designers can develop solutions that are not only visually pleasing but also functionally efficient and environmentally friendly.

Ecological Design

Ecological design is a discipline within design thinking that focuses on creating sustainable solutions that minimize harm to the environment and promote a symbiotic relationship between humans and nature. It is a holistic approach that considers the environmental, social, and economic impacts of design decisions.

Ecological design aims to address the interconnected challenges of resource depletion, pollution, and climate change by incorporating principles of ecological systems and biomimicry. It seeks inspiration from natural processes and ecosystems, recognizing their efficiency, resilience, and regenerative capabilities. By emulating these principles, ecological design seeks to create products, services, and systems that not only have a reduced negative impact on the environment but also contribute positively to the overall well-being of individuals and communities.

Ecological Sustainability

Ecological sustainability refers to the practice of designing and developing solutions that meet the needs of the present without compromising the ability of future generations to meet their own needs, while simultaneously minimizing negative impacts on the environment.

In the context of Design Thinking disciplines, ecological sustainability encompasses the consideration of the environmental consequences of any design or innovation. It involves evaluating the ecological footprint of a product, service, or system throughout its lifecycle - from raw material extraction and manufacturing, to distribution, use, and disposal. The goal is to minimize resource consumption, waste generation, and harmful emissions, while maximizing efficiency and promoting renewable and regenerative practices.

Design thinkers approach ecological sustainability by employing an iterative, human-centered approach to problem-solving. They explore alternative materials, production methods, and technologies that lessen the environmental impact of a design. This may involve incorporating recycled or biodegradable materials, designing for disassembly and recycling, optimizing energy efficiency, or promoting circular economy principles.

Furthermore, design thinkers engage stakeholders and end-users in the design process, seeking their insights and feedback to ensure the solutions developed address their needs and aspirations while promoting long-term ecological sustainability. This participatory approach encourages collaboration, innovation, and the integration of diverse perspectives, leading to more effective and sustainable outcomes.

Economic Value To The Customer (EVC)

Economic Value to the Customer (EVC) is a concept in service design that measures the financial benefit or cost savings that a customer can expect to receive from a particular service. It is a way to quantify the monetary value that a service provides to its customers, taking into account factors such as increased productivity, cost reduction, and revenue generation. EVC is determined by comparing the total cost of ownership (TCO) of a service with the potential benefits it offers. The TCO includes both the direct costs associated with using the service, such as subscription fees or maintenance costs, as well as indirect costs like training or integration expenses. On the other hand, the potential benefits can include factors such as time savings, improved efficiency, increased revenue, or competitive advantage. EVC is often used as a decision-making tool for customers when evaluating different service options. By calculating the EVC for each option, customers can compare the financial impact of each service and make an informed decision based on their specific needs and priorities. This helps them assess whether the benefits of a service outweigh its costs and determine the overall value proposition. Service providers can also use EVC to demonstrate the value of their offerings to customers. By quantifying the financial benefits that customers can expect to achieve, providers can effectively communicate the potential return on investment and justify the pricing of their services. This allows them to differentiate themselves from competitors and build trust with customers by demonstrating clear value. In conclusion, Economic Value to the Customer (EVC) is a metric that assesses the financial benefit or cost savings that a service provides to customers. It takes into account both the cost of using the service and the potential benefits it offers, helping customers make informed decisions and allowing service providers to demonstrate the value of their offerings.

Ecosystem Design

Ecosystem Design in the context of service design refers to the intentional configuration and orchestration of interconnected elements within a service ecosystem to create a harmonious and sustainable environment. It involves understanding the various components of the ecosystem, such as service providers, customers, stakeholders, technologies, and resources, and finding ways to align and integrate them effectively to deliver value to all participants. Ecosystem Design recognizes that a service is not a standalone entity but exists within a broader network of relationships and interactions.

Ecosystem Innovation

Ecosystem innovation refers to the practice of applying design thinking disciplines to create and improve the overall ecosystem in which a product, service, or organization operates. It involves a holistic approach that considers the interactions and interdependencies among various elements within the ecosystem.

In the context of design thinking, ecosystem innovation focuses on understanding the needs, behaviors, and motivations of all the stakeholders involved in the ecosystem. This includes not only the end-users but also the suppliers, partners, regulators, and other relevant actors.

The goal of ecosystem innovation is to identify and address opportunities and challenges within the ecosystem to create value for all stakeholders. This could involve designing new products or services, reconfiguring existing ones, creating new business models, or developing partnerships and collaborations.

Through ecosystem innovation, designers and innovators aim to create a more harmonious and sustainable ecosystem that benefits all stakeholders. This requires a deep understanding of the complex dynamics and relationships within the ecosystem, as well as the ability to anticipate and respond to changes and disruptions.

Overall, ecosystem innovation is a strategic approach that recognizes the interconnectedness and interdependence of all elements within a system. By leveraging design thinking principles, it enables the creation of innovative solutions that not only meet the needs of individual stakeholders but also contribute to the overall health and resilience of the ecosystem.

Ecosystem Mapping

Ecosystem mapping is a service design tool that aims to visually represent the complex relationships, interactions, and dependencies among various stakeholders, resources, and components within a specific ecosystem. It provides a holistic view of the entire ecosystem, allowing designers to identify and understand the different actors and elements involved, as well as their roles, connections, and influences on each other. The process of ecosystem mapping involves gathering extensive information through research, interviews, and observations to comprehensively identify and document all relevant stakeholders, such as service providers, users, suppliers, partners, competitors, and regulators. Additionally, it entails identifying and mapping out the various resources and components within the ecosystem, including physical assets, digital platforms, technologies, policies, and processes. Ecosystem mapping is commonly represented using visual diagrams or maps, which may include elements such as nodes, lines, labels, and icons. Nodes typically represent individual stakeholders, resources, or components, while lines indicate the relationships, connections, or flows of information, services, or resources between them. Labels and icons are used to add additional information or context to the map. By visually representing the ecosystem, designers can gain a better understanding of its overall structure, dynamics, and opportunities for improvement. They can identify key actors and components, assess their roles and influence within the ecosystem, and analyze their relationships and dependencies. This holistic view enables designers to identify potential gaps, redundancies, bottlenecks, or areas for collaboration within the ecosystem, leading to more informed decision-making and the development of more effective and sustainable service designs. Ecosystem mapping is a valuable tool for service designers as it helps them develop a deep understanding of the complex systems in which their services operate. It provides insights into the broader context and interdependencies that can inform the design process and ensure that the service aligns with the needs, goals, and capabilities of the ecosystem. By mapping out the ecosystem and visualizing the connections and relationships, designers can create more meaningful and impactful services that deliver value to all stakeholders involved.

Ecosystem Perspective

The ecosystem perspective in the context of Design Thinking disciplines refers to the holistic and interconnected view of a system and its various components, interactions, and interdependencies. It involves understanding the broader context and environment in which a problem or challenge exists, and recognizing that any solution or design should consider the impact on the entire ecosystem, rather than focusing solely on individual elements.

This perspective emphasizes the importance of considering the relationships and dynamics between different stakeholders, resources, and factors that influence or are influenced by the problem or design. It encourages designers to go beyond their immediate users or customers and consider the larger network of actors, organizations, and systems that play a role in the problem space.

By adopting an ecosystem perspective, designers can gain deeper insights into the complexities and interdependencies within a system, uncovering hidden opportunities, risks, and unintended consequences. They can identify potential synergies, collaborations, and leverage points that could enhance the effectiveness and sustainability of their solutions.

This perspective also encourages collaboration and co-creation among diverse stakeholders, fostering a collective understanding and ownership of the problem and solution. It helps designers to avoid siloed thinking and encourages them to explore multiple perspectives, disciplines, and domains to generate innovative and impactful design solutions.

Ecosystem Thinking

Ecosystem Thinking in the context of Design Thinking disciplines refers to the approach of viewing problems and solutions within a larger system or environment. It involves understanding the interconnectedness and interdependencies between various elements and stakeholders in order to create sustainable and holistic solutions.

Design Thinking, as a human-centered problem-solving methodology, traditionally focuses on understanding the needs and preferences of users to develop innovative solutions. However, Ecosystem Thinking takes this a step further by considering the broader context in which these solutions will exist. It recognizes that no problem or solution exists in isolation, and that they are influenced by a multitude of factors, such as societal, environmental, and economic variables.

Elevator Pitch

Service design is a holistic and multidisciplinary approach to designing and improving services, with the goal of creating a better user experience and delivering value to both the service provider and the service user. Using a combination of research, analysis, and co-creation, service design involves understanding the needs and behaviors of users, identifying pain points and opportunities for improvement, and designing solutions that address these challenges. It goes beyond just the physical or digital touchpoints of a service, taking into account the entire service ecosystem and the interactions between different stakeholders.

Embodied Cognition

Embodied cognition is a concept in the field of design thinking that emphasizes the role of the body in shaping and influencing cognitive processes, such as perception, understanding, and problem-solving. It suggests that our physical experiences and interactions with the environment play a significant role in shaping our thoughts, emotions, and actions.

According to embodied cognition, the mind is not separate from the body but is instead intricately intertwined with it. This means that our bodily experiences and sensations, such as movement, touch, and perception, are not passive inputs but active components of our cognitive processes. Our physical actions and interactions with the world around us shape our mental representations and understanding of the problems we are trying to solve.

Emotion Design

Emotion Design is a discipline within the broader framework of Design Thinking that focuses on incorporating emotional elements into the design process. It recognizes that emotions play a crucial role in shaping human behavior and experiences, and seeks to leverage this understanding to create more meaningful and impactful designs.

By considering how people feel and respond emotionally to products, services, and experiences, Emotion Design aims to create designs that evoke specific emotions or desired responses. It involves empathizing with the users, understanding their needs and desires, and infusing those insights into the design process.

Emotion-Centered Design

Emotion-Centered Design is a concept within the field of Design Thinking that prioritizes the emotional needs and experiences of users in the design process. It seeks to understand and address the emotional responses and feelings that users may have when interacting with a product or service. Rather than focusing solely on functionality or aesthetics, emotion-centered design aims to create a positive emotional experience for users, resulting in deeper engagement and satisfaction.

In this approach, designers conduct research and gather insights to better understand users' emotional states and needs. This may involve techniques such as empathy mapping, user interviews, and observation. By gaining a deeper understanding of the emotions and motivations that drive user behavior, designers can create more meaningful and impactful designs.

Emotion-Centered Solutions

Emotion-centered solutions in the context of Design Thinking disciplines refer to the approach of prioritizing and designing products, services, and experiences that deeply consider and address the emotional needs and desires of individuals or user groups. It involves understanding and empathizing with the emotional experiences and responses of users, and using this understanding to guide the design process.

This approach recognizes that emotions play a significant role in decision-making, behavior, and overall user satisfaction. By focusing on the emotional aspects of design, it becomes possible to create more meaningful and impactful solutions that resonate with users on a deeper level.

Emotion-Driven Solutions

Emotion-Driven Solutions refer to the approach used in the field of Design Thinking disciplines, where the design process focuses on understanding and addressing the emotional needs and experiences of users or customers. This approach acknowledges that emotions play a crucial role in shaping human behavior and decision-making, and aims to create solutions that resonate on an emotional level.

In the context of Design Thinking, Emotion-Driven Solutions involve empathizing with users to gain deep insights into their emotions, desires, and aspirations. This empathetic understanding allows designers to identify and prioritize the emotional pain points or opportunities for improvement. By considering the emotional needs of users, designers can create products, services, and experiences that establish meaningful connections, build trust, and evoke positive emotions.

Emotional Connection

A short formal definition of Emotional Connection in the context of Design Thinking disciplines:

Emotional Connection refers to the deep and meaningful bond that is established between a user and a product, service, or experience through the fulfillment of their emotional needs and desires. It is a key aspect of Design Thinking disciplines, as it focuses on creating experiences that resonate with users on a personal and emotional level.

Emotional Design

Emotional design refers to the intentional design of a service or product with the aim of evoking specific emotions or feelings in users. It acknowledges that human beings are not solely rational beings, but also emotional beings whose decisions and experiences are often influenced by their emotions. In the context of service design, emotional design seeks to create a service experience that not only meets the functional needs of users but also connects with them on an emotional level. It goes beyond providing a purely functional solution and aims to create an emotional connection and resonance with users, thereby enhancing their overall experience and satisfaction.

Emotional Intelligence

Emotional Intelligence, within the context of Design Thinking disciplines, can be defined as the ability to recognize and understand one's own emotions, as well as the emotions of others, and to effectively manage and regulate those emotions in order to enhance the design process.

Design Thinking is a human-centered approach to problem-solving that focuses on empathy, collaboration, and innovation. In this context, Emotional Intelligence plays a crucial role in the success of the design process. It enables designers to empathize with the needs and desires of the end-users, and to effectively communicate and collaborate with team members and stakeholders.

Emotionally Durable Design

Emotionally Durable Design is a concept within the discipline of Design Thinking that focuses on creating products or experiences that have a lasting emotional impact on users. It recognizes that emotions play a significant role in how people form attachments to and derive meaning from the things they interact with.

Emotionally Durable Design goes beyond simply creating aesthetically pleasing or functional designs. It seeks to design products or experiences that evoke positive emotions, foster long-lasting relationships, and inspire individuals to cherish and maintain them over time.

Empathetic Design

Empathetic Design can be defined as a key component of the Design Thinking process that focuses on understanding and addressing the needs, desires, and challenges of the end-users or stakeholders involved. It involves placing oneself in the shoes of the users to gain a deep understanding of their perspectives, emotions, and experiences, in order to create solutions that truly meet their needs and improve their lives.

Empathetic Design requires designers to conduct research, engage in active listening, and practice empathy to gather insights about the target users or stakeholders. By observing and interacting with users, designers aim to gain a deep understanding of their context, motivations, pain points, and aspirations. This understanding helps designers to develop insights that guide the design process and enable them to create innovative solutions that are truly user-centered.

Empathetic Leadership

Empathetic Leadership refers to the practice of understanding and acknowledging the needs, emotions, and perspectives of others while leading a team in the context of Design Thinking disciplines.

In the field of Design Thinking, empathetic leadership plays a crucial role in driving innovation and problem-solving. It involves the ability to put oneself in the shoes of team members, stakeholders, and end-users to gain a deep understanding of their experiences, desires, and challenges.

This type of leadership emphasizes active listening, open-mindedness, and a genuine interest in the well-being of others. It requires leaders to cultivate strong interpersonal skills, empathy, and emotional intelligence to create a collaborative and inclusive environment.

Empathetic leaders in the context of Design Thinking disciplines recognize that diverse perspectives and input lead to better outcomes. They encourage and support teams to conduct user research, engage in iterative prototyping, and use empathy-building techniques such as persona development, journey mapping, and empathy interviews. By deeply understanding the needs and emotions of stakeholders and end-users, leaders can guide the design process effectively and ensure the creation of solutions that address real problems.

In conclusion, empathetic leadership in the context of Design Thinking disciplines involves understanding and valuing the perspectives of others. It is a practice that promotes collaboration, innovation, and user-centricity. By leveraging empathy and emotional intelligence, leaders can foster a creative and inclusive environment that drives effective problem-solving and design.

Empathetic Problem Solving

Empathetic Problem Solving is a key aspect of the Design Thinking discipline that involves understanding and addressing the needs and challenges of individuals or groups through a compassionate and empathetic approach.

In this context, Empathetic Problem Solving refers to actively listening and observing people to gain insights into their experiences, emotions, and motivations. By putting oneself in the shoes of others, Design Thinkers strive to develop a deep understanding of the problems they face and the underlying reasons behind those problems.

This method emphasizes human-centeredness, ensuring that the solutions proposed are tailored to meet the actual needs and desires of the target audience. It encourages Design Thinkers to move beyond their assumptions and biases, allowing them to challenge their own perspectives and gain new insights.

Empathetic Problem Solving typically involves techniques such as interviews, observations, surveys, and empathy mapping. Through these methods, Design Thinkers strive to uncover unmet needs, pain points, and aspirations of the people they are designing for.

By combining empathy with analytical thinking, Design Thinkers are able to reframe problems, identify relevant insights, and generate innovative ideas. This approach fosters a human-centered mindset where the focus is on creating meaningful and effective solutions that truly address the needs and challenges of the end-users.

In summary, Empathetic Problem Solving in the context of Design Thinking is a process that involves understanding the needs and desires of people by actively listening, observing, and empathizing. It enables Design Thinkers to develop human-centered solutions that have a genuine impact on individuals and communities.

Empathetic Solutions

Empathetic Solutions refers to the process of developing innovative solutions to problems by deeply understanding and empathizing with the needs, desires, and pain points of the target users. It is a key component of the Design Thinking disciplines, which is a human-centered approach to problem-solving.

Design Thinking involves a series of iterative steps that include empathizing, defining, ideating, prototyping, and testing. Empathetic Solutions specifically focuses on the empathizing step, where designers seek to gain a deep understanding of the users' experiences, emotions, and challenges. This step requires the designers to step into the shoes of the users, observe their behaviors, conduct interviews, and gather insights that provide valuable context for the design process.

Empathy is crucial in the Design Thinking disciplines because it helps designers look beyond their own assumptions and biases, enabling them to uncover unmet needs that may not be evident at first. By developing a comprehensive understanding of users' perspectives, designers can identify opportunities for creating meaningful and impactful solutions.

The empathetic solutions developed in the Design Thinking disciplines are human-centered and aim to address the core needs and desires of the users. These solutions are not simply based on assumptions or guesswork, but rather on deep insights gained through empathizing with the target users. By designing with empathy, designers can create solutions that are relevant, intuitive, and emotionally resonant, thus enhancing the overall user experience and driving user adoption and satisfaction.

Empathic Design

Empathic design, in the context of service design, refers to a design approach that focuses on understanding and incorporating the emotional needs, desires, and experiences of users in order to create more meaningful and effective services. It involves deeply empathizing with users and perceiving their needs, motivations, and contexts in order to design a service that is not only functional, but also resonates with users on an emotional level. In empathic design, the designer seeks to gain a deep understanding of the users by putting themselves in their shoes, considering their motivations, beliefs, and emotional states. This understanding is achieved through various research methods such as in-depth interviews, observations, and ethnographic studies. By immersing themselves in the users' world, designers can gain valuable insights into their experiences, uncover unmet needs, and identify pain points or areas for improvement. Once the designer has gained a comprehensive understanding of the users' emotional needs and experiences, they can use this insight to inform the design of the service. This involves considering not only the functional aspects of the service, but also the interactions, touchpoints, and overall experience that users will have. The aim is to create a service that not only meets users' needs in a practical sense, but also evokes positive emotions, enhances their overall experience, and builds meaningful connections. Empathic design in service design also involves actively involving and collaborating with users throughout the design process. This can include co-creation sessions, participatory design activities, and user testing and feedback loops. By involving users directly in the design process, designers can ensure that their needs and desires are considered and incorporated into the final service. In summary, empathic design in the context of service design is an approach that places a strong emphasis on understanding and incorporating the emotional needs, desires, and experiences of users. It involves deeply empathizing with users, perceiving their needs and motivations, and designing services that not only meet their functional needs, but also resonate with them on an emotional level, ultimately creating more meaningful and effective services.

Empathic Problem Framing

Empathic problem framing refers to the process of understanding and defining problems from the perspective of the end users or stakeholders in the context of Design Thinking disciplines.

This approach involves going beyond surface-level observations and assumptions, and delving into the underlying emotions, needs, and experiences of the people who are directly or indirectly affected by the problem at hand. It aims to cultivate empathy and a deep understanding of the user's context in order to identify the core issues that need to be addressed.

Empathy Building Kits

Empathy Building Kits are tools used in the context of Design Thinking disciplines to foster and enhance empathy among individuals. Empathy, a fundamental aspect of human-centered design, is the ability to understand and share the feelings, thoughts, and experiences of another person. It plays a pivotal role in developing meaningful and innovative solutions for complex problems by putting emphasis on users' perspectives and needs.

The purpose of Empathy Building Kits is to facilitate the cultivation of empathy within design teams and individuals. These kits typically consist of a collection of materials, exercises, and prompts carefully curated to encourage participants to step into the shoes of others and develop a deep understanding of their emotions, motivations, and challenges.

By engaging in activities provided by Empathy Building Kits, participants are encouraged to observe, listen, and interact with the people they are designing for. Through role-playing, storytelling, and immersive experiences, they are able to gain insights into users' lives, needs, and aspirations, fostering a greater sense of empathy and connection.

The use of Empathy Building Kits allows design teams to move beyond assumptions and biases, enabling them to design more inclusive and impactful solutions. It helps designers uncover unmet needs, discover hidden pain points, and develop a profound comprehension of the contexts in which their users operate. Empathy Building Kits ultimately contribute to creating products, services, and experiences that truly resonate with users, providing them with valuable and meaningful solutions.

Empathy Building Workshops

Empathy Building Workshops are a fundamental component of the Design Thinking process, aimed at fostering a deep understanding and connection with users or stakeholders. These workshops provide participants with the opportunity to develop empathy, which is the ability to understand and share the feelings, thoughts, and experiences of others.

During these workshops, participants actively engage in a series of activities and exercises that encourage them to step into the shoes of the users they are designing for. They are guided to explore the perspective of the users by immersing themselves in their world, listening to their needs, and observing their behaviors. By doing so, participants gain unique insights into the users' motivations, aspirations, and challenges.

Through a combination of individual and group exercises, empathy building workshops enable participants to transcend their own perspectives and biases, allowing them to truly understand the users' emotional and functional needs. This understanding forms the foundation for designing meaningful and impactful solutions that address the users' needs effectively.

These workshops often involve activities such as storytelling, role-playing, and ethnographic research to create a safe and immersive environment for participants to develop empathy. The goal is to foster a mindset of deep curiosity, openness, and a genuine desire to address the users' unmet needs.

Overall, empathy building workshops are an essential practice within the Design Thinking process, serving as a catalyst for innovation by providing designers and other stakeholders with a human-centered perspective. By developing empathy, participants gain invaluable insights that inform the design process and result in solutions that truly resonate with users.

Empathy Cultivation

Empathy cultivation is a vital aspect within the discipline of Design Thinking. It refers to the development of the ability to understand and share the feelings, thoughts, and experiences of others, particularly the users or target audience of a design. Empathy cultivation is achieved through a deliberate and systematic approach of observation, interaction, and active listening.

Design Thinking emphasizes the principle of user-centered design, where the needs and desires of the users are at the forefront of the design process. Empathy cultivation plays a crucial role in achieving this user-centric approach. By cultivating empathy, designers are able to gain a deep understanding of the needs, motivations, and challenges faced by the target audience.

Empathy cultivation involves stepping into the shoes of the users and looking at the design problem from their perspective. It requires setting aside personal biases and assumptions and adopting a non-judgmental and open-minded attitude. Designers immerse themselves in the users' environment, observe their behaviors, and engage in meaningful conversations to uncover insights and gain a holistic understanding of the users' experiences.

By cultivating empathy, designers are able to uncover unmet needs, reveal hidden pain points, and understand the emotional aspects that influence user behavior. This empathic understanding serves as the foundation for ideation and problem-solving in Design Thinking. It enables designers to generate innovative and meaningful solutions that address the actual needs and aspirations of the target audience.

Empathy Interview Kits

Empathy Interview Kits are a tool used in the field of Design Thinking to facilitate conducting empathy interviews with users or potential users of a product or service. These kits contain a set of carefully crafted questions or prompts, along with guidance on how to conduct and document the interviews, in order to gather valuable insights and understand the needs, desires, and pain points of the interviewees.

The purpose of empathy interviews in Design Thinking is to gain a deep understanding of the user's perspective and experience. By stepping into the shoes of the users and getting to know them on a personal level, designers can uncover unmet needs and identify opportunities for innovation and improvement in their design solutions. Empathy Interview Kits help designers to conduct effective interviews by providing a structured approach, ensuring that important questions are asked and that the conversation flows smoothly.

Empathy Interview Resources

Empathy interview is a research method commonly used in the context of Design Thinking disciplines. It is a technique that allows designers to gain a deep understanding of users, their needs, and their perspectives. The goal of an empathy interview is to immerse oneself in the experiences, emotions, and motivations of the user, in order to design products or services that truly address their desires and challenges.

During an empathy interview, the designer engages in active listening and open-ended questioning to gather rich qualitative data. They strive to create a comfortable and non-judgmental environment, where the user feels free to express their thoughts and emotions freely. By actively empathizing with the user, the designer can uncover valuable insights that go beyond superficial observations.

Empathy Interview Templates

Empathy Interview Templates are a set of structured questions and prompts designed to help practitioners of Design Thinking disciplines understand and empathize with the needs, emotions, and experiences of users or customers. These templates serve as a guide for conducting interviews and gathering valuable insights that will inform the design and development process.

Empathy is a fundamental principle in Design Thinking, as it allows designers to put themselves in the shoes of the people they are designing for. By asking open-ended and probing questions, designers can uncover not only the rational needs of their users but also their deeper motivations, goals, and challenges. These interviews go beyond surface-level observations and aim to elicit emotional responses and personal stories from participants.

Empathy Interview

Empathy is a fundamental aspect of Design Thinking, encompassing understanding, sharing, and feeling the emotions, needs, and perspectives of others. It is the ability to put oneself in someone else's shoes, seeing the world through their eyes, and experiencing their challenges, values, and aspirations.

Empathy in the context of Design Thinking involves interacting directly with individuals or groups to gather insights about their experiences, preferences, and pain points. By actively listening, observing body language, and asking open-ended questions, designers can gain a deep understanding of users' behaviors, motivations, and expectations.

Empathy interviews, also known as user interviews or ethnographic research, provide an opportunity to connect with users on a personal level and build rapport, establishing trust and openness. Through these interviews, designers aim to uncover latent needs, unmet desires, and hidden challenges that may not be apparent at first glance.

Designers use empathy as a tool to identify with users, allowing them to empathize with their struggles and identify common patterns across different user groups. By immersing themselves in the user's world, designers can gain insights and uncover unique perspectives that serve as a springboard for innovation, problem-solving, and design iteration.

Empathy is the starting point of the design process, enabling designers to develop solutions that are human-centered, meaningful, and empathetic. It helps designers challenge assumptions, break down preconceived notions, and avoid biases by valuing diverse perspectives and experiences.

Empathy Interviews

Empathy interviews in the context of service design refer to the process of conducting interviews with individuals in order to gain a deep understanding of their thoughts, feelings, and experiences related to a specific service or problem. These interviews are focused on empathizing with the interviewees and gaining insights into their needs, wants, and pain points. The goal of empathy interviews is to gather rich qualitative data that can inform the design of services that truly meet the needs of users. The interviews are typically conducted in a one-on-one setting, allowing for a more intimate and personal conversation where participants feel comfortable sharing their thoughts and emotions.

Empathy Map

Empathy Map is a tool used in the Design Thinking process to understand users or customers better. It helps design teams gain insights into the emotions, thoughts, needs, and experiences of users, enabling them to develop more user-centered solutions.

Empathy Map consists of a simple framework that prompts designers and researchers to capture and organize their observations during user research interviews or observations. The framework is divided into four quadrants, each focusing on a different aspect of the user's experience:

- Says: This quadrant represents the user's spoken words and what they say about their experiences, needs, and desires. It captures direct quotes from the user that reveal their thoughts and opinions.

- Thinks: In this quadrant, designers record the internal thoughts, attitudes, and beliefs of the user. It delves into the user's underlying motivations, assumptions, and concerns that may not be explicitly expressed.

- Does: This quadrant focuses on the user's actions, behaviors, and non-verbal cues. It captures what the user does, how they behave, and the gestures they make. It helps identify patterns of behavior and actions that may inform design decisions.

- Feels: This quadrant deals with the user's emotions and feelings associated with their experiences. It captures both positive and negative emotions, as well as their intensity. Understanding the user's emotions helps designers create solutions that resonate emotionally with the user.

Empathy Mapping

Empathy mapping is a tool used in the field of service design to develop a deep understanding of customers' experiences, needs, and emotions. It helps service designers gain insights into the thoughts and feelings of users, enabling them to create products and services that meet their customers' needs effectively. Empathy mapping involves creating a visual representation of the customer's journey, capturing their experiences and interactions with a particular product or service. It focuses on understanding the customer's mindset at different stages of their journey, including what they think, feel, see, hear, say, and do. This information is gathered through research, observations, interviews, and direct interactions with customers. The empathy mapping process typically begins by identifying the target customer segment and defining the specific context or situation in which the service is being provided. This could range from using a mobile app to booking a flight or receiving healthcare services. Once the context is defined, the service designers gather relevant data and insights about the customer's experiences and emotions related to that context. The empathy map is divided into four quadrants, each representing a different aspect of the customer's experience: Think and Feel, See, Hear, and Say and Do. Under each quadrant, specific observations, quotes, or insights are documented to capture the customer's perspective accurately. The purpose of an empathy map is to uncover the underlying needs, motivations, and pain points of customers. It helps service designers gain a holistic understanding of user needs and design solutions that address those needs effectively. By putting themselves in the shoes of the customer, service designers can empathize with their experiences and identify opportunities for improvement or innovation. Empathy mapping is a collaborative process that involves cross-functional teams, including designers, researchers, and stakeholders, working together to gather insights and develop a shared understanding of the customer's experience. By leveraging empathy mapping, service designers can create meaningful and impactful solutions that meet customers' needs and enhance their overall satisfaction.

Empathy Maps

Empathy Maps are tools used in the context of Design Thinking disciplines to help understand and empathize with the experiences, emotions, needs, and behaviors of specific user groups or individuals. These maps provide a visual representation of the gathered insights and help designers and researchers gain a deeper understanding of the target users.

An Empathy Map consists of four quadrants that focus on different aspects of the user's experience: the user's thoughts and feelings, their actions and behaviors, the user's needs and desires, and the user's environment. By examining these aspects, designers can gain insights into what motivates and influences the target users, allowing them to design solutions that cater to their needs and aspirations.

Empathy Workshops

Empathy workshops in the context of Design Thinking disciplines are interactive sessions aimed at promoting and developing empathy skills among participants. Empathy, a crucial aspect of the Design Thinking process, involves understanding and sharing the feelings, thoughts, and perspectives of others. It plays a vital role in uncovering latent needs and gaining deep insights into user experiences and challenges.

Empathy workshops typically consist of a series of exercises and activities designed to foster empathy and perspective-taking. Participants engage in various hands-on exercises that challenge their assumptions, biases, and preconceived notions. These activities may include role-playing, immersive experiences, storytelling, and reflective discussions.

The workshops create a safe space for participants to step into the shoes of different stakeholders such as customers, end-users, or colleagues. By experiencing the world through their eyes, participants can develop a deeper understanding of their needs, desires, and pain points. This enables designers to create more empathetic and effective solutions that truly address the core challenges and aspirations of the target audience.

Empathy workshops enhance the overall emphasis on user-centeredness and human-centricity in Design Thinking. They cultivate a mindset of openness, curiosity, and a genuine desire to comprehend the experiences and emotions of others. By practicing empathy, designers can create products, services, and experiences that are not only visually appealing but also emotionally resonant and meaningful for the intended users.

Empathy

Empathy is a critical aspect of Design Thinking, which involves understanding and sharing the feelings, thoughts, and experiences of others. It is the practice of placing oneself in the shoes of others to gain deep insights into their perspective and emotions, ultimately enabling designers to create meaningful solutions that meet users' needs.

In the context of Design Thinking disciplines, empathy is not limited to sympathy or pity but goes beyond that by actively engaging with users and developing a true understanding of their challenges, desires, and motivations. It requires designers to step outside of their own biases and preconceived notions and develop a genuine connection with the target audience.

Employee Experience Design

Employee Experience Design, in the context of service design, refers to the deliberate and strategic approach taken by organizations to enhance and improve the overall experiences of their employees throughout their journey within the company. It involves understanding the needs, motivations, and pain points of employees and designing interventions, processes, and touchpoints that contribute to a positive and meaningful employee experience. The aim is to create an environment where employees feel valued, engaged, and empowered, leading to higher job satisfaction, productivity, and employee loyalty. Employee Experience Design encompasses various aspects of the employee journey, starting from the recruitment and onboarding process to ongoing development, performance management, and offboarding. It emphasizes taking a holistic view of the employee's interactions with the company, considering both the physical and digital aspects of the workplace environment. Key elements of Employee Experience Design include: 1. Employee Research and Understanding: Conducting research, surveys, and interviews to gain insights into the needs, preferences, and challenges faced by employees. This helps in identifying pain points and areas for improvement. 2. Journey Mapping: Mapping out the employee journey to visualize the different touchpoints and interactions employees have with the organization. This helps in identifying areas of improvement and creating a seamless and cohesive experience for employees. 3. Co-creation and Collaboration: Involving employees in the design process, seeking their feedback and ideas, and co-creating solutions. This ensures that the interventions and processes are aligned with the needs and expectations of the employees. 4. Transparent Communication: Establishing effective communication channels and practices to keep employees informed, engaged, and involved in decision-making processes. Open and transparent communication builds trust and fosters a positive employee experience. 5. Employee Empowerment: Providing employees with the necessary tools, resources, and autonomy to carry out their roles effectively. Empowered employees tend to be more engaged and motivated, leading to a better overall experience. In conclusion, Employee Experience Design is an essential aspect of service design that focuses on creating meaningful and impactful experiences for employees. By understanding their needs, designing interventions, and fostering a positive work environment, organizations can enhance employee satisfaction, productivity, and loyalty.

Employee Experience (EX)

Employee Experience (EX) is a concept within service design that focuses on creating a positive and engaging environment for employees in an organization. It encompasses the various interactions, perceptions, and emotions that employees experience throughout their journey within the company.EX aims to enhance employee satisfaction, engagement, and well-being by addressing their needs and expectations at different touchpoints. It recognizes the value of employee experience in driving organizational success, as satisfied and engaged employees are more likely to deliver exceptional customer service, improve productivity, and foster innovation.

Empowerment

Empowerment in the context of Design Thinking disciplines refers to the process of equipping individuals or groups with the knowledge, skills, and confidence to take ownership of their own creative problem-solving and decision-making processes. It involves providing people with the necessary tools and resources to explore, ideate, and implement innovative solutions to challenges they may face.

In Design Thinking, empowerment is a fundamental principle that aims to shift the traditional hierarchical approach to problem-solving and decision-making towards a more collaborative and inclusive one. It emphasizes the importance of involving all stakeholders, regardless of their role or position, in the design process. By empowering individuals or groups, Design Thinking encourages them to become active participants in the problem-solving journey and fosters a sense of ownership and accountability for the outcomes.

End-User Feedback

End-user feedback is the information or opinions provided by individuals who directly use a product or service to express their experiences, thoughts, and suggestions. In the context of service design, end-user feedback is an essential component for gathering insights and evaluating the effectiveness of a service. By collecting end-user feedback, service designers can better understand the needs, preferences, and expectations of their target audience. This feedback helps to identify any gaps or pain points in the service that may need improvement or optimization. It provides valuable insights into the customer experience, allowing service designers to make informed decisions and enhance the overall service delivery.

End-To-End Service Design

End-to-End Service Design is a comprehensive approach to the creation and delivery of a service, from its initial design and development to its implementation and ongoing improvement. It involves considering every aspect of the service, from the customer's perspective, to ensure a seamless and positive experience. This approach begins with an in-depth understanding of the customer's needs, preferences, and pain points. This includes gathering feedback, conducting research, and analyzing data to gain insights into the customer's journey and identify areas for improvement. By taking a customer-centric approach, organizations can design services that are tailored to meet the specific needs and expectations of their target audience. Once the customer's requirements have been identified, the next step is to design the service itself. This involves defining the service offerings, processes, and touchpoints, as well as establishing the roles and responsibilities of the various stakeholders involved. The aim is to create a service that is not only functional and efficient but also appealing and engaging for the customer. After the service design has been finalized, it is then implemented and delivered to the customer. This involves coordinating the necessary resources, training the staff, and putting the necessary systems and infrastructure in place to ensure the smooth delivery of the service. It also involves monitoring and measuring the performance of the service to ensure that it is meeting the desired outcomes and making adjustments as necessary. End-to-End Service Design is a continuous process, as organizations must constantly iterate and improve their services in response to changing customer needs and market conditions. This may involve gathering feedback from customers, analyzing data, and conducting user testing to identify areas for improvement and make necessary changes to the service design. In summary, End-to-End Service Design is a holistic approach to service creation and delivery that considers every aspect of the customer's journey. It involves understanding customer needs, designing the service, implementing it, and continually improving it to provide a seamless and satisfying experience for the customer.

Environmental Awareness

Environmental awareness is a crucial aspect within the context of Design Thinking disciplines. It refers to the understanding and consideration of the impact that human activities have on the natural environment and ecosystems. It involves recognizing the importance of sustainability, conservation, and reducing harm to the environment.

In the context of Design Thinking, environmental awareness plays a significant role in the ideation, development, and implementation of innovative solutions. Design thinkers recognize that their creations can have both positive and negative consequences on the environment. By being environmentally aware, designers can proactively address potential environmental issues and integrate sustainable practices into their solutions.

Ergonomics

Ergonomics is a crucial aspect of Design Thinking disciplines. It focuses on the design and arrangement of products, systems, and environments to ensure they are well-suited to the needs and abilities of individuals.

At its core, ergonomics aims to optimize human performance and well-being by considering key factors such as comfort, efficiency, and safety. By applying ergonomic principles, designers can create user-centric solutions that enhance usability and prevent potential health issues or injuries.

Ethical Consideration

Ethical consideration in the context of Design Thinking disciplines refers to the conscious and deliberate examination of the moral implications and potential consequences of the design process, solutions, and outcomes.

Design Thinking is a human-centered approach that aims to solve complex problems by understanding people's needs, generating creative ideas, prototyping solutions, and testing them empirically. It emphasizes empathy, collaboration, and iterative problem-solving. However, the pursuit of design solutions should not be isolated from ethical considerations that have significant impacts on individuals, communities, and the environment.

Ethical consideration requires designers to critically reflect on their values, motivations, and biases. It involves questioning the potential harm or benefits that their designs may have on various stakeholders. This includes considering issues such as privacy, inclusivity, fairness, transparency, sustainability, and social impact. For example, a designer developing a mobile app would need to consider the privacy implications of collecting user data and ensure that appropriate security measures are in place to protect user information.

Furthermore, ethical consideration also extends to the design process itself. Designers should promote diversity and inclusivity by involving a wide range of perspectives in their research and decision-making. They should strive for transparency and open dialogue with stakeholders, seeking their input and feedback throughout the process. Ethical consideration requires designers to continuously evaluate and improve their work to ensure it aligns with ethical standards and serves the best interests of all those affected by the design outcomes.

Ethnographic Design

Ethnographic design is a research approach commonly used in the field of design thinking disciplines. It involves studying and understanding the behaviors, experiences, and cultural context of people in order to inform the design process and create solutions that meet their needs.

Through ethnographic design, designers aim to gain deep insights into the target users of their products or services. This method goes beyond basic demographic data and focuses on understanding the cultural, social, and psychological aspects that influence people's behaviors and preferences.

Ethnographic Field Studies

Ethnographic field studies refer to a research method used in service design to gain deep insights into people's behaviors, needs, and motivations in their natural environment. This approach involves immersing oneself in the context of the users and observing their activities, interactions, and experiences firsthand. During ethnographic field studies, service designers spend considerable time in the field, interacting with users and collecting rich qualitative data. They aim to understand the social and cultural aspects that influence users' behaviors and preferences, uncovering insights that may not be evident through traditional research methods. Service designers typically employ a range of techniques during ethnographic field studies, such as participant observation, interviews, and artifact analysis. They carefully observe and document users' actions and interactions, capturing both verbal and non-verbal cues. This active engagement allows designers to grasp the context in which the service is used and discover hidden needs and pain points. The data collected through ethnographic field studies is analyzed to identify patterns, themes, and underlying drivers that shape user behavior. This analysis forms the basis for uncovering design opportunities and developing meaningful solutions that address users' needs and aspirations. Ethnographic field studies in service design have several advantages. By immersing in the users' environment, designers can gain a holistic understanding of their needs, preferences, and the challenges they face. It also enables designers to identify the discrepancies between users' stated needs and their actual behaviors, identifying opportunities for innovation. Overall, ethnographic field studies provide invaluable insights that inform service design processes. They help bridge the gap between designers and users, facilitating the creation of services that are truly user-centered and grounded in the reality of users' lives.

Ethnographic Immersion Kits

An ethnographic immersion kit refers to a collection of tools and resources that are used within the context of Design Thinking disciplines to facilitate immersive research and understanding of cultures, communities, and individuals. These kits are specifically designed to help designers, researchers, and innovators gain deep insights into the lives, behaviors, and perspectives of the people they are designing for.

Typically, an ethnographic immersion kit may include a variety of materials such as cameras, audio recording devices, observation sheets, interview guides, questionnaires, and artifacts that allow for the collection of rich qualitative data. These materials are instrumental in capturing and documenting important details, interactions, and observations during field research.

By equipping designers with the necessary tools and resources, ethnographic immersion kits empower them to immerse themselves in the context they are designing for. This immersive approach enables designers to gain a holistic and empathetic understanding of the needs, desires, challenges, and aspirations of the people they are designing for.

The use of ethnographic immersion kits within Design Thinking disciplines promotes the value of ethnography as a research method for design. By enabling designers to actively engage with the real world and develop a deep understanding of the cultural and social contexts they are designing within, ethnographic immersion kits foster more meaningful and user-centered design solutions. Ultimately, the adoption of these kits promotes a human-centered approach to design, where the needs and experiences of users are at the forefront of the design process.

Ethnographic Immersion Platforms

Ethnographic immersion platforms refer to tools or platforms that facilitate the process of conducting ethnographic research within the context of design thinking disciplines. Ethnography is a field study method that involves observing and interacting with individuals or communities in their natural environments to gain a deep understanding of their behaviors, needs, and experiences. It is commonly used in design thinking processes to inform the development of innovative solutions that address user needs. These platforms provide a structured framework for designers and researchers to immerse themselves in the cultural and social contexts of the users they are studying. They often include components such as participant observation, interviews, and cultural probes to gather rich qualitative data. By using ethnographic immersion platforms, designers and researchers can gain a holistic and empathetic understanding of the users they are designing for. This deep understanding allows them to uncover unmet needs, uncover insights, and identify opportunities for innovation. It also helps to ensure that the solutions developed are grounded in the realities of the users' lives and are therefore more likely to be meaningful, relevant, and successful. Ethnographic immersion platforms are valuable tools within design thinking disciplines because they support the human-centered approach that is at the core of the design thinking process. They enable designers and researchers to uncover user needs and generate actionable insights that inform the ideation and prototyping stages of the design process. By leveraging these platforms, they can create solutions that truly resonate with and have a positive impact on the lives of the intended users.

Ethnographic Immersion

Ethnographic immersion is a research approach within the field of Design Thinking that involves deep engagement and observation of a specific culture or community to gain insights into their behaviors, needs, and preferences. It aims to understand the social, cultural, and environmental context in which a problem or design challenge exists, in order to inform the development of more relevant and effective solutions.

During ethnographic immersion, designers or researchers spend a significant amount of time directly observing and interacting with individuals within the target culture or community. This may involve participating in their activities, attending their events, and conducting interviews or informal conversations. The immersion process allows designers to gain a holistic view of the community, including their daily routines, social dynamics, and interactions with the designed or natural environment.

Through ethnographic immersion, designers can uncover deeper insights and uncover unmet needs that may not be readily apparent through traditional research methods. By immersing themselves in the everyday lives of the people they are designing for, designers are able to develop a more empathetic, human-centered understanding of their target users.

These insights can then be used to inspire and inform the design process, helping designers to develop more meaningful and impactful solutions. Ethnographic immersion is a critical step in the Design Thinking process as it allows designers to move beyond assumptions and design for real-world contexts and users.

Ethnographic Observation

An ethnographic observation is a systematic process used by designers in the context of Design Thinking disciplines to gain a deep understanding of people's behavior, needs, and experiences within a specific cultural or social context. It involves immersing oneself in the natural environment of the participants and carefully observing their actions, interactions, and reactions.

During an ethnographic observation, designers take a non-judgmental and non-intrusive approach, aiming to observe participants in their everyday routines and activities. They may use various methods such as shadowing, participant observation, and interviews to gather qualitative data that can uncover insights and reveal unmet needs of the target audience.

Ethnographic Research Kits

Ethnographic research kits are sets of tools and resources that are designed to facilitate the process of conducting ethnographic research. Ethnography is a qualitative research method used in the field of design thinking to gain insights into the lived experiences, behaviors, and cultural contexts of individuals and communities.

These kits typically include a combination of physical and digital tools, such as interview guides, observation checklists, video cameras, note-taking materials, and data analysis software. They are carefully curated to support the various stages of the ethnographic research process, from planning and data collection to analysis and synthesis.

Ethnographic Research

Ethnographic research is a qualitative research method used in the field of service design. It involves the systematic study and observation of people and their behaviors, beliefs, and cultural practices within their natural environments. The goal of ethnographic research in service design is to gain a deep understanding of the experiences, needs, and expectations of users in order to inform the design and improvement of services. During ethnographic research, service designers immerse themselves in the users' environment, often spending extended periods of time observing and interacting with people in their natural settings, such as homes, workplaces, or public spaces. This approach allows designers to gain firsthand insights into the context in which services are used and the factors that influence user behavior and decision-making. Key methods used in ethnographic research for service design include participant observation, interviews, and artifact analysis. Participant observation involves the direct observation and documentation of people's actions, interactions, and social dynamics, while interviews provide an opportunity for in-depth conversations to uncover users' motivations, challenges, and expectations. Artifact analysis involves the examination and interpretation of physical objects, documents, or other artifacts that are relevant to the service context. The data collected through ethnographic research is typically rich and detailed, providing a holistic understanding of the user experience and the various factors shaping it. These insights can then be used to identify gaps, pain points, and opportunities for improvement within the service ecosystem. By understanding users' needs and desires, service designers can create meaningful and user-centered interactions, touchpoints, and experiences that meet and exceed user expectations. In conclusion, ethnographic research plays a crucial role in service design by providing deep and contextual insights into users' experiences, behaviors, and needs. It allows designers to gain a comprehensive understanding of the user journey and design services that effectively address user requirements and expectations.

Ethnographic Studies

Ethnographic studies refer to the research methods used in Design Thinking disciplines to gain a deep understanding of people and their behaviors within specific cultural contexts. These studies involve immersion into the target community or environment, observing and interacting with individuals to uncover their needs, values, and motivations.

Through ethnographic studies, designers collect qualitative data by conducting interviews, participant observations, and artifact analysis. By focusing on real-life experiences and cultural contexts, designers can gain valuable insights into the users' lives and the challenges they face.

Ethnographic Study

An ethnographic study is a research method within the discipline of Design Thinking that involves observing and immersing oneself in a specific culture or community to gain a deep understanding of their behaviors, beliefs, and practices. The goal of this study is to uncover insights and discover unmet needs that can inform the design process.

In an ethnographic study, researchers spend an extended period of time in the field, engaging with individuals and communities in their natural environment. They use a variety of methods, such as participant observation, interviews, and artifact analysis, to collect data and gain a holistic understanding of the culture and context they are studying.

Ethnography

Ethnography, in the context of service design, refers to a research method that involves observing and understanding the cultural and social behavior of a specific group of people to gain insights for designing better services. It involves immersing oneself in the target group's environment and studying their interactions, experiences, and needs in order to develop a deep understanding of their perspectives and challenges. The goal of ethnography is to uncover meaningful insights and discover opportunities for creating more effective and user-centered services. It provides designers with rich qualitative data that goes beyond just surface-level information, enabling them to design services that truly meet the needs of the target audience.

Evident Simplification

Design Thinking is a human-centered approach to problem-solving that involves a systematic and creative process for generating innovative solutions. It is a discipline that seeks to understand users' needs and challenges, redefine problems, and create innovative solutions in a collaborative and iterative manner. At its core, Design Thinking is driven by empathy and understanding of users' perspectives. It begins with the identification and framing of the problem, followed by extensive research and exploration of user needs and motivations. This phase typically involves conducting interviews, surveys, and observations to gain insights and develop a deep understanding of the problem. The next phase involves synthesizing and analyzing the gathered information to identify patterns, themes, and opportunities for innovation. This process often involves collaboration and brainstorming sessions to generate a wide range of ideas and perspectives. These ideas are then narrowed down and refined based on their feasibility, potential impact, and alignment with users' needs and goals. Once a set of potential solutions is identified, prototyping and testing are conducted to gather feedback and validate assumptions. Quick and iterative prototypes are created to allow users to interact with and visualize the proposed solutions. Through testing and user feedback, flaws and improvements are identified, leading to further iterations and refinements. The final phase involves implementation and evaluation of the chosen solution. This may include developing a detailed plan, seeking necessary resources, and ensuring successful implementation. Evaluation and feedback are gathered to assess the impact and effectiveness of the solution and to identify opportunities for further improvement. In summary, Design Thinking is a disciplined and creative problem-solving approach that centers around users and their needs. It involves empathetic research, ideation, prototyping, and testing to generate innovative and effective solutions. - Design Thinking is a human-centered approach to problem-solving that involves a systematic and creative process for generating innovative solutions. - It is driven by empathy and understanding of users' perspectives, and it includes phases such as problem identification and framing, research and exploration of user needs, idea generation and refinement, prototyping and testing, and implementation and evaluation of solutions.

Experience Design Platforms

An experience design platform refers to a digital tool or software that enables designers to ideate, prototype, test, and iterate on user experiences within the context of design thinking disciplines. These platforms provide a collaborative environment for designers, stakeholders, and users to come together, contribute insights, and collectively shape the design process.

By integrating various design tools, such as wireframing, visual design, prototyping, and user testing, experience design platforms enable designers to create seamless, engaging, and user-centric experiences. These platforms enable designers to transition from static representations to interactive prototypes, facilitating more accurate user feedback and iteration.

The experience design platforms typically incorporate design thinking principles, such as empathy, ideation, prototyping, and testing, into their workflows. They promote a user-centered design approach by allowing designers to gather user insights, analyze data, and iterate on designs based on user feedback. This iterative process helps designers align their solutions with the needs, behaviors, and preferences of the target audience.

Furthermore, experience design platforms often offer features for collaboration and communication, allowing designers to easily share their work, gather feedback from stakeholders, and foster a design thinking mindset throughout the project lifecycle. With these platforms, designers can involve stakeholders and users in the design process, enabling a more inclusive and holistic approach to problem-solving.

In summary, experience design platforms provide designers with a comprehensive set of digital tools and capabilities to foster collaboration, ideation, prototyping, and testing within the framework of design thinking disciplines. These platforms empower designers to create user-centered experiences by enabling iterative design cycles based on user feedback, ensuring successful solutions that meet the needs of the target audience.

Experience Design Strategy

Experience design strategy in the context of service design refers to the systematic approach and plan implemented to create meaningful and memorable experiences for users throughout their interactions with a service. It involves considering every touchpoint and aspect of the service from the user's perspective in order to provide an optimal experience. Experience design strategy aims to align the service's goals and objectives with the needs, expectations, and emotions of the users. It involves a deep understanding of user behaviors, desires, and motivations to design service experiences that meet their needs and create positive emotions.

Experience Design Thinking

Experience design thinking is a discipline within design thinking that focuses on creating meaningful and engaging experiences for users. It is a human-centered approach that aims to understand the needs, behaviors, and emotions of users to design products, services, and systems that meet their expectations and enhance their overall experience.

Experience design thinking follows a systematic process of understanding, ideating, prototyping, and testing to iteratively develop innovative solutions. It involves empathy, collaboration, and iteration to uncover insights and generate ideas that address user needs and pain points. By putting the user at the center of the design process, experience design thinking ensures that the resulting experiences are intuitive, satisfying, and delightful for users.

Experience Design

Experience Design in the context of service design refers to the intentional and systematic design of the overall experience that users have when interacting with a service. It involves understanding the needs and desires of the users, and aligning those with the goals and objectives of the service provider. Experience Design goes beyond just the functional aspects of a service, and takes into account the emotional, psychological, and sensory aspects as well.

Experience Ecosystem

The experience ecosystem refers to the interconnected network of interactions, touchpoints, and elements that collectively shape and influence an individual's overall experience with a product, service, or organization. It encompasses all the various facets and components that contribute to the user's journey and perception, from initial awareness to post-purchase satisfaction.

Within the context of design thinking disciplines, understanding and mapping the experience ecosystem is vital to creating a holistic and user-centric design solution. By comprehensively exploring and analyzing each touchpoint and interaction, designers can gain insights into the user's emotions, needs, and pain points at different stages of the experience.

Experience Journey Platforms

Experience Mapping

Experience mapping is a Design Thinking discipline that involves visually mapping out the entire journey of a customer or user, from the initial touchpoint to the final interaction. It provides a holistic view of the overall experience, capturing every step, emotion, and interaction throughout the entire journey.

Using experience mapping, designers can empathize with the user and gain a deeper understanding of their needs and pain points. The process involves gathering both qualitative and quantitative data, conducting user interviews, and observing user behaviors. By analyzing this data, designers can identify key moments that impact the user's experience and identify opportunities for improvement.

The mapping process typically starts by identifying the different stages of the journey and creating a timeline. Each stage is then divided into different touchpoints, such as online interactions, physical interactions, or customer service interactions. Designers can then visualize the user's emotions and thoughts at each touchpoint, using color or symbols to represent positive, negative, or neutral experiences.

Experience mapping helps designers identify pain points, bottlenecks, and areas for improvement. It enables them to prioritize design efforts based on the user's needs and expectations. By visualizing the entire journey, designers can uncover often overlooked moments that have a significant impact on the user experience.

Experience Metrics Dashboards

Experience Metrics Dashboards are visual representations of data that provide a comprehensive view of a user's experience with a product or service. These dashboards are designed to capture and display key metrics and measurements that are relevant to the design thinking disciplines.

By analyzing the data presented in the experience metrics dashboard, design thinkers can gain insights into the effectiveness of their solutions and make informed decisions to improve the user experience. The dashboard helps to identify patterns, trends, and areas of improvement based on user interactions and feedback.

Experience Metrics Kits

Experience Metrics Kits refer to a set of tools and methodologies used within the context of Design Thinking disciplines to measure and evaluate the user experience and gather data for further analysis and improvements. These kits are typically comprised of a combination of quantitative and qualitative metrics and techniques, aimed at capturing diverse aspects of user behavior, perceptions, and interactions with a product or service.

The primary objective of Experience Metrics Kits is to provide designers and researchers with actionable insights into how users engage with a particular design, enabling them to make informed decisions and iterate upon their designs. These kits often incorporate a mix of both standardized and customized metrics, allowing for a comprehensive evaluation of the user experience across various dimensions.

Experience Metrics Platforms

Experience Metrics Platforms are tools or software used in the context of Design Thinking disciplines to track, measure, and analyze user experiences and interactions with a product, service, or system. They provide quantifiable data and insights that inform design decisions and help improve the overall user experience.

These platforms enable designers to collect and analyze various types of experience metrics, such as user behavior, preferences, satisfaction, and performance. Through the use of surveys, feedback forms, user testing, and data analytics, designers can gain a deep understanding of how users engage with their designs and identify areas for improvement.

Experience Prototype

An experience prototype is a design thinking discipline that involves creating a simplified representation of a proposed product or service. It allows designers to test and gather feedback on the user experience before investing resources in fully developing the final solution. This type of prototype focuses on simulating the interactions and emotions that users may experience when using a product or service. It is not intended to be a functional or complete version of the final solution, but rather a tool for exploring and refining the user experience. Experience prototypes can take various forms, such as storyboards, videos, or physical models. The key is to create a representation that effectively communicates the intended experience to stakeholders and users. The purpose of an experience prototype is to uncover potential issues and opportunities early in the design process. By simulating the user experience, designers can gain insights into how users might respond and identify areas for improvement. This allows for iterative testing and refinement, ensuring that the final product or service meets the needs and expectations of the users. Overall, an experience prototype provides a means to visually and experientially communicate a design concept, validate assumptions, and gain valuable insights in order to create a better user experience. As a crucial step in the design thinking process, it empowers designers to make informed decisions and create meaningful solutions that address user needs and desires.

Experience Prototyping Kits

An Experience Prototyping Kit is a set of tools and materials designed to facilitate the creation of interactive prototypes in the field of design thinking. It is primarily used to bring ideas and concepts to life, enabling designers to test and refine their designs through hands-on user experiences.

The purpose of an Experience Prototyping Kit is to bridge the gap between the abstract and tangible, allowing designers to quickly iterate and iterate their ideas in order to gain valuable feedback and insights. These kits are often used in the early stages of the design process, where low-fidelity prototypes can help designers explore different possibilities and uncover potential design challenges or opportunities.

The components of an Experience Prototyping Kit can vary widely depending on the specific needs of the project and the desired level of fidelity. Common elements may include materials such as cardboard, foam, or clay, as well as various tools and accessories like markers, scissors, and adhesive. Additionally, electronic components such as sensors, microcontrollers, or actuators may be included in advanced kits to create more interactive and immersive prototypes.

Experience Prototyping Kits are essential tools for design thinking practitioners, as they facilitate the rapid testing and refinement of ideas and concepts. By creating tangible, interactive prototypes, designers can gather valuable user feedback, generate new insights, and make informed design decisions. These kits not only foster collaboration and creativity within design teams but also enable designers to empathize with and better understand users' needs, leading to more effective and user-centered solutions.

Experience Prototyping Software

Experience prototyping software is a design thinking tool that allows designers to create interactive and immersive mockups or simulations of a product or service. It enables designers to test and refine their ideas in a real-world context before investing time and resources into full-scale development.

By using experience prototyping software, designers can quickly and easily create digital prototypes that simulate the user experience, allowing them to gather feedback and validate their design decisions. This software typically includes features that enable designers to add interactive elements such as buttons, sliders, and animations, as well as simulate user interactions and scenarios.

Experience Prototyping Tools

Experience prototyping tools are a set of techniques and materials used in the field of Design Thinking disciplines to create tangible representations of user experiences and interactions in order to gather feedback and iterate on design concepts. These tools enable designers to simulate and communicate the intended user experience and test its feasibility before investing resources in developing a final product or service.

The primary purpose of experience prototyping is to shift the focus from abstract ideas to concrete and tangible solutions. By creating prototypes that users can interact with, designers can gather rich insights about user needs, preferences, and pain points. This iterative process allows designers to identify areas for improvement and make informed design decisions.

Experience Prototyping

Experience prototyping is a method used in the field of service design to simulate and test service experiences before they are fully developed and implemented. It involves creating tangible representations or prototypes of the service, allowing designers and users to interact with and experience the service in a realistic way. Unlike other forms of prototyping that focus on creating physical or digital products, experience prototyping focuses on designing and evaluating the entire service journey. It enables designers to understand and refine the different touchpoints, interactions, and emotions that users may encounter throughout their service experience.

Experience Sampling Method (ESM)

The Experience Sampling Method (ESM) is a research technique commonly used in service design to collect data about individuals' experiences and perceptions in real-time. It involves participants being prompted to record their thoughts, feelings, and activities at random or predetermined intervals throughout the day. ESM is designed to capture data about individuals' subjective experiences as they occur, providing a more accurate reflection of their day-to-day lives compared to traditional retrospective methods. It allows researchers to collect rich, detailed, and contextual information about individuals' interactions with services, enabling a deeper understanding of their needs, preferences, and challenges.

Experience Testing

Experience testing is a method used in service design to evaluate the quality and effectiveness of a service from the perspective of the end-users. It involves observing and documenting the interactions between users and the service, as well as gathering their feedback and opinions. The goal of experience testing is to identify any issues, pain points, or areas for improvement in the service design. By directly involving users in the evaluation process, designers can gain valuable insights into how their service is perceived and experienced in real-world scenarios.

Experience-Centered Design

Experience-Centered Design is a design approach that focuses on creating products, services, or systems that prioritize the user experience. It is a discipline within Design Thinking that seeks to understand and empathize with the users, in order to develop solutions that address their needs and enhance their overall experience.

Experience-Centered Design places the user at the center of the design process, emphasizing the importance of understanding their behaviors, motivations, and emotions. By gaining insights into the user's journey, from the initial interaction with a product or service to the final outcome, designers can create experiences that are intuitive, enjoyable, and meaningful.

Experience-Centric Approach

An experience-centric approach is a key principle of design thinking disciplines that prioritize understanding and addressing the needs, desires, and emotions of users throughout the design process.

This approach recognizes that the ultimate goal of any design is to create a positive and impactful experience for the user. By putting the user at the center, designers aim to deeply understand their needs, empathize with their challenges, and uncover opportunities for innovation.

Designers adopting an experience-centric approach employ various methods to gather qualitative and quantitative data about user behaviors, preferences, and pain points. They may conduct user research through interviews, observations, or surveys to gain insights into users' motivations and frustrations.

Using these insights, designers can then ideate, prototype, and test potential solutions that address the identified needs and provide a seamless and satisfying user experience. This iterative process allows for constant refinement and improvement based on user feedback.

Moreover, an experience-centric approach emphasizes the emotional and sensory aspects of design. It considers not only the functionality and aesthetics but also how the design makes the user feel. By focusing on emotional delight and positive engagement, designers can create memorable experiences that foster user loyalty and advocacy.

In summary, an experience-centric approach in design thinking disciplines places the user experience as the primary consideration. It enables designers to deeply understand and empathize with users, iterate on solutions based on user feedback, and create designs that fulfill both functional needs and emotional desires.

Experience-Centric Design Thinking

Experience-centric design thinking is a discipline within the broader field of design thinking that focuses on creating products, services, and experiences that prioritize the users' emotional, psychological, and sensory interactions. It places a heavy emphasis on understanding the needs, desires, and behaviors of the users, and aims to design experiences that are intuitive, engaging, and meaningful.

This approach recognizes that people's perceptions and emotions play a critical role in their overall satisfaction and adoption of a product or service. By deeply empathizing with users, designers can gain insights into their experiences and identify opportunities to improve and innovate. They seek to uncover unmet needs, pain points, and desires, and use these insights to inform the design process.

Experience-Centric Design

Experience-Centric Design, in the context of Design Thinking disciplines, refers to a design approach that prioritizes the user's experience throughout the design process. It places the user at the center of the design, taking into consideration their needs, preferences, and behaviors. This approach aims to create products, services, and systems that provide seamless, meaningful, and enjoyable experiences for the users.

Experience-Centric Design involves understanding and empathizing with the users, anticipating their wants and needs, and designing solutions that meet those needs in a user-friendly and intuitive manner. It emphasizes the importance of human-centered design, where the focus is on designing for the user rather than designing to meet specific technical or business requirements.

Experiential Design

Experiential design, within the context of Design Thinking disciplines, refers to the intentional creation of meaningful and engaging experiences for people. It involves an iterative and human-centered approach to designing products, services, systems, or environments that prioritize user needs and desires. This design approach aims to promote positive and memorable experiences that resonate with individuals on an emotional and sensory level.

Experiential design incorporates empathy and observation to gain deep insights into users' behaviors, motivations, and aspirations. By understanding their context, designers can develop solutions that not only solve problems but also create enjoyable and valuable experiences. This involves considering the physical, cognitive, social, and emotional aspects of the experience, allowing users to connect with the design in a meaningful and personal way.

Through prototyping and testing, designers can refine and improve the experiential design, ensuring it aligns with user expectations and desires. This iterative process allows for continuous learning and adaptation, as designers gather feedback and insights from users.

Experiential design also recognizes the importance of storytelling and narrative in creating immersive experiences. By incorporating elements such as visual aesthetics, interaction design, and sensory stimuli, designers can craft narratives that captivate and engage users, enhancing the overall experience.

Experiential Learning

Experiential learning is a pedagogical approach that emphasizes hands-on and practical experiences as a means of acquiring knowledge and understanding in the context of design thinking disciplines.

In the context of design thinking disciplines, experiential learning involves actively engaging students in real-world experiences and challenges. It encourages them to explore, experiment, and learn through direct involvement and observation. This approach recognizes that design thinking is not solely a theoretical concept, but rather a practical and iterative process that requires active participation and experimentation.

Experimental Iteration

Experimental Iteration is a core principle within Design Thinking disciplines that involves the process of iteratively refining and improving a design through multiple rounds of testing and evaluation. It emphasizes the importance of learning from failures, recognizing that each iteration of the design provides valuable insights and opportunities for improvement.

The process of Experimental Iteration typically begins with the creation of a prototype or initial design concept. This prototype is then tested with users or stakeholders in order to gather feedback and identify areas for improvement. By involving users early on in the design process, designers are able to gain a deeper understanding of their needs and preferences, ultimately leading to a more user-centered design.

Based on the feedback received, designers then make iterative changes to the design, addressing the identified areas for improvement. This process is repeated multiple times, with each iteration building upon the previous one. Each round of testing and evaluation provides designers with new insights and learnings, allowing them to refine and enhance the design as they progress.

Experimental Iteration is an essential component of Design Thinking as it encourages designers to embrace a mindset of continuous learning and improvement. By actively seeking feedback, designers are able to create designs that are more aligned with user needs and expectations, resulting in better overall experiences. Through the iterative process of Experimental Iteration, designers are able to take calculated risks, test assumptions, and make evidence-based decisions, ultimately leading to more innovative and successful outcomes.

Experimental Iterations

Experimental iterations refer to the repetitive process of testing and iterating a design solution through experimentation. It is a key component of the Design Thinking discipline, which is a problem-solving approach that aims to understand and address people's needs and desires.

In the context of Design Thinking, experimental iterations involve creating prototypes or mock-ups of a design solution and then testing it with users or stakeholders to gather feedback and insights. These prototypes can be physical or digital representations of the design, ranging from simple sketches to interactive models. Through these experiments, designers can uncover what works and what doesn't, and make informed adjustments and refinements to improve the solution.

Experimental Learning

Experimental learning refers to the process of acquiring knowledge and skills through hands-on experiences, active experimentation, and reflection. It is a central component of Design Thinking, a problem-solving approach that emphasizes empathy, creativity, and iteratively refining solutions.

In the context of Design Thinking, experimental learning involves actively engaging with the problem or challenge at hand, rather than relying solely on theoretical knowledge or passive observation. It encourages designers to generate ideas, prototype solutions, and test them in real-world situations to gather valuable feedback and insights.

This approach recognizes that failure is an essential part of the learning process. Designers actively embrace setbacks and use them as opportunities for growth and improvement. By experimenting and iterating, designers can uncover new possibilities, challenge assumptions, and uncover unexpected insights that lead to innovative solutions.

At its core, experimental learning in Design Thinking is rooted in a human-centered approach. It involves interacting with users, stakeholders, and the broader context to understand their needs, uncover hidden motivations, and gain a deep understanding of the problem space. This empathetic understanding allows designers to create solutions that truly address user needs and provide meaningful experiences.

Experimentation Culture

Experimentation culture refers to a mindset and approach within the context of Design Thinking disciplines that encourages and values experimentation as an integral part of the design process. It is a culture that promotes a willingness to take risks, learn from failures, and iterate on ideas through rapid prototyping and testing.

In an experimentation culture, designers and teams embrace the idea that the best solutions are often discovered through a process of trial and error. They understand that not all ideas will work out as intended, and that's okay. Failure is seen as an opportunity for growth and learning rather than a setback.

Explorative Interviews

Explorative interviews are a qualitative research method used in the context of Design Thinking disciplines. They involve conducting in-depth conversations with individuals or groups to gain a deep understanding of their experiences, perspectives, needs, and desires. This approach allows designers to explore the problem space, generate insights, and inform the design process.

During explorative interviews, designers use open-ended questions and active listening techniques to encourage participants to share their thoughts and experiences freely. The goal is to uncover underlying motivations, challenges, and opportunities that may not be apparent through traditional research methods. By delving into the participants' emotions, values, and behaviors, designers can gain empathy for their target users and discover innovative solutions.

Eye-Tracking Studies

Eye-tracking studies are a method used in service design to understand and analyze user behavior by tracking and measuring where and how users look at a given screen or visual stimulus. This technique involves using specialized eye-tracking technology, such as eye-tracking glasses or software, to capture and record data related to eye movements, fixations, and gaze points. Through eye-tracking studies, service designers can gain valuable insights into how users interact with digital interfaces, physical spaces, and other visual elements. By precisely examining and analyzing user eye movements, designers can uncover patterns, preferences, and areas of focus. This information helps to inform the design and development of user-centric services and interfaces that better meet the needs and expectations of users.

Fail Fast

Fail Fast is a principle employed in Design Thinking that encourages quickly testing and learning from ideas and prototypes, with the goal of identifying potential flaws and minimizing the impact of those flaws early in the design process.

By deliberately embracing and seeking out failure, teams can gain valuable insights and make more informed decisions as they iterate and improve their designs. The Fail Fast approach helps to avoid investing significant time and resources in ideas or solutions that may ultimately prove ineffective or unsuccessful.

Failure Analysis

A failure analysis in the context of Design Thinking disciplines is a systematic evaluation and examination of a failed design or innovation, aiming to understand the root causes of the failure and identify opportunities for improvement. It involves a structured investigation process that focuses on identifying and analyzing both technical and non-technical factors that contributed to the failure.

The analysis begins by gathering relevant data and information about the failed design, including its purpose, intended users, context, and intended outcomes. This data is then analyzed to identify potential failure points and underlying issues. The examination may involve reviewing documentation, conducting interviews with stakeholders, and studying usage patterns and feedback.

Once the failure points and issues are identified, further analysis is conducted to understand the underlying causes. This involves examining factors such as inadequate research, poor problem framing, incorrect assumptions, ineffective collaboration, or inadequate testing and iteration. The goal is to uncover the systemic weaknesses that led to the failure and highlight areas for improvement.

The analysis concludes by generating insights and recommendations for future design iterations or alternative approaches. These insights can inform the development of new design concepts, the refinement of existing designs, or the adjustment of the innovation strategy. By learning from failures, Design Thinking practitioners can iteratively improve their designs and increase the chances of success in subsequent iterations or innovations.

Feasibility Study

A feasibility study, in the context of service design, refers to a systematic evaluation of a

113

proposed service to determine its practicality and viability. It analyzes various factors such as financial, technical, operational, and market aspects to assess the feasibility of implementing the service successfully. The purpose of conducting a feasibility study is to gather relevant data and information to make informed decisions about the potential service. It helps in identifying any potential challenges, risks, or limitations that may impact the service's successful implementation. By carefully evaluating these factors, service designers can assess whether the proposed service is achievable within the given constraints and resources. The first step in conducting a feasibility study is to define the objectives and goals of the proposed service. This helps in setting a clear direction and understanding the desired outcomes. Once the objectives are established, the study focuses on evaluating the technical feasibility, which involves assessing whether the required technology, infrastructure, and resources are available to support the service. The financial feasibility analysis involves determining the costs associated with developing, operating, and maintaining the service. It includes conducting a cost-benefit analysis to compare the financial gains with the investment required. This analysis helps in understanding the profitability and long-term sustainability of the service. Operational feasibility evaluates the service's practicality and compatibility with existing systems, processes, and resources. It assesses the potential impact on daily operations and identifies any necessary changes or modifications required for seamless integration. Market feasibility involves analyzing the target market and assessing the demand for the service. It examines the competition, customer preferences, and market trends to determine whether there is a viable market for the proposed service. The feasibility study concludes by providing recommendations and insights based on the analysis conducted. It helps in decision-making, allowing stakeholders to determine whether to proceed with the service implementation, modify the service concept, or abandon it altogether. In summary, a feasibility study in service design is a comprehensive evaluation that assesses the practicality and viability of a proposed service. It takes into account various factors such as financial, technical, operational, and market aspects to determine the service's feasibility and potential for success.

Feedback Integration

Feedback integration is a crucial aspect within the discipline of Design Thinking. It involves the continuous incorporation and utilization of feedback throughout the design process in order to refine and improve a solution.

The process of Design Thinking typically involves empathizing with users, defining the problem, ideating potential solutions, prototyping, and testing. At each stage, feedback plays a vital role in informing the design decisions. Feedback can be gathered through various methods such as user interviews, surveys, usability testing, and observations.

During the empathize stage, feedback helps designers gain insights into the needs, pain points, and aspirations of the users. By understanding the users' perspectives, designers can create solutions that truly address their problems. The feedback collected during this stage helps in defining the problem more accurately.

During the ideate and prototype stages, feedback helps designers evaluate the potential of their ideas and prototypes. It helps identify flaws, areas of improvement, and opportunities for innovation. Feedback is used to refine and iterate on the design solutions, ensuring that they align with the users' needs and expectations.

Feedback integration continues during the testing stage, where prototypes are evaluated by users. This feedback helps designers validate their assumptions and make necessary adjustments to the design. Testing also provides an opportunity to gather additional feedback for further improvement.

In summary, feedback integration in Design Thinking is a continuous process that enables designers to gather valuable insights, refine their solutions, and create products or services that effectively meet the users' needs and preferences.

Feedback Loop

A feedback loop in the context of Design Thinking disciplines refers to the iterative process of obtaining user feedback, analyzing it, and incorporating it into the design process. It is a crucial element in the iterative and user-centered approach of Design Thinking.

The feedback loop typically consists of several stages:

1. Empathize: In this stage, designers gather insights and understand the needs, wants, and challenges of the users. Feedback from users and stakeholders is collected through various methods such as interviews, surveys, and observations.

2. Define: Once the feedback is collected, designers analyze and synthesize the information to define the problem or the opportunity for improvement. This stage involves identifying patterns, themes, and key insights from the feedback received.

3. Ideate: Using the defined problem or opportunity, designers brainstorm and generate a wide range of ideas and potential solutions. Feedback from users is crucial at this stage to ensure that the ideas align with their needs and expectations.

4. Prototype: Designers create low-fidelity prototypes or mock-ups of their ideas, which can be tested and evaluated by users for feedback. This stage allows designers to gather insights on how well their concepts meet users' expectations and make necessary iterations.

5. Test: The prototypes are tested with potential users and stakeholders, and their feedback is collected and analyzed. This feedback informs further iterations and improvements to the design. The testing process helps in validating assumptions, confirming or revising design decisions, and identifying areas that require refinement.

By continuously iterating through these stages, the feedback loop enables designers to refine and improve their designs based on users' feedback and needs. It ensures that the final solution addresses the identified problem or opportunity effectively and meets the users' expectations.

Field Observations

Field Observations (Design Thinking):

Field observations are a key practice in the field of Design Thinking, which involves the systematic study and analysis of real-world situations to inform the design process. It is a discipline that emphasizes empathetic understanding of users and their needs, and field observations provide designers with direct insights into the context in which their designs will be used.

Field Research

Field research, within the context of Design Thinking disciplines, refers to the process of gathering firsthand knowledge and insights through direct observation, interaction, and immersing oneself in the real-world environment relevant to the design problem or challenge at hand.

This hands-on approach involves going out into the field, whether it be a physical location or a virtual space, to gain a deep understanding of the users, their needs, behaviors, and the various contextual factors that impact their experiences. Field research enables designers to uncover rich, nuanced information that cannot be obtained through surveys or secondary sources alone.

Field Studies

Field studies refer to the research method used in the context of Design Thinking disciplines where the researcher directly observes and gathers data by immersing themselves in the real-world environment of the users or participants. This approach involves going out into the field, which may include various settings such as homes, workplaces, or public spaces, and actively engaging with the individuals or groups being studied.

The aim of field studies is to gain a deep understanding of the users, their needs, behaviors, and challenges, in order to inform the design process and facilitate the creation of innovative and user-centered solutions. By observing and interacting with users in their natural settings, researchers can uncover valuable insights that may not be apparent through traditional research methods.

Five Whys

The Five Whys is a problem-solving technique commonly used in service design to identify the root cause of a problem. It involves asking "why" five times to get to the underlying issue causing a specific problem or challenge. The basic concept behind the Five Whys is to probe deeper into the reasons behind a problem by asking a series of "why" questions. Each time a "why" question is asked, the answer is used as the basis for the next question. By repeating this process five times, it is believed that the root cause of the problem can be uncovered. The Five Whys technique is particularly useful in service design as it helps designers gain a better understanding of the underlying issues that may be impacting the customer experience. By getting to the root cause of a problem, designers can then develop more effective solutions that address the core issues. Using pure HTML format, the essence of the Five Whys technique can be summarized as follows: The Five Whys is a problem-solving technique commonly used in service design to identify the root cause of a problem. It involves asking "why" five times to get to the underlying issue causing a specific problem or challenge. The basic concept behind the Five Whys is to probe deeper into the reasons behind a problem by asking a series of "why" questions. Each time a "why" question is asked, the answer is used as the basis for the next question. By repeating this process five times, it is believed that the root cause of the problem can be uncovered.

Flexibility In Interpretation

Flexibility in interpretation refers to the ability to approach problems, ideas, and concepts from multiple perspectives and adapt one's understanding and viewpoint according to different contexts and situations within the Design Thinking discipline.

In the context of Design Thinking, flexibility in interpretation enables designers and practitioners to embrace a diverse range of viewpoints, experiences, and opinions. It encourages the exploration of different possibilities and allows for the examination of multiple solutions to a problem.

Flexibility In Process

Flexibility in process refers to the ability to adapt and modify the steps and approaches followed in Design Thinking disciplines to suit the specific needs and challenges of a particular project or situation.

Design Thinking is a human-centered approach that emphasizes empathy, experimentation, and iterative problem-solving. It involves a structured process that typically consists of several stages, such as understanding the problem, researching and gathering insights, ideating and brainstorming, prototyping, and testing. However, flexibility in process recognizes that each project is unique and may require adjustments to the traditional stages or incorporation of additional steps.

Flexibility

Flexibility in the context of Design Thinking disciplines refers to the ability to adapt and adjust throughout the design process in order to meet the evolving needs and requirements of the project. It involves being open to change, embracing new ideas, and willing to explore different possibilities.

In the initial stages of the design process, flexibility allows for the exploration of various problem-solving approaches. Designers can generate multiple ideas and concepts, considering various perspectives and potential solutions. Flexibility enables them to test and refine these ideas, making adjustments as needed based on feedback and new insights.

Throughout the design process, flexibility also allows for iteration and refinement. Designers may need to revisit and revise their work in response to new information, user feedback, or

116

changing project constraints. They should be willing to let go of ideas that are not working and adapt their approach to better meet the design goals.

Flexibility is closely linked to an iterative and collaborative mindset. Designers should be open to collaboration and feedback from stakeholders, clients, and users. They should be able to integrate new ideas and perspectives into their work, adjusting their designs accordingly.

Overall, flexibility is a crucial mindset in Design Thinking disciplines as it enables designers to navigate the complex and ever-changing landscape of design projects. It allows for innovation, responsiveness, and continuous improvement throughout the design process.

Flow State

The flow state, in the context of Design Thinking disciplines, refers to an optimal state of consciousness where individuals are fully immersed and focused in an activity. It is characterized by a deep sense of enjoyment, effortless concentration, and a heightened state of creativity and productivity.

When designers are in a flow state, they experience a sense of timelessness, and lose awareness of their surroundings and distractions. They are fully absorbed in the task at hand, and their skills and abilities are aligned with the challenges they face. In this state, designers enter a state of "flow" where they feel a sense of control, mastery, and deep engagement with their work.

Flowcharts

Flowcharts are visual representations used in service design to illustrate the sequence and interaction of steps, decisions, and activities within a process. They consist of different types of symbols and connectors that represent various elements and relationships within the process. Flowcharts provide a way to understand, analyze, and communicate the flow of activities and decisions in a service design process. They help to visualize the logical connections between different actions and decision points, and highlight the dependencies and conditions that affect the journey of a service user. The symbols used in a flowchart have specific meanings. Rectangles represent process steps or activities, such as gathering customer information or providing a service. Diamonds represent decision points, where different paths or outcomes are possible based on specific conditions or criteria. Arrows and lines link the symbols and indicate the flow and direction of the process. Flowcharts not only show the sequential order of activities but also highlight loops, iterations, and branches within the process. They allow service designers to identify bottlenecks, redundancies, or potential inefficiencies in a service journey. By visually representing the process, flowcharts enable designers to identify areas for improvement, streamline processes, and enhance the overall service experience. In service design, flowcharts are commonly used during the initial stages of designing and mapping out a service experience. They are useful for brainstorming and capturing ideas, as well as for communicating and collaborating with different stakeholders involved in the service design process. Overall, flowcharts provide a structured and visual way to understand and communicate the flow of activities, decisions, and interactions within a service design process. They help service designers analyze and improve the service experience, ensuring that it is efficient, effective, and user-centric.

Focus Groups

Focus Groups are a service design research method that involves gathering a small group of individuals to provide feedback, opinions, and insights on a specific topic or service. The purpose of focus groups is to understand the needs, preferences, and expectations of the target audience in order to improve the design and delivery of a service. Focus groups typically consist of 6-10 participants who are selected based on their relevance to the topic or their potential as representative users. The participants are carefully recruited to ensure diversity in terms of demographics, backgrounds, and experiences, allowing for a comprehensive understanding of different perspectives. During the focus group session, a moderator facilitates a group discussion and encourages participants to share their thoughts, feelings, and reactions related to the service or topic at hand. The discussions are typically structured around open-ended questions or specific prompts to stimulate meaningful conversations and elicit valuable insights. The role of the moderator is crucial in guiding the discussion, managing dynamics among participants, and ensuring that all relevant topics and perspectives are covered. The moderator also needs to create a safe and inclusive environment where participants feel comfortable expressing their opinions and ideas. Focus groups provide a rich source of qualitative data, allowing designers and researchers to gain in-depth insights into the participants' perceptions, expectations, and behaviors. The discussions can reveal valuable information about usability issues, pain points, unmet needs, as well as opportunities for service improvement or innovation. In addition to capturing individual perspectives, focus groups also facilitate interaction and group dynamics, enabling participants to build upon each other's ideas and generate new insights collectively. This collaborative aspect can lead to a deeper understanding of the social and cultural contexts in which the service is situated. However, it is important to note that focus groups have limitations as well. The small sample size may not represent the entire target audience or the diversity within it. Additionally, participants' responses may be influenced by social desirability bias or the presence of dominant individuals within the group. Therefore, focus groups are often used in conjunction with other research methods to gain a more comprehensive and nuanced understanding of users' needs and preferences.

Follow-Me-Homes

Follow-Me-Homes is a service design technique used to gain deep insights into user needs and behaviors. It involves observing and interacting with users in their natural environment to understand their daily routines, challenges, and preferences. This approach allows service designers to develop a more holistic understanding of users' experiences and identify opportunities for improvement in the design of products, services, or systems. During a Follow-Me-Home session, a service designer visits the user's home or workplace and observes their activities firsthand. The user is encouraged to go about their usual tasks and routines while the designer quietly observes and takes notes. This approach provides valuable context that may be missed in a controlled lab or interview setting, allowing designers to see how users interact with various elements of their environment and uncover pain points or areas for improvement. By observing users in their natural environment, service designers can gain a deeper understanding of their needs, motivations, and expectations. They can observe how users interact with technology, physical objects, and other people, as well as identify any barriers or frustrations they may encounter. This information can then be used to inform the design of products, services, or systems that better meet users' needs and enhance their experiences. Follow-Me-Homes can be particularly useful in the early stages of the design process when researchers are seeking to generate insights and ideas. It allows designers to empathize with users and gain a firsthand understanding of their context, which can lead to more innovative and user-centered solutions. Additionally, this technique enables designers to identify potential gaps or inconsistencies between user expectations and current offerings, which can inform future iterations or improvements.

Framing Assumptions

Framing assumptions in the context of Design Thinking disciplines refer to the underlying beliefs, expectations, and limitations that shape the problem space and guide the design process. These assumptions serve as a starting point for designers to understand the problem, define the scope of their work, and identify potential solutions.

When framing assumptions, designers acknowledge that their understanding of the problem is based on certain preconceived notions about the users, context, and constraints involved. These assumptions can come from various sources, including user research, market analysis, or personal experiences. However, they are recognized as fallible and open to validation and refinement as the design process progresses.

Framing Design Challenges

Framing design challenges is an essential step in the design thinking discipline. It involves defining and refining the problem or opportunity that the design team aims to solve or explore. By properly framing the design challenge, designers can set a clear direction and focus their efforts on generating innovative and effective solutions.

118

The process of framing design challenges typically includes identifying the main user needs, goals, and pain points, as well as considering the broader context in which the design will exist. This involves conducting research, gathering insights, and analyzing the gathered information to gain a deep understanding of the problem or opportunity at hand.

Framing

Framing, in the context of service design, refers to the act of defining the problem or opportunity that a service aims to address. It involves defining the boundaries, scope, and objectives of the service design project. When framing a service design project, designers need to clearly articulate what needs to be achieved and why. This helps stakeholders understand the purpose and potential outcomes of the project, and aligns everyone involved in a shared understanding of the problem or opportunity at hand.

Front-Stage And Back-Stage Design

Front-Stage Design: Front-stage design in the context of service design refers to the intentional and deliberate creation of the physical and virtual touchpoints that customers directly interact with during their service experience. It focuses on designing the visible and tangible aspects of the service that customers engage with, such as the interface of a website, the layout and signage in a physical store, or the appearance and functionality of a mobile app. Front-stage design aims to create a positive and seamless service experience by carefully considering the needs, preferences, and expectations of the customers. It involves a deep understanding of user behavior, preferences, and technological affordances to design interfaces, processes, and interactions that are intuitive, engaging, and user-friendly. Back-Stage Design: Back-stage design in the context of service design refers to the behind-the-scenes processes, systems, and activities that support and enable the front-stage service experience. Unlike the front-stage, which is visible to customers, the back-stage is hidden and involves the internal operations of the service provider. Back-stage design focuses on optimizing the efficiency, effectiveness, and reliability of the service delivery system. It involves designing the processes, resources, and technologies that enable seamless and sustainable service delivery. This includes everything from inventory management, supply chain logistics, IT infrastructure, and employee training, to name a few.

Functional Prototype

A functional prototype is a tangible representation of a product or solution that is created during the design thinking process. It serves as a working model that allows designers and stakeholders to explore, test, and evaluate the functionality and usability of the product before fully developing it.

The main purpose of a functional prototype is to gather feedback and gain insights into how the product will perform in real-world scenarios. By building a prototype, designers can identify potential flaws, usability issues, or other challenges that may arise once the product is implemented. This iterative approach enables them to make informed design decisions and refine the product to better meet user needs and expectations.

Future Scenarios

Future scenarios in the context of service design refer to potential future states or situations that businesses or organizations may encounter. These scenarios explore different possible futures that could emerge based on various factors such as technological advancements, societal changes, economic developments, and market trends. They are used as a tool to anticipate and prepare for the future, enabling businesses to adapt their services to meet the evolving needs and preferences of their customers. Future scenarios in service design are created through a systematic and collaborative process that involves researching, analyzing, and synthesizing information from various sources. This process helps uncover emerging trends, identify potential opportunities and challenges, and generate insights about the future landscape of the industry or market in which the service operates. The scenarios are typically developed through a combination of qualitative and quantitative methods, including trend analysis, scenario planning, user research, and market analysis.

Future-Oriented

Future-Oriented is a mindset and approach within the Design Thinking disciplines that focuses on anticipating, envisioning, and designing for the future. It involves considering the long-term impacts and implications of design decisions and innovations, and proactively shaping future possibilities.

This mindset is rooted in the understanding that the world is constantly evolving, and that design solutions should adapt and anticipate this evolution. Future-Oriented designers embrace uncertainty and ambiguity, seeking to understand emerging trends, technologies, and social changes in order to design with relevance and foresight.

Futures Exploration

Futures exploration in the context of Design Thinking disciplines refers to the process of envisioning and understanding possible future scenarios to inform the design and development of innovative solutions. It involves seeking a deep understanding of the current and emerging trends, technologies, and societal shifts that may impact the problem at hand.

This exploration is driven by the recognition that the future is uncertain and that designing for the present may not be sufficient for long-term success. By engaging in futures exploration, designers aim to anticipate and prepare for potential changes and disruptions, enabling them to create more robust and adaptable solutions.

Futures Thinking

Futures thinking is a discipline within Design Thinking that focuses on anticipating and understanding potential future scenarios and their implications. It involves investigating and exploring different possibilities, trends, and patterns to envision multiple futures and make informed decisions in the present.

This approach encourages designers and innovators to look beyond the immediate needs and problems, and instead, consider the long-term consequences and effects of their designs. By anticipating and preparing for various potential futures, designers can create more robust and adaptable solutions that can withstand uncertainties and changing circumstances over time.

Gameful Design

Gameful Design is a concept within design thinking disciplines that focuses on applying principles and elements of game design to create engaging and motivating experiences for users. It involves incorporating game-like elements such as challenges, rewards, feedback, and competition into non-game contexts, such as educational systems, healthcare, or productivity tools.

The goal of gameful design is to enhance user motivation, engagement, and overall experience by borrowing techniques from game design, which is known for its ability to captivate and sustain players' interest. By introducing these game-like elements, designers aim to promote desirable behaviors, increase participation, and foster a sense of mastery and achievement in users.

Gamification Approaches

Gamification approaches are strategies that leverage game principles and mechanics to enhance the engagement and motivation of users in non-game contexts, particularly in the field of Design Thinking disciplines. By incorporating elements such as points, badges, leaderboards, challenges, and rewards, gamification can promote deeper involvement, generate a sense of achievement, and foster a positive behavioral change among participants.

In the context of Design Thinking disciplines, gamification techniques can be applied to various stages of the innovation process to stimulate creativity, collaboration, and problem-solving. The use of game-like experiences encourages participants to explore multiple perspectives, think divergently, and experiment with alternative solutions, leading to more innovative outcomes.

Gamification can also facilitate the co-creation process by encouraging active participation and interaction among team members.

Gamification Strategies

Gamification strategies refer to the implementation of game elements, mechanics, and dynamics in non-game contexts to engage and motivate users in achieving desired outcomes. It is a design thinking discipline that leverages the principles of game design to solve problems and enhance user experiences.

Incorporating gamification strategies involves identifying the target audience's motivations, designing meaningful challenges, and providing rewards and feedback to encourage desired behaviors. By tapping into people's natural inclination for play and competition, gamification can increase participation, foster learning, and drive desired actions.

Gamification

Gamification is a technique used in the context of Design Thinking disciplines to enhance user engagement and motivation by incorporating game elements and mechanics into non-game contexts. It involves applying game design principles, such as competition, rewards, challenges, and feedback loops, to non-game experiences to make them more enjoyable and interactive.

The goal of gamification is to tap into the intrinsic human desire for achievement, recognition, and competition, encouraging users to actively participate and adopt desired behaviors. By introducing game elements, such as points, levels, badges, and leaderboards, designers can create a sense of progress, status, and competition, which motivates users to engage more deeply with the experience.

Gamification can be implemented in various fields, including education, marketing, healthcare, and workplace environments. In education, gamification can make learning more engaging, encouraging students to actively participate and retain information. In marketing, it can be used to create interactive campaigns and reward customer loyalty. In healthcare, it can motivate individuals to adopt healthier habits and adhere to medical treatments. In the workplace, gamification can improve employee engagement, productivity, and collaboration.

However, it is crucial to balance the game elements with the overall user experience and the desired outcomes. Gamification should not overshadow the core purpose of the experience or become a mere gimmick. It should be strategically implemented to align with the users' goals, provide meaningful challenges, and offer relevant rewards and feedback. Successful gamification requires a deep understanding of the target audience, their motivations, and the context in which the experience is taking place.

Gamified Solutions

Gamified Solutions are design thinking disciplines that incorporate game elements and mechanics into non-game contexts, with the goal of engaging and motivating users to achieve specific objectives.

These solutions leverage the inherent characteristics of games, such as competition, rewards, challenges, and feedback, to enhance user experiences, drive desired behaviors, and solve problems effectively.

Generative Design

Generative design is a methodology in the field of design thinking disciplines that leverages computational algorithms to explore multiple design possibilities and generate innovative solutions. It involves using powerful software and machines to generate and evaluate a large number of design variations based on defined parameters and constraints.

The process of generative design begins with defining the problem statement, desired outcomes, and constraints. These constraints can include factors such as material properties, manufacturing capabilities, budget limitations, and functional requirements. The designer then sets up a generative design software or environment, which uses algorithms to generate a wide range of design options.

This approach allows designers to quickly explore numerous design solutions that they may not have considered otherwise. By systematically iterating through different design possibilities, generative design enables the discovery of innovative solutions that can fulfill multiple objectives and push the boundaries of creativity.

Generative design helps designers uncover unexpected patterns, forms, and configurations, leading to optimized and efficient designs. It enables designers to balance multiple variables and find optimal solutions that meet complex requirements. This methodology encourages designers to embrace iterative problem-solving and pushes them to think beyond traditional design constraints.

In summary, generative design is a powerful tool that employs computational algorithms to explore a vast design space, generate diverse solutions, and optimize the design process. It encourages creativity, efficiency, and innovation by allowing designers to quickly iterate through multiple design options and discover optimal solutions.

Generative Research

Generative research is a crucial method used in service design to gain a deep understanding of user needs, preferences, and behaviors. It involves gathering insights directly from the target audience through various qualitative research techniques. The goal of generative research is to inform the design process by uncovering the underlying motivations, desires, and pain points of users. Through generative research, service designers aim to identify users' unmet needs and identify opportunities for innovation. This type of research is exploratory in nature and focuses on providing rich, contextual information that goes beyond surface-level observations. It helps designers gain empathy for the users and develop a holistic understanding of their experiences.

Gestalt Principles

The Gestalt Principles in the context of Design Thinking disciplines refer to a set of principles that explain how humans perceive and make sense of visual information. These principles are based on the Gestalt psychology, which suggests that humans have a tendency to organize stimuli into meaningful patterns and structures.

There are several Gestalt Principles that are commonly applied in design, including:

1. Closure: This principle states that humans tend to perceive incomplete objects as whole by mentally filling in missing information. In design, closure can be used to create visual stimuli that encourage viewers to complete the missing parts.

2. Proximity: According to this principle, elements that are close to each other in space are perceived as a group. Designers often use proximity to visually organize information and indicate relationships between elements.

3. Similarity: The principle of similarity suggests that elements that share similar characteristics, such as shape, color, or size, are perceived as belonging to the same group. Designers can use similarity to group related elements and create visual hierarchy.

These principles provide designers with a framework for understanding how people perceive and interpret visual information. By applying the Gestalt Principles, designers can create visually cohesive and engaging designs that effectively communicate their intended message.

Goal-Directed Design

Goal-Directed Design in the context of service design refers to a user-centered approach that aims to create services that fulfill specific user goals or objectives. It involves understanding and incorporating the needs, desires, and motivations of users into the design process to ensure the end result meets their expectations and provides value. The goal of Goal-Directed Design is to deliver a service that supports users in achieving their desired outcomes or completing a specific task efficiently and effectively. To achieve this, designers need to conduct thorough research to gain insights into user behaviors, preferences, and pain points. This research helps identify the goals and objectives users have when interacting with a service, and provides valuable information for informing the design process. Once user goals have been identified, designers can use this information to inform the creation of service interactions, experiences, and touchpoints that align with these goals. This can involve mapping out user journeys, designing intuitive user interfaces, and ensuring that the service flows seamlessly from start to finish. By considering user goals throughout the design process, designers have a better chance of creating a service that is intuitive, user-friendly, and ultimately successful in meeting the needs of its users. Goal-Directed Design also emphasizes the importance of iterative testing and feedback throughout the design process. By involving users in the evaluation and improvement of the service design, designers can gain insights into how well the service aligns with their goals and make necessary adjustments to enhance the overall user experience. In summary, Goal-Directed Design in service design focuses on understanding, incorporating, and aligning with the goals and objectives of users. It involves conducting research to gain insights into user needs, designing experiences that support these needs, and involving users in the evaluation and improvement of the service to ensure it meets their expectations and provides value.

Guerilla Testing

Guerilla testing is a method used in service design to gather quick and actionable insights by conducting user research in an informal and unstructured manner. This approach involves conducting user testing sessions with a small number of participants, typically around 5 to 10, in a non-traditional or ad-hoc setting. Unlike traditional usability testing that is conducted in a controlled lab environment, guerilla testing takes place in real-world situations, such as cafes, parks, or public spaces, where the target users are present. This allows for more natural and contextual interaction between the users and the service being tested.

Habitual Design

Habitual Design refers to the practice of incorporating sustainable and ethical principles into the design process to create products, services, and systems that promote long-term wellbeing for individuals, communities, and the environment. It is a discipline within Design Thinking that explores the intersection of human-centered design and sustainability, aiming to shift the focus from short-term gains to long-term impact.

In Habitual Design, designers consider not only the immediate needs and desires of users but also the broader social and ecological implications of their creations. This involves conducting thorough research to understand the current social and environmental challenges, identifying opportunities for positive change, and iteratively prototyping and testing solutions that align with sustainable principles.

By practicing Habitual Design, designers strive to minimize negative impacts, such as resource depletion, pollution, and social inequality, while maximizing positive outcomes, such as resource efficiency, regenerative practices, and social equity. This requires a holistic approach that considers the entire lifecycle of a product or service, from raw material sourcing and manufacturing to distribution, use, and end-of-life disposal.

Habitual Design also encourages collaboration and interdisciplinary thinking, as addressing complex sustainability challenges often requires insights and expertise from various fields, including engineering, sociology, psychology, and policy. By embracing diverse perspectives and engaging stakeholders throughout the design process, designers can create more inclusive and impactful solutions.

In conclusion, Habitual Design is a methodology within Design Thinking that integrates sustainable and ethical considerations into the design process. By adopting a long-term perspective and prioritizing social and environmental wellbeing, designers can contribute to a more sustainable and equitable future.

Heuristic Evaluation

Heuristic Evaluation, in the context of service design, refers to the systematic inspection and assessment of a service's interface and interaction design using a set of pre-defined usability heuristics or principles. It involves the evaluation of a service's user interface by expert evaluators, who compare the design against established usability guidelines to identify potential usability issues and areas for improvement. This evaluation method is based on the concept of heuristics, which are rules of thumb or best practices that have been found to be effective in identifying usability problems. The evaluators apply these heuristics to evaluate the service's interface and interaction design and identify any deviations or violations from these established principles.

Hierarchical Task Analysis (HTA)

Hierarchical Task Analysis (HTA) is a method used in service design to systematically analyze and organize complex tasks performed by individuals or groups in order to improve the overall efficiency and effectiveness of a service. HTA breaks down a service into its constituent tasks and sub-tasks, creating a hierarchical structure that represents the relationships between these tasks. This analysis helps designers understand how a service is currently performed, identify potential bottlenecks or inefficiencies, and suggest changes that can enhance user experience and service delivery.

Holistic Approach

A holistic approach in the context of Design Thinking disciplines refers to an inclusive and comprehensive approach that considers all aspects of a problem or situation in order to develop effective solutions. It involves examining the problem from multiple perspectives, understanding the underlying causes and interconnectedness of various factors, and considering the broader context in which the problem exists.

By adopting a holistic approach, designers are able to gain a deeper understanding of the problem and its root causes, which in turn allows them to generate more innovative and targeted solutions. This approach requires designers to go beyond surface-level observations and consider the social, cultural, economic, and environmental factors that impact the problem. It encourages interdisciplinary collaboration and engagement with stakeholders to ensure that all relevant perspectives are taken into account.

Holistic Design

Holistic design is a problem-solving approach within the realm of design thinking disciplines that aims to create comprehensive solutions by considering the entire ecosystem and context in which a problem exists, rather than focusing on individual components or isolated aspects. It embraces a holistic view of the problem, recognizing that all aspects are interconnected and interdependent, and seeks to design solutions that optimize the overall system rather than just its individual parts.

This approach requires a deep understanding of the problem space, including the needs, desires, behaviors, and constraints of all stakeholders involved. It involves gathering and synthesizing diverse perspectives, integrating various disciplines and domains of knowledge, and considering the environmental, social, economic, and cultural implications of design decisions.

Holistic Perspective

A holistic perspective in the context of design thinking disciplines refers to a comprehensive and integrated approach to problem-solving and innovation. It takes into account the interconnectedness and interdependencies of various factors and stakeholders involved in the design process.

Design thinking is a human-centered approach that emphasizes empathy, collaboration, and iterative problem-solving. A holistic perspective goes beyond considering individual components or elements of a design solution and instead takes a broader view of the entire system or ecosystem in which the design exists.

This perspective encourages designers to consider the context, environment, and larger social,

124

cultural, and economic factors that may influence the success or effectiveness of a design solution. It involves a deep understanding of the needs, desires, and motivations of the end users or target audience, as well as the goals and objectives of the organization or stakeholders involved.

A holistic perspective also recognizes the importance of interdisciplinary collaboration and the integration of diverse perspectives and expertise. It encourages designers to work closely with individuals from different backgrounds, disciplines, and areas of expertise to gain insights, generate ideas, and test and refine design solutions.

By considering the holistic perspective, designers can create innovative and impactful solutions that address the underlying challenges and opportunities in a more comprehensive and sustainable way. It enables them to create designs that not only meet the functional requirements but also consider the broader social, environmental, and ethical implications.

Holistic Service Design

Holistic Service Design is a comprehensive approach to designing services that takes into consideration the entire service ecosystem, including all touchpoints and stakeholders involved in the service delivery process. It aims to create a seamless and meaningful experience for both the service provider and the service user by understanding and addressing their needs, goals, and expectations. At its core, Holistic Service Design is focused on understanding the complex interactions between various components of a service system and designing interventions that optimize the overall service experience. This approach recognizes that a service is not just a standalone offering but an interconnected system of people, processes, technologies, and physical and digital touchpoints.

Holistic User Understanding

Holistic User Understanding is a concept within the discipline of Design Thinking that involves gaining a comprehensive and empathetic understanding of the target users of a product or service. It goes beyond simply identifying demographic information or conducting market research and delves into the deeper layers of user experiences, needs, and desires.

By adopting a holistic approach, designers strive to understand the users on a personal and emotional level, recognizing that their experiences, motivations, and values greatly influence their behaviors and decisions. This understanding is essential for creating a product or service that truly meets the needs of the users and addresses the challenges they face.

Human Factors

Human factors in the context of service design refer to the understanding and consideration of the capabilities, limitations, and behaviors of individuals when designing and implementing services. It involves studying how people interact with systems, products, and services and incorporating that knowledge into the design process to ensure that the service is user-friendly, efficient, and meets the needs and expectations of its users. The primary goal of considering human factors in service design is to create services that are intuitive, easy to use, and effective in helping users achieve their goals. By understanding the characteristics and behaviors of the intended users, designers can identify potential pain points, barriers, and challenges that may arise during the service interaction. This understanding allows them to make informed design decisions that can help mitigate these issues and improve the overall user experience. Human factors encompass various aspects such as cognitive abilities, physical capabilities, emotional responses, and social interactions. For example, designers should consider how individuals process information, make decisions, and solve problems when designing the information architecture of a website or app. They should also understand the physical limitations of users, such as dexterity, vision, and hearing, and ensure that the service is accessible and usable for individuals with diverse abilities. Additionally, human factors also involve considering the emotional and social aspects of service interactions. Designers should strive to create services that evoke positive emotions, such as satisfaction and delight, and facilitate positive social interactions between users. This can be achieved through well-designed interfaces, clear communication, and effective feedback mechanisms. Incorporating human factors in service design requires a systematic and iterative approach. Designers should conduct user research, such as user interviews, observations, and usability testing, to gather insights about users' needs, expectations, and pain points. These insights should then inform the design decisions and be validated through testing and feedback loops. In conclusion, human factors in service design involve understanding and considering the capabilities, limitations, and behaviors of individuals when designing and implementing services. By taking into account cognitive, physical, emotional, and social aspects, designers can create user-friendly and effective services that meet the needs and expectations of their users.

Human-Centered Approach

A human-centered approach refers to the design thinking discipline that places the needs, desires, and behaviors of humans at the core of the design process. It involves deeply understanding the perspectives, motivations, and challenges of individuals to create solutions that are meaningful and relevant to them.

This approach starts by engaging directly with the end-users or stakeholders through empathy building techniques such as interviews, observations, and immersive experiences. By listening and observing, designers gain valuable insights into the emotions, thoughts, and experiences of the people they are designing for.

Once these insights are gathered, designers analyze and synthesize the information to identify patterns and themes. This helps them define the problem and frame it in a way that aligns with the users' needs and aspirations. The users become active participants in the design process, contributing their unique perspectives and co-creating solutions.

The human-centered approach also emphasizes iterative and prototyping methods, allowing designers to constantly gather feedback and refine their solutions. This ensures that the final design is informed by continuous learning and iteration rather than assumptions or expert opinions.

Ultimately, a human-centered approach aims to create designs that are not only aesthetically pleasing but also genuinely improve the lives of people. By understanding the people they are designing for and involving them throughout the process, designers can create solutions that are intuitive, inclusive, and impactful.

Human-Centered Design Solutions

Human-Centered Design Solutions refer to approaches and solutions that are developed with a deep understanding of human needs, desires, and behaviors. It is a discipline within Design Thinking that places the needs and experiences of users at the center of the design process.

The aim of Human-Centered Design is to create solutions that are not only functional but also meaningful and delightful for the users. It involves extensive research and empathizing with the users to gain insights into their thoughts, emotions, and experiences. Through this understanding, designers can identify the underlying problems and challenges that users face and develop solutions that address these needs directly.

Human-Centered Design

Human-Centered Design (HCD) is an iterative approach used in service design that focuses on understanding the needs, behaviors, and experiences of people in order to create effective and meaningful solutions. It places the target users at the center of the design process, ensuring that the services are tailored to their specific needs and desires. HCD involves gathering insights and empathy from users through various techniques such as interviews, observations, and surveys. These insights form the basis for defining the problem and identifying opportunities for improvement. By understanding the users' goals, motivations, and pain points, designers can develop solutions that meet their needs and address their challenges.

Human-Centered Innovation

Human-Centered Innovation is a key principle of the Design Thinking discipline, which emphasizes the understanding and consideration of human needs, desires, and experiences in the innovation process. It involves putting the needs and wishes of people at the center of the problem-solving and ideation process, with the goal of creating innovative solutions that truly resonate with their target audience.

By adopting a human-centered approach, Design Thinkers seek to gain empathy and deep insights into the lives, behaviors, and motivations of the people they are designing for. They engage in thorough qualitative research to uncover unmet needs, pain points, and desires of the target users or customers. This process involves conducting interviews, observations, and immersive experiences to gain a holistic understanding of the user's context, concerns, and aspirations.

Design Thinkers then use this rich qualitative data to inspire and inform their ideation and innovation processes. They generate multiple ideas and concepts, always keeping in mind the human perspective and the positive impact their solutions can have on people's lives. Prototyping and testing are also crucial components of human-centered design, allowing designers to iterate and refine their solutions based on continuous feedback from users.

In conclusion, Human-Centered Innovation is a design approach that prioritizes the needs and experiences of people throughout the innovation process. By gaining empathy, conducting thorough research, and involving users in the design process, Design Thinkers can create solutions that truly address human needs and bring positive change to individuals and communities.

Human-Centered Solutions

Human-Centered Solutions refer to the design thinking approach that places the needs, desires, and behaviors of users at the core of problem-solving and innovation. It involves empathizing with users, defining their problems, ideating potential solutions, prototyping, and testing them. This process is iterative and collaborative, involving multiple stakeholders such as designers, researchers, engineers, and users themselves.

The key principles underlying human-centered solutions are to understand the perspectives, motivations, and challenges of the users; involve them in the design process to ensure their needs are adequately addressed; and continuously iterate and refine solutions based on user feedback and insights.

The human-centered design approach recognizes that solutions should be tailored to the specific context and goals of the users. It emphasizes the importance of observations, interviews, and other research methods to gain a deep understanding of user needs. By focusing on users' experiences, behaviors, and emotions, human-centered solutions aim to create products, services, and environments that are usable, meaningful, and desirable.

Human-centered solutions are especially relevant in addressing complex problems that require innovative and sustainable solutions. By placing the human experience at the forefront, design thinking enables the creation of solutions that not only meet functional requirements but also resonate with users on a deeper level. This approach has been successfully applied in various fields, including product design, healthcare, education, and social entrepreneurship, to create transformative and impactful solutions.

Human-Centered Technology

Human-Centered Technology is an approach in the field of Design Thinking that puts the needs, desires, and experiences of users at the forefront of the design and development process. It aims to create technology that enhances and enriches the lives of individuals by understanding their behaviors, motivations, and challenges.

This approach involves conducting extensive research and gathering insights about users through methods such as interviews, observations, and usability testing. These findings are then used to inform the design and development of technology solutions that are intuitive, accessible, and meaningful to users.

Human-Centered

Human-centered design is a discipline within design thinking that focuses on creating solutions that meet the specific needs, desires, and behaviors of the target users or customers. This approach places humans, their experiences, and their perspectives at the center of the design process.

In human-centered design, the first step is to gain a deep understanding of the people for whom the solution is being designed. This involves conducting research, such as interviews, observations, and surveys, to uncover the users' needs, preferences, and pain points. By empathizing with users, designers can gain insights into their problems and motivations.

Once the insights are gathered, designers can start ideating and prototyping potential solutions. These solutions are continuously tested and refined in collaboration with users to ensure they align with their needs and expectations. The iterative process allows designers to learn from failures and make improvements. It places an emphasis on rapid experimentation and quick feedback loops.

By focusing on the human element, human-centered design aims to create innovative and user-friendly solutions that address real-world problems. It recognizes that successful designs are not just visually pleasing, but also functional and intuitive. By involving users throughout the design process, it helps ensure that the final product or service meets their expectations and delivers value.

Human-Centric Design Thinking

Human-Centric Design Thinking refers to a problem-solving approach that emphasizes the needs, preferences, and experiences of humans or end-users. It is a discipline within the broader framework of Design Thinking, which seeks to understand and address complex problems through a user-centered perspective.

In the context of Human-Centric Design Thinking, the focus is on empathizing with users, gaining insights into their motivations and challenges, and incorporating these understandings into the design process. This approach recognizes that successful solutions are not just based on functional requirements but also on the emotional and psychological needs of users.

By adopting a Human-Centric Design Thinking approach, designers can create more meaningful and impactful solutions that truly resonate with the intended users. The process typically involves several stages, including research, ideation, prototyping, and testing. Throughout these stages, designers continuously gather feedback from users, allowing them to iteratively refine and improve their designs.

The goal of Human-Centric Design Thinking is to design products, services, or experiences that are intuitive, enjoyable, and relevant to users' lives. It prioritizes the development of solutions that solve real problems and add value to users' experiences. By placing human needs at the center of the design process, designers can create solutions that are not only functional but also meaningful and impactful.

Hypothesis Testing

Hypothesis testing is a key concept in the field of Design Thinking disciplines. It is a statistical method used to assess the validity of a proposed hypothesis or claim about a population based on sample data. The process involves formulating a null hypothesis, which assumes that there is no significant difference or relationship between variables, and an alternative hypothesis, which suggests that there is a significant difference or relationship. The steps of hypothesis testing typically involve selecting a level of significance, collecting and analyzing sample data, and drawing conclusions based on the evidence. The level of significance, often denoted as α, is the threshold at which the null hypothesis is rejected. If the calculated p-value (the probability of observing the data given the null hypothesis) is below the chosen level of significance, the null hypothesis is rejected in favor of the alternative hypothesis. Otherwise, the null hypothesis is not rejected. Hypothesis testing is essential in Design Thinking disciplines as it allows researchers to make informed decisions and draw meaningful conclusions based on objective evidence. By applying statistical methods, designers can test their assumptions about user needs and preferences, evaluate the effectiveness of design solutions, and validate design decisions. This iterative process helps refine and improve designs, ensuring that they effectively meet user requirements and provide a positive user experience.

Hypothesis-Driven

A hypothesis-driven approach is a fundamental aspect of Design Thinking disciplines. It involves formulating and testing hypotheses as a means to drive the problem-solving process, understand user needs, and identify potential solutions.

In Design Thinking, a hypothesis is a proposed explanation or solution based on limited evidence or preliminary understanding. Design thinkers use hypotheses to explore various possibilities and generate insights. These hypotheses serve as guiding principles that structure the research, ideation, and prototyping phases of the design process.

Idea Generation Techniques

Idea generation techniques are methods or approaches used within the discipline of Design Thinking to stimulate creativity and generate new ideas. These techniques help designers and teams to think outside the box, explore different perspectives, and come up with innovative solutions to challenges or problems they are trying to address.

One commonly used idea generation technique is brainstorming. This involves gathering a group of individuals and encouraging them to freely share their ideas and thoughts on a particular topic. The goal is to generate a large number of ideas without judgment or criticism. Another technique is mind mapping, which involves creating a visual representation of ideas and concepts in a non-linear way to explore connections and relationships between them.

Designers also use techniques such as role playing to put themselves in the shoes of end users or stakeholders, which helps them gain a deeper understanding of their needs and priorities. Another method is analogies, where designers draw on similarities between unrelated concepts to generate new ideas and solutions.

Furthermore, prototyping and iteration are important idea generation techniques in Design Thinking. By creating quick, low-resolution prototypes, designers can test and refine their ideas, leading to new iterations and improvements. This process allows for exploration and ideation through hands-on experimentation rather than solely relying on theoretical thinking.

Idea Generation

Design Thinking is a problem-solving and innovation approach that emphasizes a human-centered perspective. It aims to generate creative and practical solutions by understanding the needs and perspectives of users, identifying opportunities for improvement, and iteratively experimenting and refining ideas.

Design Thinking involves multiple disciplines and stages. The first stage is empathizing, which involves gaining a deep understanding of the end-users and their needs, goals, and challenges. This is done through methods such as interviews, observations, and surveys. The second stage is defining, where the problem or opportunity is defined based on the insights gained in the empathizing stage. This involves synthesizing the data and identifying the key issues to be addressed. The third stage is ideating, which is the process of generating a wide range of ideas and concepts for potential solutions. This can be done through brainstorming sessions or other creative techniques. The fourth stage is prototyping, where the best ideas from the ideation stage are transformed into tangible prototypes or representations that are used for testing and feedback. The final stage is testing, where the prototypes are tested with users to gather feedback and insights. This feedback is used to refine and improve the prototypes and eventually develop the final solution.

Idea Management Platforms

Idea Management Platforms refer to digital tools or software that facilitate the collection, organization, and evaluation of ideas in the context of Design Thinking disciplines. These platforms provide a centralized space where individuals or teams can submit their ideas, collaborate, and collectively contribute to problem-solving and innovation.

The primary goal of an Idea Management Platform is to enhance the ideation and innovation process by enabling a diverse range of stakeholders to contribute their ideas and insights. With these platforms, design teams can harness the collective intelligence of participants and leverage their diverse perspectives to arrive at more creative and effective solutions.

Idea Management Software

Idea Management Software is a digital tool that facilitates the process of generating, capturing, organizing, and implementing ideas within the context of Design Thinking disciplines. It enables the efficient management of ideas from inception to execution, promoting collaboration and innovation among multidisciplinary teams.

Within Design Thinking, the software serves as a centralized platform for idea collection, evaluation, and development. It allows participants to submit ideas, share insights, and provide feedback, fostering a culture of creativity and open communication. The software typically provides features such as idea generation templates, brainstorming tools, and collaborative workspaces to support the various stages of the design process.

Ideation Diversity

Ideation diversity in the context of Design Thinking disciplines refers to the inclusion of a wide range of perspectives, experiences, and backgrounds during the process of generating ideas and solutions for a design challenge. It emphasizes the importance of gathering diverse inputs and viewpoints from individuals with different skill sets, knowledge, cultural backgrounds, and disciplinary expertise.

By embracing ideation diversity, design thinkers aim to foster an environment that encourages brainstorming and collaboration from a diverse group of stakeholders. This approach recognizes that diverse inputs lead to more innovative and creative ideas, as each individual brings their unique insights, problem-solving abilities, and perspectives to the table.

Ideation Session

In the context of Design Thinking disciplines, an ideation session can be defined as a collaborative process that encourages the generation and exploration of various ideas and solutions for a specific problem or challenge. This session serves as a platform for individuals or teams to engage in creative thinking, brainstorming, and idea sharing in order to foster innovation and uncover novel approaches.

During an ideation session, participants are encouraged to suspend judgment and embrace a mindset of open-mindedness and curiosity. The main objective is to generate a wide range of ideas, regardless of their feasibility or practicality, as this can spark new perspectives and insights. Facilitators often use various techniques and tools, such as mind mapping, role-playing, or sketching, to stimulate creativity and encourage out-of-the-box thinking.

The ideation session typically involves multiple rounds of idea generation and refinement. Participants can build upon each other's ideas, modify existing concepts, or even combine multiple ideas to create innovative solutions. The emphasis is on quantity rather than quality at this stage, as a large pool of ideas can lead to breakthroughs and unexpected solutions.

At the end of an ideation session, participants evaluate and prioritize the generated ideas based on certain criteria, such as feasibility, desirability, or alignment with the problem statement. The most promising ideas are then selected for further development and prototyping in subsequent stages of the design thinking process.

Ideation Sessions

Ideation sessions refer to collaborative brainstorming sessions that are conducted in the field of service design. These sessions involve a group of individuals, typically including designers, stakeholders, and users, who come together to generate innovative ideas and concepts for designing or improving services. The main objective of ideation sessions is to foster creativity and generate a wide range of ideas that can be used to address various challenges and opportunities in the design of services. These sessions often follow a structured approach and incorporate different techniques and methods to encourage participants to think outside the box and explore new possibilities.

Ideation Software

Ideation software refers to a digital tool or application used within the context of Design Thinking disciplines to facilitate and enhance the ideation stage of the design process. Design Thinking is a problem-solving approach that focuses on understanding user needs, generating creative ideas, and prototyping and testing solutions. The ideation stage is crucial in this process as it involves generating a wide range of ideas and possibilities before selecting the most promising ones for further development.

Ideation software allows individuals or teams to brainstorm and generate ideas in a structured and collaborative manner. It provides a platform for capturing, organizing, and sharing ideas, enabling participants to build upon each other's contributions and foster creativity. The software often includes features such as virtual whiteboards, digital sticky notes, and mind maps, which allow for visual representation and organization of thoughts.

One of the key advantages of ideation software is its ability to encourage divergent thinking, where participants are free to explore multiple perspectives and possibilities. The digital nature of the software also facilitates the easy manipulation and reorganization of ideas, supporting the convergence of thoughts towards more refined and viable concepts.

Moreover, ideation software often includes collaboration features such as real-time editing, commenting, and voting, which foster a collective and inclusive approach to ideation. This promotes active participation and engagement among team members, regardless of their geographical location.

In summary, ideation software plays a vital role in the Design Thinking process by providing a digital platform for structured and collaborative idea generation. It enables the exploration of diverse perspectives, facilitates the organization of thoughts, and promotes collective creativity and participation.

Ideation Space

Ideation Space refers to the phase in Design Thinking disciplines where a team or individual generates a wide range of ideas and concepts to address a specific problem or challenge. It is a collaborative and open-minded environment that encourages creativity, brainstorming, and experimentation.

The ideation space is characterized by a non-judgmental atmosphere, where all ideas are considered valid and valuable. The objective is to explore as many possibilities as possible, without any constraints or limitations. This allows for the exploration of unconventional and disruptive ideas that may lead to innovative solutions.

The ideation space often involves various techniques and methods to stimulate creative thinking, such as brainstorming sessions, mind mapping, role playing, and sketching. It encourages participants to think outside the box and challenge conventional assumptions, fostering a culture of innovation and continuous improvement.

During the ideation phase, teams generate a large quantity of ideas, ranging from wild and ambitious concepts to more practical and feasible solutions. These ideas are then evaluated and refined in subsequent stages of the Design Thinking process, such as prototyping and testing.

The ideation space is a crucial component of Design Thinking, as it is the stage where innovative and disruptive ideas are born. By fostering collaboration, creativity, and experimentation, it helps teams to uncover new insights and create solutions that address complex challenges in a human-centered and sustainable manner.

Ideation Techniques

Ideation techniques are methods used within the Design Thinking discipline to generate creative ideas and solutions. These techniques facilitate the exploration and generation of new possibilities, allowing designers to break through mental barriers and think outside the box.

One common ideation technique is brainstorming, where a group of individuals come together to generate a large quantity of ideas in a short amount of time. This technique encourages participants to build on each other's ideas, creating a collaborative and energetic environment. Another technique is mind mapping, where thoughts and concepts are visually represented in a diagram, allowing for the exploration of connections and associations between ideas.

Ideation Workbooks

Ideation workbooks are tools used in design thinking disciplines to help generate and refine creative ideas. They provide a structured and organized approach to the ideation process, helping individuals and teams think outside the box and come up with innovative solutions to design challenges.

These workbooks typically consist of a series of exercises and prompts that encourage brainstorming, problem-solving, and collaboration. They may include activities such as mind mapping, sketching, storytelling, role-playing, and prototyping. The exercises are designed to stimulate diverse perspectives, encourage free thinking, and foster a culture of experimentation.

Ideation workbooks serve as a guide and reference for design thinkers throughout the ideation phase of the design process. They help practitioners to explore multiple possibilities, overcome creative blocks, and generate a wide range of ideas. By providing a structured format, the workbooks ensure that the ideation process is productive and efficient. They help to capture and document ideas, making it easier to review, evaluate, and select the most promising concepts for further development.

Overall, ideation workbooks are valuable tools for designers and design teams who are seeking to generate innovative and user-centered solutions. They provide a framework for ideation activities, encourage collaboration, and facilitate the creative thinking and problem-solving skills necessary for successful design outcomes.

Ideation

Ideation is a key step in the process of service design, involving the generation and exploration of new ideas for the improvement or creation of services. It is a creative and collaborative process that aims to uncover innovative solutions to address user needs and enhance the overall user experience. During ideation, multidisciplinary teams come together to brainstorm and generate a diverse range of ideas. This can involve techniques such as brainstorming, mind mapping, and design thinking exercises. The focus is on generating a large quantity of ideas without judgment or evaluation, fostering a culture of creativity and experimentation.

Impact Mapping

Impact Mapping is a technique in service design that helps identify the desired outcomes and impacts of a service or product by creating a visual map of these goals and their underlying assumptions. It is a collaborative approach that brings together stakeholders, such as customers, users, and team members, to align their understanding of the service's purpose and its expected outcomes. The main purpose of Impact Mapping is to ensure that the development and delivery of a service or product are focused on achieving specific business or user goals, rather than merely implementing features. It provides a structured framework to explore the potential impacts of the service and helps prioritize activities based on the value they bring in meeting these goals.

Implementation Plan

An implementation plan, in the context of service design, refers to a detailed blueprint or roadmap outlining the steps and resources required to execute a service design project successfully. It provides a systematic approach to implementing the designed service solution and ensures efficient coordination and communication among stakeholders involved in the implementation process. The implementation plan typically includes a set of activities, timelines, responsibilities, and resources needed to accomplish each task. It serves as a guideline for the service design team, helping them stay organized and focused on achieving the desired outcomes.

Inclusive Design

Inclusive design, in the context of service design, refers to the deliberate and thoughtful consideration of diversity and inclusivity principles throughout the entire design process of a service. It aims to create services that are accessible and usable by as many people as possible, regardless of their abilities, age, gender, cultural background, or other characteristics. By adopting an inclusive design approach, service designers seek to eliminate barriers and provide equal opportunities for all individuals to access and engage with the service. This involves understanding and addressing various dimensions of diversity, including physical, sensory, cognitive, and emotional aspects.

Information Architecture

Information Architecture (IA) refers to the structural design and organization of information within a service. It focuses on creating a clear and intuitive navigation system that allows users to easily find and access relevant information. IA plays a crucial role in service design as it helps improve the overall user experience and ensures that information is presented in a logical and meaningful way. By organizing information into a coherent structure, IA enables users to quickly understand the relationship between different pieces of information and navigate through the service with ease.

Information Visualization

Information visualization in the context of service design refers to the visual representation of complex data and information in a clear and intuitive way, aimed at facilitating understanding, analysis, and decision-making. Through the use of various visual techniques such as charts, graphs, maps, and diagrams, information visualization simplifies and condenses the data, making it more accessible and digestible for users. The primary goal is to translate raw information into meaningful visual patterns, relationships, and insights.

Innovation Framework

In the context of service design, the innovation framework refers to a structured approach or methodology that enables the creation, development, and implementation of new and improved service offerings within an organization. It provides a systematic process for generating and cultivating innovative ideas, evaluating their feasibility and potential impact, and ultimately translating them into tangible service solutions. The innovation framework typically encompasses several key stages or components. Firstly, it involves the identification and understanding of customer needs and pain points through various research methods such as user interviews, surveys, or observations. This step helps to uncover insights and opportunities for innovation within the context of the service being designed. Once the customer needs have been identified, the framework involves ideation and brainstorming sessions to generate a wide range of potential ideas and concepts. This creative phase encourages thinking beyond the constraints of current service offerings and exploring radical or disruptive ideas that have the potential to meet the identified customer needs more effectively. Following the ideation phase, the innovation framework incorporates a rigorous evaluation and selection process. This stage entails analyzing the feasibility and viability of each idea in terms of technical requirements, resource availability, market demand, and potential business impact. Through careful evaluation, the most promising ideas are chosen for further development. The next step within the innovation framework involves the prototyping and testing of the selected concepts. This iterative process allows for the exploration of different design solutions and the gathering of feedback from users or stakeholders. Prototypes can range from simple low-fidelity mock-ups to interactive simulations, providing a tangible representation of the envisioned service experience. After validating and refining the prototype, the innovation framework moves towards the implementation and scaling of the new service offering. This phase requires careful planning, coordination, and collaboration across various departments to ensure the successful integration of the innovative solution into the existing service ecosystem. Ultimately, the innovation framework serves as a guide, providing structure and direction throughout the service design process. By employing this systematic approach, organizations can foster a culture of innovation, increase their ability to adapt to changing customer needs and market dynamics, and ultimately deliver enhanced service experiences.

Innovation Games

Innovation Games refer to a set of collaborative activities and methodologies used in the context of service design. They are designed to facilitate ideation, problem-solving, and decision-making processes, allowing teams to gather valuable insights and generate innovative solutions for designing or improving services. These games are typically played with diverse groups of stakeholders, including service providers, customers, and other relevant parties, in order to ensure a holistic and inclusive approach to service design. The games employ various interactive techniques to encourage active participation, creativity, and effective communication among participants.

Insight Generation Workshops

Insight Generation Workshops in the context of service design are collaborative sessions aimed at uncovering key insights and understanding about a particular problem or challenge. These workshops bring together a diverse group of stakeholders, including designers, researchers, and users, to collectively generate ideas, explore possibilities, and gain a deeper understanding of the problem space. During an Insight Generation Workshop, participants engage in a series of interactive activities and exercises that encourage divergent thinking and facilitate open discussions. These activities may include brainstorming, storytelling, role-playing, or utilizing design thinking methodologies such as empathy mapping or journey mapping. The goal is to foster an environment of creativity and innovation, allowing participants to explore different perspectives and generate new insights that can inform the design process. The workshop facilitator plays a crucial role in guiding the session and ensuring that all voices are heard. They create a safe and inclusive space for participants to freely express their ideas, opinions, and experiences. By fostering collaboration and active participation, the facilitator encourages the group to challenge assumptions, question existing beliefs, and think outside the box. Insight Generation Workshops typically result in a range of valuable outputs, including user personas, customer journeys, or design principles. These outputs are based on the collective insights and understandings derived from the workshop discussions and activities. They provide a foundation for further ideation, prototyping, and decision-making in the service design process. Overall, Insight Generation Workshops are a powerful tool for service designers to gain a holistic understanding of the problem space and to generate meaningful insights that drive the design process. By harnessing the collective intelligence and creativity of diverse stakeholders, these workshops enable designers to uncover unique perspectives and to develop solutions that meet the needs and aspirations of users.

Interaction Design

Interaction design, in the context of service design, refers to the process of creating meaningful and intuitive user experiences by designing the way users interact with a service or system. It is a user-centered approach that focuses on understanding and addressing the needs, goals, and expectations of users. Interaction design involves the design of both the physical and digital aspects of a service, including its interfaces, interactions, and workflows. It is concerned with creating seamless, efficient, and enjoyable interactions that enable users to easily and effectively accomplish their tasks and achieve their goals.

Iterative Design

Iterative design is a systematic approach to service design that involves repeating a series of design iterations to continuously improve, refine, and enhance the service being developed. It is a collaborative and cyclical process that allows designers and stakeholders to gather feedback, make adjustments, and test out new ideas to create a more effective and user-centric service. In the context of service design, the iterative design process typically begins with a thorough understanding of the users' needs, goals, and preferences. This initial research phase allows designers to identify potential pain points, areas for improvement, and opportunities for innovation. Based on these insights, the design team develops a prototype or a test service that embodies the desired experience. The iterative design process then moves into the evaluation phase, where the prototype or test service is presented to users and stakeholders. Through observations, interviews, surveys, and other research methods, valuable feedback is gathered to assess the strengths, weaknesses, and potential areas of improvement. This feedback is carefully analyzed to inform the next design iteration. Building on the insights gained from the evaluation phase, the service design team makes iterative refinements and enhancements to the prototype or test service. These refinements often involve adjusting the service's functionality, user interface, features, or processes to better align with the users' needs and expectations. The refined version is then subjected to further evaluation and feedback, and the iterative cycle continues until the desired level of satisfaction is achieved. Iterative design is particularly valuable in service design as it allows for continuous learning and adaptation. It enables designers to validate assumptions, mitigate risks, and address any design flaws or usability issues gradually. By involving users and stakeholders throughout the design process, iterative design ensures that the final service delivered is both useful and meaningful to those who will be using it. It empowers designers to make informed design decisions based on real-user insights rather than assumptions or guesswork, leading to more successful, user-centric services.

Job Stories

Job Stories are a technique used in service design to understand user needs and expectations by framing them in the context of a specific job or task that the user wants to accomplish. Unlike traditional user stories that typically focus on the features or functionalities of a product or service, job stories focus on the underlying motivation and desired outcomes of the user. Job Stories follow a simple template: When [situation], I want to [motivation], so I can [expected outcome]. The situation represents the context or scenario in which the user finds themselves, the motivation represents the reason or goal they have in mind, and the expected outcome represents the result they hope to achieve.

Jobs To Be Done Framework

The Jobs To Be Done (JTBD) framework is a customer-centered approach to service design that focuses on uncovering the underlying motivations and needs of customers when they "hire" a product or service to get a job done. It provides a structured methodology for understanding customer behavior and creating solutions that meet their needs.The premise of the JTBD framework is that customers "hire" products or services to help them accomplish specific goals or jobs in their lives. These jobs can range from functional tasks (e.g., fixing a leaky faucet) to social or emotional needs (e.g., impressing others with a stylish outfit). By identifying the specific jobs that customers are trying to accomplish, service designers can gain insights into the customer's context, goals, and pain points.

Journey Mapping

Journey mapping is a method used in service design to visually represent the customer experience throughout their interactions with a service or product. It provides a detailed understanding of the user's perspective, emotions, and pain points at each touchpoint, enabling service designers to identify areas for improvement and create a more seamless and satisfying experience. A journey map typically consists of a timeline that illustrates the customer's journey from the initial engagement to the final outcome. It incorporates various factors such as the customer's goals, actions, and emotions at each stage, as well as the channels and touchpoints they encounter along the way. These touchpoints include physical, digital, and human interactions, which collectively shape the overall experience. The purpose of journey mapping is to uncover insights about the customer's experience and align it with business goals. By analyzing the customer's journey, service designers can identify pain points, bottlenecks, and areas of friction that may negatively impact the overall experience. They can also identify moments of delight and areas of opportunity to differentiate the service and exceed customer expectations. Journey mapping involves qualitative research methods such as interviews, observations, and customer feedback to gather data about the customer's journey. This information is then synthesized and visualized in a journey map, which can be shared and communicated to stakeholders for better understanding and collaboration. Service design teams can use journey maps as a tool for ideation, problem-solving, and decision-making. They can prioritize improvements and design interventions that address specific pain points and enhance the overall customer experience. Journey maps also provide a holistic view of the service ecosystem, revealing the interconnectedness of touchpoints and interactions, allowing teams to identify dependencies and potential areas for optimization. In conclusion, journey mapping is an essential method in service design that helps uncover insights about the customer's experience. By visually representing the customer's journey, service designers can identify pain points, delight moments, and opportunities for improvement to create a more seamless and satisfying experience.

KJ Technique

The KJ Technique, also known as the Affinity Technique or the Affinity Diagram, is a method used in service design to organize and categorize large amounts of data or information generated during a brainstorming or research session. This technique was developed by Jiro Kawakita, a Japanese anthropologist, in the 1960s as a way to facilitate team collaboration and decision-making. The goal of the KJ Technique is to help teams make sense of complex ideas, identify patterns, and derive insights to inform the design process. The process starts with individuals generating ideas or insights on sticky notes or small pieces of paper. These ideas could be related to customer needs, pain points, service improvements, or any other relevant aspect of the service design process. Each idea is written down as briefly as possible to capture the essence of the thought. Once all the ideas are generated, the team members take turns presenting their ideas one by one. As each idea is presented, it is collected on a wall or a large surface, creating a visual representation of the collective input. This step is performed silently to encourage unbiased presentation and avoid influencing other team members. After all the ideas are presented and collected, the team members collaboratively group similar ideas together based on common themes or patterns. This process involves discussing and negotiating potential connections and relationships between the ideas. The goal is to create natural clusters of ideas that are related to each other. Once the ideas are grouped, the team can label each cluster to summarize the underlying theme or concept. These labels are typically brief phrases that capture the essence of the ideas in the group. The team can also prioritize the clusters or identify the most important insights that emerge from the analysis. The KJ Technique provides a visual and collaborative way to make sense of a large amount of data or information. It helps teams to go beyond individual perspectives and uncover patterns and connections that may not have been apparent initially. By organizing the data into clusters, this technique enables teams to extract valuable insights and inform the subsequent steps in the service design process.

Kano Analysis

Kano Analysis is a service design tool used to prioritize and categorize customer requirements based on their impact on customer satisfaction. It helps in understanding which features or attributes of a service are considered basic necessities, which ones are expected, and which ones would provide delight or exceed customer expectations. This analysis enables service designers to make informed decisions about resource allocation and feature development. The Kano model classifies customer requirements into five categories: Must-be, One-dimensional, Attractive, Indifferent, and Reverse. These categories are represented on a two-dimensional graph, with customer satisfaction on the y-axis and the degree of functionality or presence of a certain feature on the x-axis. The Must-be category includes basic requirements that customers expect as a given. If these requirements are not met, customers will be extremely dissatisfied. However, meeting these requirements does not necessarily lead to increased customer satisfaction. The One-dimensional category includes requirements that directly correlate with customer satisfaction. The more a service provider fulfills these requirements, the more satisfied the customers will be. These requirements are typically stated explicitly by customers and can be easily prioritized and implemented. The Attractive category includes requirements that customers may not explicitly mention but can lead to delight when met. These requirements are unexpected, and their fulfillment can significantly differentiate a service from its competitors.

Identifying and incorporating attractive features can build customer loyalty and create a competitive advantage. The Indifferent category includes requirements that do not significantly impact customer satisfaction. Customers are not particularly interested in these requirements, and their fulfillment does not result in increased satisfaction. These requirements can be evaluated as lower priority in terms of resource allocation. The Reverse category includes requirements that, when fulfilled, actually decrease customer satisfaction. These requirements may be perceived by some customers as unnecessary or even undesirable. Identifying and eliminating reverse features is crucial for avoiding negative impact on customer satisfaction. By conducting Kano Analysis, service designers can prioritize resources and investments based on the categories and understand which features are essential for meeting customer expectations, which ones are opportunities for differentiation, and which ones can be omitted without negative consequences. This analysis ultimately helps in designing services that maximize customer satisfaction and business success.

Kano Model

The Kano Model is a framework used in service design to understand and prioritize customer requirements and preferences. It was developed by Professor Noriaki Kano in the 1980s and is widely used by businesses to enhance customer satisfaction and drive product/service innovation. The model categorizes customer needs into five distinct categories: Basic, Performance, Excitement, Indifferent, and Reverse. These categories are based on the relationship between customer satisfaction and the degree to which a particular attribute or feature is present in a product or service. The Basic needs are the fundamental requirements that customers expect as a minimum standard. These needs are considered mandatory and their absence or failure to meet them can lead to complete customer dissatisfaction. An example would be a hotel providing clean and comfortable rooms. The Performance needs are the features or attributes that customers explicitly articulate and are typically expressed in terms of "more is better." These needs directly influence customer satisfaction and are usually the focus of improvement efforts. An example would be a hotel providing free Wi-Fi or a faster check-in process. The Excitement needs are unexpected or innovative features that delight customers and generate positive emotions. They are often referred to as "delighters" or "wow factors" and can differentiate a product or service from its competitors. These needs are not explicitly expressed by customers but can lead to increased customer loyalty and advocacy. An example would be a hotel providing personalized welcome gifts or surprise discounts. The Indifferent needs are features or attributes that do not significantly impact overall customer satisfaction. Customers are generally indifferent to their presence, absence, or level of performance. These needs are typically considered "nice to have" but not essential. An example would be a hotel offering a variety of TV channels that are seldom watched by guests. The Reverse needs are attributes that customers prefer to be absent from a product or service. Meeting these needs may actually decrease customer satisfaction. An example would be a hotel providing loud background music in public areas.

Kansei Engineering

Kansei Engineering is a methodology used in service design to understand and incorporate customers' emotional responses and preferences into the development of products or services. It is a user-oriented approach that aims to enhance user satisfaction by identifying and addressing their emotional needs and expectations. In Kansei Engineering, the term "kansei" refers to the customers' subjective psychological experiences, including their feelings, emotions, and sensory perceptions. These subjective experiences are considered essential factors in shaping customers' perceptions and overall satisfaction with a service. By using Kansei Engineering, service designers can explore and map the emotional dimensions associated with a service and then use this knowledge to create and improve the service design. The process typically involves the following steps: 1. Identification of Kansei Words: Kansei words are specific terms used to express customers' subjective feelings and emotions towards a particular service. Through surveys, interviews, or other research methods, designers gather these words to understand the emotional aspects of the service. 2. Development of a Kansei Space: The collected Kansei words are then organized and visualized in a Kansei space, which represents the emotional landscape associated with the service. The Kansei space helps designers identify patterns, relationships, and priority areas for improvement. 3. Translation into Design Elements: Based on the insights gained from the Kansei space, designers translate the identified emotional aspects into tangible design elements. These elements can include visual cues, sounds, scents, or other sensory stimuli that evoke the desired emotional response in customers. 4. Testing and Refining: The designed elements are implemented in the service, and their impact on customer emotions is evaluated through surveys or usability tests. This feedback is then used to refine and further optimize the service design. Kansei Engineering enables service designers to go beyond functional aspects and consider the holistic customer experience. By understanding and integrating customers' emotional needs, designers can create services that resonate with users on a deeper level, resulting in enhanced satisfaction and loyalty.

Key Performance Indicators (KPIs)

Key Performance Indicators (KPIs) are measurable values used to evaluate the success of a service design strategy and its respective service offerings. KPIs provide organizations with quantifiable insights into the performance and effectiveness of their services, facilitating continuous improvement and informed decision-making. Essentially, KPIs serve as performance benchmarks that reflect the progress made towards achieving service design objectives. They allow organizations to assess how well their services are meeting customer needs, meeting business goals, and delivering value to stakeholders. By monitoring KPIs, organizations can gain valuable insights into service performance, identify areas for improvement, and make data-driven adjustments to enhance customer experiences and increase the overall quality of their services.

Laddering Technique

The laddering technique in the context of service design is a research method used to uncover customers' underlying motivations and beliefs in relation to a particular service or product. It involves conducting in-depth interviews to understand the hierarchy of customer values and the connections between these values and the features or attributes of the service being evaluated. Through the laddering technique, service designers aim to go beyond surface-level descriptions or preferences expressed by customers and delve into their deeper values and motivations. The method is based on the assumption that customers have a hierarchy of values that guide their decision-making processes. By understanding this hierarchy, designers can gain insights into the true drivers behind customer behavior and preferences.

Landscape Assessment

A landscape assessment, in the context of service design, refers to the comprehensive analysis and evaluation of the external environment or market in which a service or organization operates. It involves examining various factors and components that can potentially influence the design and delivery of a service, such as economic, social, technological, political, and environmental aspects. The primary purpose of conducting a landscape assessment is to gain a deeper understanding of the current state of the market or industry, identify opportunities, challenges, and risks, and inform the design and development of new services or the improvement of existing ones. Through a landscape assessment, service designers can gather relevant data and insights and use them to inform decision-making processes and strategic planning.

Lean Service Blueprinting

Lean Service Blueprinting is a service design methodology that aims to improve the efficiency and effectiveness of service delivery by visually mapping out the customer journey and highlighting areas for improvement. It is rooted in the principles of Lean Six Sigma, which focuses on reducing waste and improving process flow. The process begins by identifying the key steps in the service delivery process and understanding the customer's journey from start to finish. This includes mapping out all the touchpoints and interactions that the customer has with the service provider, both online and offline. Once the customer journey is mapped out, the next step is to identify areas for improvement. This could include eliminating unnecessary steps, reducing wait times, or streamlining communication between different departments or stakeholders. The goal is to create a more seamless and efficient experience for the customer while also reducing costs and improving service quality. Lean Service Blueprinting also involves identifying potential pain points and areas of friction in the customer journey. These could be bottlenecks in the process, unclear instructions or information, or gaps in communication. By highlighting these pain points, service providers can then brainstorm and implement solutions to address them and enhance the overall customer experience. The visual representation of the service blueprint is a key component of Lean Service Blueprinting. It allows service providers to easily see the entire customer journey at a glance and identify areas for improvement. This visual mapping also helps to facilitate collaboration and communication between different teams and stakeholders, as everyone can clearly see and understand the process flow. In summary, Lean Service Blueprinting is a service design methodology that focuses on improving the efficiency and effectiveness of service delivery by visually mapping out the customer journey, identifying areas for improvement, and implementing solutions. It is an essential tool for service providers looking to enhance the customer experience, reduce waste, and drive continuous improvement.

Lean Startup

The Lean Startup is a methodology that aims to help companies design and deliver innovative services or products by emphasizing continuous experimentation and learning. By following the Lean Startup approach, service designers focus on developing a minimum viable product (MVP) as quickly as possible and then gathering feedback from users. This feedback is used to iterate and improve the service in small increments, with the overall goal of creating a service that meets the needs and desires of customers.

Life Cycle Assessment (LCA)

The Life Cycle Assessment (LCA) is a systematic method used to evaluate the environmental impacts of a service design throughout its entire life cycle. It examines the entire lifecycle of a service, from the extraction of raw materials and production processes, through distribution and use, to disposal and end-of-life treatment. LCA takes into account all the inputs and outputs associated with each stage of the service's life cycle, including energy consumption, material usage, waste generation, and emissions to air, water, and soil. It considers both direct and indirect environmental impacts, such as those resulting from the production of raw materials, the supply chain, and the use of the service by customers. LCA is based on a comprehensive and holistic approach that considers all stages of a service's life cycle, including upstream and downstream processes. It enables service designers to identify and assess the potential environmental impacts associated with different design choices and to make informed decisions that minimize environmental harm. The LCA methodology typically consists of four main steps: goal and scope definition, inventory analysis, impact assessment, and interpretation. In the goal and scope definition phase, the objectives and boundaries of the study are established, as well as the functional unit and system boundaries. The inventory analysis stage involves collecting data on inputs and outputs, including energy and material flows, emissions, and waste generated. The impact assessment phase evaluates the potential environmental impacts associated with the inputs and outputs identified in the inventory analysis. Finally, in the interpretation stage, the results of the LCA study are analyzed, and conclusions and recommendations are drawn. LCA is a valuable tool for service designers as it helps them identify opportunities for improvement and innovation to minimize the environmental footprint of their designs. By assessing the environmental impacts of different design options, service designers can make informed decisions that promote sustainability and support the transition to a circular economy.

Living Labs

Living Labs are collaborative spaces where users, stakeholders, and researchers engage in the co-creation and evaluation of innovative products, services, and systems in real-life contexts. They serve as an interactive platform for service design, allowing for the development, testing, and refinement of user-centered solutions. In a Living Lab, a diverse group of participants actively participate in the design process, bridging the gap between producers and users. These labs are characterized by their openness, flexibility, and interdisciplinary nature, incorporating a wide range of perspectives and expertise.

Market Research

Market research is the process of gathering, analyzing, and interpreting data to obtain insights and understanding about a specific market and its customers, competitors, and trends. It involves systematic collection and examination of information to support decision-making, strategy development, and problem-solving in service design. Market research plays a crucial role in service design as it provides valuable information about customer needs, preferences, and behaviors. By conducting thorough research, service designers can gain a deep understanding of market dynamics, identify potential opportunities, and develop strategies to meet customer demands effectively.

Mental Models

A mental model, in the context of service design, refers to a cognitive framework or representation that individuals use to understand, interpret, and make sense of the world around them. It is a mental tool that helps individuals organize and process information, as well as predict and anticipate outcomes. Mental models play a critical role in service design as they influence how individuals perceive and interact with a service. Service designers must take into consideration the mental models of both service providers and service users to ensure effective and efficient service delivery. By understanding and aligning with the mental models of the target audience, service designers can design services that are intuitive, user-friendly, and meet the needs and expectations of the users.

Mind Mapping

Mind Mapping is a visual method used in service design to organize and structure information in a non-linear and creative way. It involves creating a visual representation of thoughts, ideas, and concepts, allowing designers to explore different connections and relationships between them. By using Mind Maps, designers can capture and organize complex information in a clear and concise manner. The central idea or problem is placed at the center of the map, and related ideas branch out from it, forming a web-like structure. This helps in understanding the overall context and identifying key elements of a service design project.

Mindful Design

Mindful Design, in the context of service design, refers to the intentional and thoughtful creation of services that consider the needs, preferences, and experiences of users. It involves a human-centered approach, where designers aim to understand the users by empathizing with them, gaining insights into their motivations and behaviors, and using this understanding to develop services that meet their needs effectively and efficiently.

Minimum Viable Product (MVP)

A Minimum Viable Product (MVP) is a core version of a service that allows for quick validation and learning in the early stages of service design. It is the smallest, most essential version of a service that can be released to customers to gather feedback and validate assumptions. The purpose of an MVP is to test hypotheses and gather insights about customer needs, preferences, and pain points. By launching an MVP, service designers can learn from real user interactions and feedback, which enables them to make informed decisions and iterate on the service design.

Mobile Ethnography

Mobile ethnography is a research methodology used in service design to understand user behavior, needs, and preferences in the context of mobile technology. It involves gathering qualitative data by observing and interacting with users in their natural mobile environments, such as their homes, workplaces, or on the go. By using mobile devices as research tools, researchers can gain insights into users' experiences in real-time and in their everyday contexts. This method allows for a deeper understanding of how users engage with mobile services, what motivations drive their behaviors, and how they navigate through different touchpoints and channels.

Multi-Channel Integration

Multi-channel integration in the context of service design refers to the seamless integration of various communication channels, platforms, and touchpoints to provide a consistent and unified experience to customers. It involves the coordination and synchronization of channels such as websites, mobile applications, social media, physical stores, call centers, and more, in order to deliver a cohesive and integrated customer journey.

Mystery Shopping

Mystery shopping is a research technique used in service design that involves deploying trained individuals, referred to as mystery shoppers, to evaluate the quality of service provided by businesses. These mystery shoppers act as regular customers and interact with the business anonymously, thus creating a realistic customer experience. The purpose of mystery shopping is to assess various aspects of the customer journey, such as customer service, product knowledge, and overall satisfaction. By posing as ordinary customers, mystery shoppers observe and evaluate interactions with service staff, the physical environment, and other elements of the service process.

Narrative Inquiry

Narrative inquiry is a research method commonly used in the field of service design to explore and understand individuals' and communities' experiences, perspectives, and stories. It involves collecting and analyzing personal narratives or stories to gain a deeper insight into the meaning and significance of service encounters and interactions. This research approach recognizes the value of subjective experiences and the role of stories in shaping people's understanding and interpretation of their own experiences. It aims to capture the complexity and richness of human experiences and emotions, allowing researchers to uncover hidden patterns, themes, and meanings that may not be apparent through traditional quantitative methods.

Narrative Storytelling

Narrative storytelling refers to the practice of using narratives or stories to communicate and convey information in the context of service design. In service design, narrative storytelling is a powerful tool that helps designers understand and empathize with users' experiences, needs, and desires. By capturing and sharing stories, designers can gain valuable insights into the challenges and opportunities that users face when interacting with a service. Through narrative storytelling, designers can also communicate their ideas, concepts, and solutions to stakeholders and team members. Stories provide a framework for articulating complex concepts and ideas in a relatable and engaging manner. When using narrative storytelling in service design, it is important to consider the following elements: 1. Context: Stories should be set in a relevant and relatable context. This helps users and stakeholders connect with the narrative and understand its relevance to the overall service design process. 2. Characters: Stories should involve characters that represent the users or stakeholders involved in the service. By creating relatable and well-developed characters, designers can evoke empathy and understanding from the audience. 3. Plot: Stories should have a clear structure and plot that effectively communicates the key message or objective. This helps ensure that the narrative is coherent, engaging, and impactful. 4. Emotion: Stories should evoke emotions and create a connection with the audience. By tapping into the emotional aspect of storytelling, designers can create a memorable and meaningful experience that resonates with users and stakeholders. Overall, narrative storytelling plays a crucial role in service design by facilitating the understanding, communication, and engagement of users and stakeholders. By leveraging the power of storytelling, designers can create impactful and meaningful experiences that drive innovation and improvement in service design processes.

Needs Assessment

A needs assessment in the context of service design refers to the systematic process of identifying and evaluating the needs, challenges, and expectations of individuals or groups who will be using or benefitting from a service. It is a vital step in the service design process as it helps ensure that the resulting service is tailored to meet the specific needs of its users. The needs assessment typically involves conducting thorough research and analysis to gather relevant information about the target users and their requirements. This may include collecting

141

data through surveys, interviews, focus groups, or direct observation. The gathered information is then analyzed to gain insights into the users' preferences, behaviors, goals, and pain points. The main objectives of a needs assessment are to identify the specific features and functionalities that should be included in the service, as well as to determine any barriers or obstacles that may hinder its successful implementation. It helps service designers gain a deep understanding of the context in which the service will be used, enabling them to make informed decisions about how to best meet users' needs. By conducting a needs assessment, service designers can gain valuable insights into the user experience and ensure that the service is designed in a way that maximizes its usability, efficiency, and effectiveness. This process helps bridge the gap between user expectations and the actual service delivery, increasing user satisfaction and improving the overall service quality. A needs assessment is an ongoing process that may continue throughout the service design journey. As new information and insights are gathered, designers can refine and iterate their service concepts to better match the evolving needs of the users.

Net Promoter Score (NPS)

The Net Promoter Score (NPS) is a key metric used in service design to measure customer loyalty and satisfaction. It is based on the simple premise that by asking customers a single question, their likelihood to recommend a product or service can provide valuable insights into their overall experience and future behavior. The NPS is derived from a survey question that asks customers to rate, on a scale of 0 to 10, how likely they would be to recommend a company, product, or service to a friend or colleague. Based on their responses, customers are categorized into three groups: Promoters (score 9-10), Passives (score 7-8), and Detractors (score 0-6). Promoters are highly satisfied customers who actively promote and recommend a product or service to others. They are likely to be repeat customers and have a positive impact on business growth. Passives are moderately satisfied customers who are indifferent and may be easily swayed by competitors. Detractors are unsatisfied customers who are likely to share negative experiences and may negatively impact business reputation. The NPS is calculated by subtracting the percentage of Detractors from the percentage of Promoters. The resulting score can range from -100 to +100. A positive NPS indicates a majority of Promoters, while a negative NPS indicates a majority of Detractors. The closer the NPS is to +100, the higher the customer loyalty and satisfaction. The NPS provides service designers with valuable insights into customer sentiment, enabling them to identify areas of improvement and prioritize efforts to deliver exceptional customer experiences. By monitoring the NPS over time, designers can track the effectiveness of their service design interventions and gauge customer loyalty and satisfaction trends.

Netnography

Netnography is a research methodology used in the field of service design to study and analyze the online communities and social interactions of individuals. It involves observing and interpreting the behaviors, attitudes, and opinions of people within online platforms, such as social media, forums, and blogs, with the aim of gaining insights into their experiences and perceptions related to a specific service or product. Netnography is primarily based on ethnography, which is a qualitative research method traditionally used in anthropology to study cultures and social groups. However, netnography focuses specifically on online communities and virtual environments. It utilizes a variety of data collection techniques, including participant observation and content analysis, to gain a deep understanding of the participants' practices, rituals, and interactions within their online communities.

Observational Research

Observational research, in the context of service design, refers to a qualitative research method where the researcher observes and analyzes user behavior, interactions, and experiences in a natural setting without manipulating variables or directly interacting with the participants. It aims to gain insight into how users engage with a service, identify pain points, and uncover opportunities for improvement. This type of research is valuable in service design as it allows designers to understand the service from the perspective of the user. By observing users in their natural environment, researchers can gain rich and nuanced insights that may not be captured through other research methods like surveys or interviews.

Opportunity Assessment

An opportunity assessment is a systematic and structured process used in service design to identify and evaluate potential opportunities for improvement or innovation within a service. It involves gathering and analyzing data, identifying pain points and areas of inefficiency, and exploring potential solutions. The purpose of an opportunity assessment is to gain insights into the current state of a service and identify areas where changes can be made to enhance the customer experience, increase efficiency, or generate new revenue streams. It is an essential step in the design thinking process, as it helps service designers understand the needs and expectations of customers and stakeholders, and identify opportunities to create value.

PIE Framework (Purpose, Importance, Ease)

The PIE Framework is a service design tool that enables organizations to evaluate and prioritize their initiatives based on three key factors: Purpose, Importance, and Ease. Firstly, Purpose refers to the alignment of an initiative with the overall goals and objectives of the organization. It evaluates whether the initiative is in line with the mission and vision, and whether it contributes to solving a relevant problem or addressing a customer need. By considering the purpose of an initiative, organizations can ensure that their resources are directed towards initiatives that create value and support their strategic direction. The second factor, Importance, evaluates the significance and impact of an initiative. It examines the potential benefits and outcomes that the initiative can generate, both for the organization and its customers. Importance takes into account factors such as market demand, customer value proposition, and competitive advantage. By assessing the importance of an initiative, organizations can prioritize those that have the potential for high impact and value creation. The third factor, Ease, assesses the feasibility and practicality of implementing an initiative. It considers factors such as technological readiness, resource availability, and implementation complexity. Evaluating the ease of an initiative helps organizations identify potential barriers or challenges that may hinder successful implementation. It also helps in identifying initiatives that can be implemented quickly and efficiently, contributing to the overall effectiveness of the service design process. The PIE Framework provides a structured approach for evaluating and prioritizing service design initiatives. By considering the purpose, importance, and ease of each initiative, organizations can make informed decisions about resource allocation and focus their efforts on initiatives that align with their strategic objectives, have high impact, and are feasible to implement. The framework enables organizations to optimize their service design efforts and maximize the value created for both the organization and its customers.

Parallel Prototyping

Parallel prototyping in the context of service design refers to a methodological approach that involves the simultaneous creation and testing of multiple design solutions or prototypes. It is a collaborative process that allows designers and stakeholders to explore different possibilities and refine their ideas based on user feedback and iterative improvements. This approach recognizes that service design is a complex and dynamic process that requires continuous refinement and adaptation. By creating multiple prototypes in parallel, designers can explore various design directions and evaluate their effectiveness in addressing user needs and business goals.

Pareto Analysis

Pareto Analysis is a decision-making technique used in service design to identify and prioritize the most significant factors or issues that contribute to a problem or outcome. It is named after Vilfredo Pareto, an Italian economist, who observed that 80% of the wealth was owned by 20% of the population, which led to the principle known as the Pareto Principle or the 80/20 rule. The Pareto Analysis involves analyzing data and categorizing it based on the frequency or impact of each factor. The goal is to identify the few vital factors that have the most significant influence on the problem or outcome in question. By focusing on these key factors, service designers can effectively allocate their resources and efforts to address the root causes and achieve optimal results. To conduct a Pareto Analysis, service designers follow a systematic approach: 1. Define the Problem: Clearly define the problem or outcome that needs to be addressed. This step ensures a focused and targeted analysis. 2. Gather Data: Collect relevant data related to the problem or outcome. This could include customer feedback, process data, performance indicators, or any other quantifiable information. 3. Categorize the Data: Group the data into categories based on the different factors contributing to the problem or outcome. For example, if the problem is customer dissatisfaction, the categories could be product quality, service responsiveness, billing issues, etc. 4. Analyze and Rank: Analyze the data within each category to determine the frequency or impact of each factor. Rank the factors from most to least significant. 5. Focus on the Vital Few: Identify the top-ranked factors that account for a significant portion of the problem or outcome. These are the vital few factors that require immediate attention and intervention. Pareto Analysis provides a structured approach to prioritize issues and allocate resources effectively. By focusing on the vital few factors, service designers can make informed decisions and devise targeted strategies for improvement. It ensures that efforts are directed towards the factors that will yield the maximum impact and ultimately drive better service design outcomes.

Participatory Action Research (PAR)

Participatory Action Research (PAR) is an approach used in service design that engages stakeholders in active participation throughout the research process. It is a collaborative method that empowers individuals and communities to take ownership of their service experiences and co-create solutions to address issues or improve services.PAR is characterized by its emphasis on collaboration, collective learning, and social change. It goes beyond traditional research methods by involving those directly affected by the service in the research process, allowing their voices and experiences to shape the design and implementation of interventions.In the context of service design, PAR is particularly relevant as it enables a deeper understanding of the people who use or are affected by the service. By involving stakeholders in the research process, designers gain valuable insights into their needs, preferences, and pain points. This participatory approach helps uncover hidden issues and challenges that may not have been apparent through traditional research methods.PAR typically involves several stages: problem identification, data collection, analysis, interpretation, action planning, and implementation. Throughout these stages, stakeholders actively contribute their knowledge and expertise, becoming co-researchers alongside designers. This co-creation process not only generates richer data but also fosters a sense of ownership and commitment among stakeholders.One key aspect of PAR is its focus on promoting social change. By involving stakeholders in decision-making, PAR empowers marginalized or underrepresented groups to have a voice and influence in shaping their services. It aims to address social inequalities and promote equity by including diverse perspectives in the design and delivery of services.PAR is a powerful tool in service design as it helps designers create more effective and user-centered solutions. By actively involving stakeholders in the research process, designers can better understand the context in which the service operates, identify areas for improvement, and co-create innovative interventions that meet the needs and expectations of users.Overall, Participatory Action Research is a collaborative and inclusive approach in service design that empowers stakeholders, fosters collective learning, and drives social change. It is a powerful tool for designers to create meaningful and impactful services.

Participatory Design Workshops

Participatory Design Workshops are collaborative sessions conducted in the context of service design that involve end-users, stakeholders, and design professionals. These workshops aim to include all relevant stakeholders in the design process to ensure that the final service solution meets their needs and expectations. In Participatory Design Workshops, participants are engaged in various exercises and activities to gather their insights, ideas, and feedback. These could include brainstorming sessions, design games, role-playing exercises, and interactive discussions. The facilitators guide the participants through these activities to ensure maximum engagement and inclusivity.

Participatory Design

Participatory Design, in the context of service design, is a methodological approach that involves actively engaging end-users, stakeholders, and designers in the design process of a service. It emphasizes inclusivity, collaboration, and co-creation to ensure that the final service meets the needs and expectations of the target users. The main aim of Participatory Design is to empower and give voice to all stakeholders involved in the design process. By involving end-users and stakeholders from the early stages of service design, it helps to gather valuable insights, knowledge, and perspectives that inform the design decisions. This approach recognizes that the end-users are the real experts when it comes to their needs, preferences, and experiences.

Pattern Libraries

A pattern library, in the context of service design, refers to a collection of reusable design components and guidelines that facilitate the consistent and efficient creation of user interfaces and experiences for a service. It serves as a centralized repository of design patterns, which are common solutions to recurring design problems that have been proven to be effective and user-friendly. The pattern library is typically created by a design team or organization to establish and maintain a cohesive visual language and user experience across different touchpoints of a service. It provides designers, developers, and other stakeholders with a shared vocabulary and set of tools to ensure consistency, reduce duplication of efforts, and improve overall design quality.

Pen-And-Paper Prototyping

Pen-and-paper prototyping is a method used in the field of service design to create and test service concepts, interactions, and experiences. It involves using simple materials such as paper, pens, and sometimes other tangible objects to simulate and visualize the different stages of a service. During the early stages of service design, pen-and-paper prototyping is commonly employed to quickly explore and iterate upon ideas without the need for extensive technical development. By sketching out the various elements and touchpoints of a service on paper, designers can easily make modifications and gather feedback from stakeholders and potential users. This low-fidelity approach allows for rapid ideation and iteration, saving time and resources in the long run.

Perceptual Mapping

Perceptual mapping in the context of service design refers to a technique used to visually represent how customers perceive different services or service providers in relation to each other. This tool helps service designers gain insights into customers' perceptions and preferences, allowing them to identify opportunities for improvement and make informed decisions when designing or modifying services. Perceptual mapping is typically based on customer feedback or market research data, which is collected through surveys, focus groups, or other research methods. The data collected usually includes customers' perceptions of various service attributes or factors, such as quality, reliability, price, convenience, and customer support. These attributes are then plotted on a two-dimensional graph, with each axis representing a different attribute, and the position of each service or service provider representing its perceived performance or positioning in relation to those attributes. The graph created through perceptual mapping allows service designers to visualize the relationships between different services or service providers and their key attributes. By examining the positioning of different services on the map, designers can identify gaps or spaces that exist in the market, where there may be unmet customer needs or opportunities for differentiation. They can also compare their own service's position to competitors' positions to understand how they are perceived by customers relative to others in the market. Perceptual mapping is a valuable tool for service designers because it provides a clear and concise visual representation of complex data, enabling them to make data-driven decisions. By understanding how customers perceive different services and their key attributes, designers can prioritize improvements or modifications to their own services that align with customer preferences and expectations. They can also identify areas of competitive advantage or uniqueness that can be leveraged to differentiate their services in the market.

Performance Metrics

A performance metric, in the context of service design, refers to a quantifiable measure used to assess the efficiency, effectiveness, and quality of a service. It provides objective data and insights that help in evaluating the performance of a service against predefined goals and benchmarks. Performance metrics play a crucial role in service design as they aid in monitoring and improving the overall service delivery and customer experience. By tracking these metrics, organizations can identify areas of improvement, make data-driven decisions, and enhance the value they deliver to customers.

Persona Development

Persona development is a crucial part of service design, aiming to create fictional but realistic representations of target user groups or customer segments. These personas are detailed profiles that encompass key characteristics, motivations, behaviors, and needs of specific user groups or customers, helping service designers gain a deep understanding of their target audience. Personas are created through a research process that involves collecting and analyzing data from various sources such as user interviews, surveys, and market research. This information is then synthesized and transformed into a persona profile that represents a typical user within a target user group. The persona profiles are often accompanied by a name, a photograph, and a brief personal background, enhancing their relatability and creating empathy among the design team. By using personas, service designers can develop a user-centered approach to design, ensuring that the needs and wants of real users are considered throughout the design process. Personas enable designers to make informed decisions about various aspects of the service, such as features, interactions, and even the overall service concept. Personas help designers empathize with users and adopt their perspectives, allowing for the creation of services that truly meet their needs. They provide a reference point throughout the design process, ensuring that design decisions are aligned with the goals and expectations of the target audience. Personas contribute to the overall user experience by enabling designers to identify pain points, uncover opportunities, and design solutions that cater to specific user groups. Furthermore, personas facilitate collaboration within design teams and stakeholders, serving as a communication tool that aligns everyone's understanding of the target audience. They help create a shared language and mindset among team members, fostering discussions and decision-making based on user needs rather than personal opinions. In conclusion, persona development is a fundamental technique in service design that enables designers to understand, empathize with, and design for their target users or customers. By creating fictional but realistic user profiles, personas provide insights that guide the design process and ensure that services are tailored to meet the needs of specific user groups.

Personas And Scenarios

Personas:Personas are fictional characters that represent different user groups or target audiences. In the context of service design, personas are used to understand and empathize with users' needs, aspirations, and behaviors. They are based on research and analysis of real user data and are created to help design teams gain insights into how different users might interact with a product or service.Personas provide a way to gather and synthesize information about user demographics, behaviors, motivations, and goals. They are typically created through user research methods such as interviews, surveys, or observational studies. The information collected is then used to create realistic personas that have specific names, backgrounds, goals, and characteristics.Personas help service design teams to humanize the design process and make more informed decisions. By embodying specific user profiles, personas bring users to life and enable designers to step into the shoes of their target audience. This deep understanding of users' needs and contexts enables designers to create solutions that are tailored to the specific requirements of different user groups. Scenarios:Scenarios are narrative descriptions that portray how a user might interact with a product, service, or system in a specific situation. In the context of service design, scenarios are used to test and visualize user experiences, identify pain points and opportunities, and inform the design process.Scenarios are typically created based on personas and are designed to be realistic and relatable. They describe the user's goals, motivations, and tasks, as well as the context in which the interaction takes place. Scenarios often include details such as the user's environment, emotional state, and any constraints or challenges they might face.Scenarios provide a valuable tool for service design teams to anticipate and address user needs. By envisioning and exploring different scenarios, designers can identify potential pitfalls or opportunities for improvement in their service. Scenarios also allow designers to test and validate their design ideas by simulating how users would interact with the service and assessing its effectiveness in meeting their needs.

Personas

Personas in the context of service design refer to fictional representations or archetypes of the target users or customers of a product or service. These personas are created based on research and data to accurately represent the characteristics, needs, behaviors, and goals of different user groups. Personas are used as a tool to understand and empathize with the end-users, enabling service designers to design products and services that meet their specific needs and preferences. By personifying the users, designers can better relate to them and make informed decisions about design elements, features, and overall user experience.

Pilot Testing

Pilot testing in service design refers to a method used to assess the feasibility and effectiveness of a new service or service improvement before its full-scale implementation. It involves conducting a small-scale trial or test of the service with a select group of users or customers. The purpose of pilot testing is to gather feedback, identify any potential issues or areas for improvement, and ensure that the service is designed to meet the needs and expectations of the target audience. It allows designers to evaluate and refine the service based on user feedback and make necessary adjustments before fully launching it.

Preference Testing

Preference testing, in the context of service design, refers to a method of gathering feedback from users or customers to determine their preferences or opinions regarding specific aspects of a service. This type of testing aims to understand user preferences on different options or features in order to create a service that aligns with their needs and desires. During preference testing, participants are presented with a variety of options or scenarios and asked to indicate their preferred choice. This can be done through surveys, interviews, or interactive tasks. The aim is to capture the subjective opinions and preferences of users, which can then be used to inform decisions and improvements in the design of the service. The goal of preference testing is to gain insights into what users value, what features they find appealing or useful, and what aspects of the service can be improved or optimized. By understanding user preferences, service designers can make informed decisions about how to allocate resources, prioritize features, and shape the overall experience to maximize user satisfaction. Preference testing can be used at various stages of service design, from the early exploration and concept development phases to the refinement and optimization stages. It can help identify potential pain points or areas of improvement, uncover hidden opportunities, and guide decision-making processes to create a service that resonates with users. Overall, preference testing is an essential tool in the service design toolkit, allowing designers to gather and analyze user feedback to inform the creation of services that meet user preferences and expectations.

Process Mapping

Process mapping in the context of service design is a systematic technique used to visually represent and analyze the flow of activities, interactions, and information involved in delivering a service. It is a tool that helps stakeholders gain a clear understanding of the current service delivery process and identify areas for improvement. The process mapping approach involves depicting the sequence of steps, decision points, and dependencies that occur during the service delivery process. This can be done using various visual representations, such as flowcharts, swimlane diagrams, or value stream maps. The chosen format depends on the complexity and nature of the service being mapped.

Product Roadmapping

Product roadmapping in the context of service design refers to the strategic planning process that outlines the development and evolution of a specific product or service. It involves creating a timeline or pathway that outlines the steps, stages, and key milestones in the product's lifecycle, from ideation to launch and beyond. The product roadmap serves as a visual guide for the entire team involved in the service design process, including managers, designers, developers, and stakeholders. It provides a clear overview of the product's strategic direction, helping to align everyone's efforts and ensure a shared understanding of the product's goals and objectives.

Prototype Testing

147

Prototype testing in the context of service design refers to the process of evaluating and validating a service concept or design by creating and testing a preliminary version of the service. This involves gathering feedback from potential users and stakeholders to identify areas of improvement and make necessary adjustments before fully developing and implementing the service. The purpose of prototype testing is to uncover potential issues or shortcomings in the service design early on, in order to reduce risks and costs associated with developing a service that does not meet user needs or expectations. By testing a prototype, designers can gain valuable insights into the usability, feasibility, and desirability of the service, allowing them to make informed decisions and iterate on the design to create a better end product. Prototype testing typically involves creating a simplified or scaled-down version of the service, often using low-fidelity materials such as sketches, wireframes, or interactive mockups. This allows designers to quickly and cost-effectively gather feedback from users without investing significant time and resources in developing a fully functional service. By presenting the prototype to users, designers can observe their interactions, collect feedback, and gain a better understanding of how the service would be perceived and used in real-life situations. During prototype testing, designers may use various evaluation methods such as usability testing, feedback surveys, or interviews to gather user insights. By observing users' reactions, preferences, and challenges encountered during the testing process, designers can identify areas for improvement and refine the service concept to ensure a better user experience. The feedback and data collected during prototype testing are used to inform the next steps in the design process. Designers can analyze the results, identify patterns or recurring issues, and make appropriate modifications to the service concept or design. This iterative process of testing and refining the prototype helps to ensure that the final service meets the needs and expectations of its intended users. In summary, prototype testing is a crucial step in service design that allows designers to evaluate, validate, and refine a service concept or design. By involving users early on in the design process, designers can gather valuable feedback, identify potential issues, and make necessary adjustments to create a more user-centered and successful service.

Prototyping

Prototyping is a critical process in service design that involves creating a tangible representation of a service concept or idea. It is an iterative approach that allows designers to quickly test and refine their concepts, gather feedback, and make improvements before fully implementing the service. Through prototyping, designers can evaluate the feasibility, usability, and desirability of a service, as well as identify any potential challenges or areas for improvement. It serves as a visual and interactive tool that helps stakeholders and users better understand and experience the proposed service, fostering collaboration and co-creation.

Qualitative Data Analysis

Qualitative data analysis refers to the process of examining and interpreting non-numeric data in service design. It involves systematically organizing, categorizing, and making sense of qualitative information obtained through observations, interviews, focus groups, and other qualitative research methods. Unlike quantitative data analysis, which focuses on numerical data, qualitative data analysis focuses on understanding the meanings, themes, patterns, and rich contextual details inherent in qualitative data. Qualitative data analysis in service design aims to uncover insights, generate knowledge, and inform decision-making by carefully analyzing qualitative data collected from various sources. Service designers use this analysis to understand customers' needs, behaviors, expectations, and experiences to improve the design, delivery, and evaluation of services. By examining the qualitative data, service designers can identify common themes, issues, and trends that emerge from the data, which can then inform the design of customer-centric services.

Quality Function Deployment (QFD)

Quality Function Deployment (QFD) is a systematic method used in service design to translate customer requirements into specific, measurable, and actionable design characteristics. It is a process that ensures that the voice of the customer (VOC) is effectively incorporated into the service design process. QFD starts by capturing and organizing customer needs, expectations, and desires. These inputs are typically gathered through surveys, interviews, focus groups, and feedback channels. The customer requirements are then prioritized based on their importance and significance, using techniques such as customer surveys, market research, and statistical analysis. The next step in QFD is to identify the technical features or service attributes that will satisfy the customer requirements. These are often referred to as technical descriptors or service characteristics. The technical descriptors are derived through brainstorming sessions, experts' opinions, and engineering analysis. Each technical descriptor is linked to one or more customer requirements, creating a matrix that shows the relationships between the customer requirements and the technical descriptors. This matrix, known as the "House of Quality," is a visual representation of the interrelations between the voice of the customer and the design characteristics. Once the House of Quality is completed, QFD moves to the deployment phase. In this phase, the technical descriptors are assigned specific design targets and measures. These targets are usually determined based on engineering specifications, industry standards, and best practices. The deployment phase also involves identifying the process elements, resources, and technologies needed to achieve the desired design characteristics. This ensures that the service design is technically feasible and can be implemented within the organization's capabilities. The final step of QFD is the verification and testing of the design. This involves evaluating the performance of the service design against the customer requirements and design targets. Feedback from customers, field tests, and user trials are used to validate the effectiveness of the design and make necessary improvements. This iterative process helps in refining the design, reducing potential risks, and enhancing customer satisfaction. In conclusion, QFD is a valuable tool in service design that enables organizations to align their offerings with customer needs and expectations. By systematically capturing, prioritizing, and translating customer requirements into design characteristics, QFD helps in delivering high-quality services that meet customer satisfaction and drive business success.

Quantitative Data Analysis

Quantitative Data Analysis refers to the process of collecting, organizing, and analyzing numerical data to gain meaningful insights in the context of service design. When designing services, it is important to have a clear understanding of the quantitative data that is available and to analyze it effectively. Quantitative data is collected through various methods such as surveys, questionnaires, observations, or existing databases. This data is typically numerical in nature, allowing for statistical analysis to be performed. The analysis of quantitative data involves several steps. Firstly, the data needs to be organized and cleaned to ensure accuracy and consistency. This may include removing any outliers or errors in the dataset. Once the data is cleaned, it can be summarized using descriptive statistics such as mean, median, mode, or standard deviation. These summary statistics provide a snapshot of the data and can be used to understand key trends or patterns. In addition to descriptive statistics, quantitative data analysis often includes inferential statistics. Inferential statistics are used to make predictions or draw conclusions about a larger population based on a sample. This can be useful in service design to make informed decisions about how to improve or optimize a service based on data from a smaller group. Common inferential statistical techniques include hypothesis testing and regression analysis. Quantitative data analysis is a rigorous process that requires a strong understanding of statistical principles and analytical techniques. It enables service designers to make data-driven decisions and identify areas for improvement in the design and delivery of services. By examining numerical data, patterns and trends can be identified, allowing for targeted interventions and improvements to be made. Ultimately, quantitative data analysis is a valuable tool in the service design process, providing evidence-based insights that can drive meaningful change.

Rapid Ethnography

Rapid Ethnography can be defined as a research method used in service design to gain deep insights into the needs, behaviors, and experiences of users within a short period of time. It involves immersing researchers in the users' natural environment and observing their actions and interactions with the service or product being studied. This method typically involves a small team of researchers who spend a brief but intensive period of time with the users, often ranging from a few hours to a few days. The researchers aim to understand the users' needs, motivations, and pain points by observing their behaviors, listening to their stories, and engaging in informal conversations. Rapid Ethnography differs from traditional ethnographic research in that it focuses on quickly generating insights rather than producing an in-depth, comprehensive study. The goal is not to provide an exhaustive analysis of the users' culture or way of life, but to identify key patterns and insights that inform the design process. This method is particularly valuable in the context of service design, where understanding the users' experiences and perspectives is crucial for creating meaningful and effective services. By gaining rich qualitative data quickly, service designers can iterate and improve their designs based on real user needs and behaviors. Rapid Ethnography can be conducted through a variety of methods, including direct observation, interviewing, and diary studies. It often involves a combination of these methods to capture a holistic understanding of the user experience. In summary, Rapid Ethnography is a research method used in service design to quickly gain insights into user needs and behaviors. By immersing researchers in the users' natural environment and engaging in direct observation and informal conversations, rapid ethnography provides valuable qualitative data that informs the design process.

Rapid Iterative Testing And Evaluation (RITE)

Rapid Iterative Testing and Evaluation (RITE) is a user-centered design approach that involves iteratively testing and evaluating a service throughout its development process. This method aims to identify and address any usability issues or areas for improvement as early as possible, resulting in a more user-friendly and effective service. RITE involves conducting frequent and rapid testing sessions with users, where they interact with prototypes or early versions of the service. These tests are typically conducted in a controlled setting, such as a usability lab, and involve users performing specific tasks or scenarios related to the service. During the testing sessions, users' interactions with the service are closely observed and recorded, providing valuable insights into their needs, preferences, and pain points. The feedback collected from users is then used to continuously refine and enhance the service, making it more intuitive, efficient, and satisfying to use. The iterative nature of RITE allows for the quick identification and resolution of usability issues. After each testing session, the findings are analyzed, and necessary changes or updates are made to the service. These improvements are then tested again in subsequent sessions to validate their effectiveness. RITE also emphasizes the involvement of cross-functional teams throughout the testing and evaluation process. This collaborative approach ensures that different perspectives and expertise are considered, leading to a holistic understanding of the service and its users. It also facilitates better communication and alignment between the various stakeholders involved in the service design process. Overall, the RITE approach enables service designers to continuously learn from users' feedback and iterate on the service's design and features. By regularly testing and evaluating the service, designers can uncover hidden opportunities, address usability issues, and ultimately deliver a more user-centric and impactful service.

Rapid Prototyping

Rapid prototyping, in the context of service design, refers to the iterative process of quickly creating and testing tangible representations or mock-ups of a service concept or experience. It is a method used to gather feedback, learn from users, and improve the design before investing significant resources into the final implementation. The goal of rapid prototyping is to validate assumptions and gain insights into user needs, preferences, and pain points. By creating low-fidelity prototypes that simulate the key interactions and touchpoints of the service, designers can gather valuable feedback from users and stakeholders early in the design process.

Rapid Visualization

Rapid Visualization is a technique used in service design to quickly visualize ideas and concepts in order to facilitate communication and decision-making within a design team or with stakeholders. It involves the creation of visual representations, such as sketches, diagrams, or storyboards, to convey design solutions and illustrate the user experience. The main purpose of rapid visualization is to provide a tangible and visual representation of ideas, allowing designers and stakeholders to better understand and evaluate concepts. By creating quick visualizations, designers are able to explore different design possibilities, communicate their ideas effectively, and gain feedback from stakeholders in a timely manner.

Remote User Testing

Remote User Testing is a service design process that involves gathering data and insights related to user behavior, preferences, and expectations through online testing methods. It allows designers, researchers, and product teams to observe and understand user interactions with a digital product or service, without being physically present with the users. This testing method involves recruiting participants who remotely access the digital product or service to perform specific tasks or scenarios. These participants may be located in different geographical locations and can access the product using their own devices and internet connections. They are provided with clear instructions and tasks to complete while their interactions and experiences are recorded and analyzed. Remote User Testing enables researchers to evaluate the effectiveness, usability, and overall user experience of a digital product or service. By capturing real-time user behavior, feedback, and preferences, designers can identify pain points, areas of improvement, and opportunities for innovation. During remote user testing, researchers typically use various techniques to collect data and insights. These may include screen recording software, eye-tracking technology, surveys, interviews, and think-aloud protocols. By gathering data from multiple sources, designers are able to gain a holistic understanding of user interactions and experiences. The advantages of remote user testing include cost-effectiveness, convenience, and scalability. It eliminates geographical limitations and reduces the need for physical facilities or equipment. Remote testing allows for a larger pool of participants, representing diverse demographics and user profiles. However, remote user testing also has its limitations. It may lack the richness of in-person testing, as researchers are unable to observe non-verbal cues or provide immediate assistance. Technical issues, such as internet connectivity or device compatibility, may also impact the reliability and validity of the test results. In summary, Remote User Testing is a service design process that involves gathering data and insights through online testing methods. It enables designers to evaluate user interactions, preferences, and experiences with a digital product or service, without being physically present. Although it has advantages in terms of cost-effectiveness and scalability, it also has limitations in terms of richness and technical reliability.

Repertory Grid Technique

The Repertory Grid Technique in the context of service design is a qualitative research method used to explore and understand people's perceptions and evaluations of services. It is a tool that allows service designers to uncover and analyze the underlying factors and dimensions that influence customers' experiences and satisfaction with a service. The technique consists of a series of structured interviews with participants, in which they are shown a grid and asked to compare and evaluate a set of elements (e.g., service attributes, touchpoints, customer interactions) based on their personal experiences and preferences. The elements are typically represented as rows in the grid, while the columns represent the dimensions or factors that participants use to evaluate the elements. During the interview, participants are asked to articulate their reasoning behind the comparisons they make, helping the service designer gain insights into their mental models and decision-making processes. This qualitative data is then analyzed to identify patterns, themes, and relationships that can inform the design and improvement of service experiences. The Repertory Grid Technique offers several advantages in the context of service design. It provides a structured framework for capturing and organizing qualitative data, making it easier to compare and analyze participants' perceptions. By allowing participants to articulate their reasoning, it helps uncover the hidden dimensions and factors that shape their evaluations, providing a deeper understanding of their needs and expectations. This method also allows for the exploration of subjective and context-dependent factors that may not be captured by traditional quantitative measures. However, it is important to note that the Repertory Grid Technique also has its limitations. The results are based on participants' subjective opinions and may not necessarily reflect objective reality or generalizable patterns. The technique requires skilled facilitators who can effectively guide participants through the process and elicit meaningful insights. Additionally, the analysis of the qualitative data can be time-consuming and subjective, relying heavily on the interpretation and judgment of the service designer. In conclusion, the Repertory Grid Technique is a valuable tool in service design research, providing a structured approach to understanding and analyzing customers' perceptions and evaluations. It offers insights into the underlying dimensions and factors that shape their experiences, informing the design and improvement of service offerings. By incorporating this technique into the service design process, designers can gain a deeper understanding of their target audience and create more engaging and satisfying service experiences.

Requirements Gathering

Requirements gathering is a systematic process in service design that involves collecting and documenting information about the needs, expectations, and preferences of the stakeholders. It is a crucial step in the service design process as it helps in understanding the purpose, scope, and constraints of the service being designed, and informing the subsequent design decisions. During the requirements gathering phase, the service design team engages with various stakeholders such as customers, users, internal staff, and subject matter experts to elicit their requirements. This can be done through various techniques such as interviews, surveys, observations, and workshops. The goal is to obtain a comprehensive understanding of the stakeholders' needs, which can then be analyzed to identify common patterns, prioritize requirements, and define the scope of the service. The requirements gathered during this process typically include both functional and non-functional requirements. Functional requirements specify the features, tasks, and actions that the service should support to meet the stakeholders' needs. Non-functional requirements, on the other hand, describe the qualities, characteristics, and constraints that the service should possess, such as performance, security, usability, and compliance. Once the requirements have been gathered, they are documented in a clear and concise manner, ensuring that they are easily understandable by all stakeholders. This documentation serves as a reference for the service design team throughout the design and development process, guiding their decisions and ensuring that the final service meets the stakeholders' expectations. Effective requirements gathering requires strong communication and listening skills, as well as the ability to ask the right questions. It is important to involve all relevant stakeholders and encourage their active participation to ensure that their needs are accurately captured. Additionally, the requirements gathering process should be iterative and flexible, allowing for adjustments and refinements as new insights and information emerge.

Responsive Web Design

Responsive Web Design is a design approach that aims to create websites that provide optimal viewing and interaction experience across a wide range of devices and screen sizes. It is a service design practice that focuses on designing websites that automatically adjust their layout and appearance based on the device being used to access them, ensuring that users have a consistent and intuitive experience regardless of whether they are using a desktop computer, laptop, tablet, or smartphone. One of the key principles of responsive web design is flexibility. This means that the design and layout of a website should automatically adapt and adjust to fit the screen size and resolution of the device being used. This involves using fluid grids, flexible images, and media queries to ensure that the content of the website is displayed in a way that is visually appealing and easy to navigate, regardless of the device being used. Responsive web design also prioritizes the content of the website, ensuring that it is easily accessible and readable on any device. This involves using techniques such as font scaling and optimized typography to ensure that text is legible and images are clear and sharp, regardless of the screen size. It also involves organizing and structuring content in a way that is intuitive and user-friendly, making it easy for users to find the information they are looking for and complete desired actions, such as making a purchase or submitting a form. By adopting responsive web design principles, service designers can create websites that provide a consistent and optimal user experience, regardless of the device being used. This not only improves user satisfaction and engagement but also increases accessibility and reach, as websites can be easily accessed and viewed on a wide variety of devices. Additionally, responsive web design can also have positive SEO implications, as search engines tend to favor mobile-friendly websites in their search results. In conclusion, responsive web design is a service design practice that focuses on creating websites that adapt and adjust their layout and appearance based on the device being used. By prioritizing flexibility and content accessibility, designers can create websites that provide an optimal user experience, regardless of the screen size or device.

Role-Playing Exercises

Role-playing exercises in the context of service design refer to interactive activities that simulate real-life scenarios and allow individuals or teams to assume and act out specific roles. These exercises are used as a means to understand, develop, or improve services by exploring different perspectives, challenging assumptions, and promoting collaboration. During role-playing exercises, participants are assigned specific roles, such as service providers, customers, or stakeholders, and are given a scenario or problem to solve within the context of service design. They then act out these roles, engaging in dialogue, making decisions, and exploring various options and outcomes. The exercises may involve scripted or improvisational elements, depending on the objectives and complexity of the scenario.

Role-Playing

Role-playing is a method used in service design to simulate and explore different scenarios and interactions that may occur within a service. It involves individuals taking on specific roles and acting out situations to gain a deeper understanding of the service and its impact on users. During a role-playing session, participants are assigned specific roles, such as a service provider, a customer, or any other relevant role within the service ecosystem. They are then given a set of instructions and guidelines on how to behave and interact with others in their assigned roles. The main goal of role-playing in service design is to provide a realistic and immersive experience that allows participants to empathize with different perspectives and uncover potential challenges, opportunities, and areas for improvement within the service. By embodying different roles, participants can explore diverse viewpoints and gain insights into how different users may experience the service. Role-playing also allows service designers to test and validate service concepts, touchpoints, and processes in a safe and controlled environment. It helps identify any gaps or issues in the service delivery and customer experience, and provides an opportunity to iterate and refine the design accordingly. Role-playing sessions can be facilitated using various tools and techniques, such as scripts, props, and improvised scenarios. It is important to create a supportive and non-judgmental atmosphere to encourage active participation and open communication among participants. Overall, role-playing is a valuable tool in service design as it enables designers and stakeholders to gain a deeper understanding of the service ecosystem, user needs, and potential pain points. It helps create empathy, uncover insights, and inform the design process to create meaningful and user-centered services.

Root Cause Analysis

Root Cause Analysis in the context of service design is a systematic approach to identify and address the underlying causes of service failures or problems. It involves analyzing the various factors and events that contribute to a service issue to determine the primary cause or causes, rather than just treating the symptoms. The objective of Root Cause Analysis is to prevent the recurrence of service issues by understanding and rectifying the fundamental reasons behind them. It aims to go beyond the immediate or surface-level causes and delve deeper into the root causes that are often hidden or overlooked.

SME Interviews

SME Interviews in the context of service design refer to the process of conducting interviews with Subject Matter Experts (SMEs) to gather valuable insights, knowledge, and expertise that can contribute to the design and improvement of a service. During SME interviews, designers or researchers engage with individuals who possess in-depth knowledge and experience in a particular domain or industry. These SMEs may be employees, managers, or external consultants who have a deep understanding of the service being developed or enhanced. The primary objective of SME interviews is to leverage the expertise of these individuals to gain insights into various aspects of the service, such as its current state, challenges, user needs, expectations, and potential areas for improvement. By conducting structured or semi-structured interviews, designers can explore specific topics with SMEs and capture their insights effectively. SME interviews typically involve asking open-ended questions and encouraging SMEs to share their knowledge, experiences, and suggestions freely. Designers may also use various techniques, such as brainstorming sessions or storyboarding, to facilitate a more productive dialogue and extract valuable insights from the SMEs. The information gathered from SME interviews plays a critical role in informing the design process. It helps designers gain a deeper understanding of the service's ecosystem, identify pain points, uncover opportunities for innovation, and generate ideas for service improvements. SME interviews also enable designers to validate assumptions, clarify requirements, and ensure that the design aligns with the needs of both users and business stakeholders. In conclusion, SME interviews are a crucial part of the service design process. They provide designers with access to the knowledge and expertise of

SMEs, enabling them to make informed decisions and create user-centric services that meet the needs of the target audience.

SWOT Analysis

A SWOT analysis is a strategic tool used in service design to assess the strengths, weaknesses, opportunities, and threats of a particular service or organization. It provides a comprehensive overview of both the internal and external factors that can impact the success of a service. The strengths component of a SWOT analysis focuses on the positive attributes of the service. This could include factors such as a strong brand reputation, a highly skilled workforce, or a unique selling proposition. By identifying these strengths, service designers can leverage them to their advantage and differentiate themselves from competitors. On the other hand, weaknesses are internal factors that may hinder the success of the service. These could include things like subpar customer service, outdated technology, or a lack of resources. Recognizing these weaknesses allows service designers to address them and make necessary improvements to enhance the overall service experience. Opportunities refer to external factors that can positively impact the service. This could include emerging market trends, changes in consumer behavior, or new technologies. By capitalizing on these opportunities, service designers can stay ahead of the curve and adapt their services to meet evolving customer needs and expectations. Lastly, threats are external factors that can pose challenges to the service. This could include factors such as intense competition, changing regulations, or economic downturns. Understanding these threats helps service designers to develop contingency plans and mitigate potential risks. A SWOT analysis is a valuable tool in service design as it enables service designers to identify and capitalize on their strengths, improve upon their weaknesses, take advantage of opportunities, and navigate potential threats. It provides a comprehensive understanding of the internal and external factors that can influence the success of a service, guiding service designers in making informed decisions and designing impactful services that meet the needs of their target audience.

Scenario Mapping

Scenario mapping is a technique used in service design to visually represent the various steps and interactions that occur within a specific service scenario or user journey. It involves the creation of a sequence of interconnected events, actions, and touchpoints, which help designers gain a deeper understanding of the entire user experience. By mapping out scenarios, service designers can identify pain points, areas for improvement, and potential opportunities for innovation. It allows them to explore different possibilities and test potential solutions, ultimately leading to the creation of more user-centered services.

Scenario Planning

Scenario planning is a strategic tool used in the context of service design to envision and prepare for possible future scenarios that may impact a service or organization. It involves the identification, exploration, and analysis of various alternative futures to assess their potential impact and inform strategic decision-making. By considering multiple scenarios, service designers can develop a broader understanding of the uncertainties and complexities that may arise in the future. This helps them build resilience and adaptability into their service design, enabling them to better respond to changing circumstances and customer needs.

Scenarios And Storyboarding

Scenarios and storyboarding are important tools in the field of service design, used to visualize and communicate the user experience and journey within a service system. These tools help designers understand user needs, identify pain points, and iterate on service concepts to improve usability and overall user satisfaction. A scenario is a narrative that describes a specific user interaction or journey within a service system. It provides a detailed account of the steps a user takes, the actions they perform, and the outcomes they achieve while using the service. Scenarios allow designers to walk in the shoes of the user, gaining insights into their motivations, goals, and frustrations. By exploring various scenarios, designers can identify opportunities for improvement and design services that better meet user needs. Storyboarding is the process of visually representing scenarios using a series of frames or panels. Each frame depicts a specific point in the scenario, capturing key moments and interactions. Storyboards help designers visualize the flow of the user experience, highlighting key touchpoints and showing how different elements of the service interact. They provide a tangible representation of the user journey and enable designers to analyze and improve the service design. Storyboards are usually created using simple sketches, drawings, or digital mockups. They can be used to communicate ideas and concepts to stakeholders and team members, allowing for feedback and iteration. Storyboarding helps designers think through the details of the user experience, considering factors such as user interface, information flow, and overall service coherence. It allows for a visual exploration of different design possibilities and helps teams align on a shared understanding of the desired user experience. Overall, scenarios and storyboarding are essential tools in the service design process. They enable designers to understand user needs, identify opportunities for improvement, and visualize the user experience in a tangible and communicative way. By employing scenarios and storyboards, designers can create services that are intuitive, seamless, and ultimately more satisfying for users.

Scenarios And Storytelling

Scenarios and storytelling are methods used in service design to better understand and communicate the user experience and the journey through a service. They involve creating narratives or stories that depict how a user would interact with a service in various situations or contexts. A scenario is a detailed description of a specific situation in which a user would engage with a service. It outlines the user's goals, actions, and interactions throughout the service journey. Scenarios are often developed based on user research, personas, and user needs to ensure they accurately represent the target audience and their expectations. By outlining different scenarios, service designers can identify pain points, areas of improvement, and opportunities to enhance the user experience. Storytelling, on the other hand, focuses on creating compelling narratives or stories that bring the scenarios to life. These stories may be in written form, visualized through storyboards or sketches, or even acted out as role plays. The purpose of storytelling is to engage stakeholders and communicate the user experience in a memorable and immersive way. It allows designers to portray the service journey, highlight potential issues, and illustrate the intended outcomes or desired user behaviors. Both scenarios and storytelling play critical roles in service design as they provide designers and stakeholders with a shared understanding of the service experience. They enable designers to empathize with users, identify pain points, and design solutions that best meet user needs. Additionally, scenarios and storytelling help bridge the gap between different stakeholders by communicating complex service interactions and behaviors in a concise and accessible manner. In conclusion, scenarios and storytelling are vital tools in service design, as they allow designers to understand and communicate the user experience effectively. Scenarios outline specific user situations, while storytelling brings these scenarios to life through compelling narratives. Together, they help designers empathize with users, identify pain points, and design services that meet user needs.

Scenarios

A scenario, in the context of service design, refers to a detailed description or narrative of a specific situation or interaction that represents a user's journey and experience with a particular service. It offers a way to understand and analyze the different touchpoints, actions, and emotions that users may encounter during their interaction with the service. A scenario typically includes information about the user's context, their goals, the steps they take to achieve those goals, the interactions they have with the service, and the outcomes or results of their actions. It helps service designers visualize the user's experience and identify pain points, opportunities for improvement, and areas where the service can be optimized.

Semi-Structured Interviews

Semi-structured interviews in the context of service design refer to a research method that combines elements of both structured and unstructured interviews. These interviews provide a flexible framework for collecting qualitative data from individuals, allowing for a deeper understanding of their perspectives, experiences, needs, and expectations in relation to a specific service or service-related issues. In a semi-structured interview, the interviewer follows a predefined set of questions or topics while also allowing for open-ended discussions and exploration of unforeseen areas of interest. This approach provides a balance between the structure of guided questions and the flexibility to capture valuable insights that may arise during the conversation.

Sensory Evaluation

Sensory evaluation is a systematic method used in service design to assess and measure the sensory aspects of a service experience. It involves gathering data and feedback from users to evaluate how the service appeals to their senses, such as taste, smell, sight, touch, and sound. The main objective of sensory evaluation in service design is to understand how different sensory stimuli impact the perception and overall experience of the service. By analyzing the sensory dimensions of a service, designers can identify strengths, weaknesses, and areas for improvement.

Service Blueprint

A service blueprint is a visual representation of the entire service process, highlighting all the steps, actions, and interactions that take place between the service provider and the customer. It maps out the different touchpoints, physical and digital, and outlines the behind-the-scenes activities and support systems involved in delivering a service. Typically, a service blueprint consists of several layers or sections. The top layer presents the customer's journey, starting from the initial point of contact with the service provider and progressing through various stages until the service is complete. This layer focuses on the customer's actions, needs, and emotions throughout the process. The middle layer of the blueprint describes the physical evidence or tangible elements required to support the service delivery. It includes the visible elements that customers interact with, such as websites, mobile apps, self-service machines, or physical spaces. This layer helps to ensure that the customer's experience is cohesive and consistent across different touchpoints. The bottom layer reveals the backstage activities necessary to deliver the service effectively. It includes all the internal processes, resources, and employee actions involved in fulfilling the customer's needs. This layer helps identify potential bottlenecks, points of failure, or areas where improvements can be made to enhance the overall service experience. Service blueprints are valuable tools for service design as they provide a comprehensive overview of the service system. They enable service designers to identify pain points in the customer journey, opportunities for innovation, and areas where the service can be optimized. By visually representing the service process and its supporting elements, service blueprints help align stakeholders' understanding, foster collaboration, and facilitate the design of seamless and customer-centric services.

Service Blueprinting

Service Blueprinting is a visual tool used in service design to map the customer journey and the corresponding actions and interactions of both customers and service providers. It provides a comprehensive overview of the service process, highlighting the different touchpoints and identifying potential areas for improvement. Service Blueprinting consists of several key elements. The first element is the customer journey, which outlines the steps the customer takes to complete a service. This includes both front-stage activities that are visible to the customer and backstage activities that happen behind the scenes. The second element is the line of visibility, which separates the actions and interactions that are visible to the customer from those that are not. This helps to identify areas where the customer may need more support or information. The third element is the interaction points, which are the moments where the customer and service provider interact. These interactions can be in person, over the phone, or through digital channels. The fourth element is the supporting processes, which are the activities and systems that enable the service to be delivered. These can include technology, training, and documentation. The final element is the physical evidence, which refers to the tangible aspects of the service, such as the service environment or the physical products used during the service.

Service Design Blueprint

A service design blueprint is a visual representation of a service that is used to understand, analyze, and improve the various touchpoints and interactions between the customer and the service provider throughout the service journey. It is a detailed and comprehensive map that captures the entire service experience, from the initial customer contact to the final outcome. The blueprint provides a holistic view of the service by illustrating the various components involved, including physical and digital elements, people, processes, and systems. It identifies the different customer touchpoints and highlights the interactions, emotions, and expectations that arise at each stage of the service journey. The purpose of creating a service design blueprint is to identify pain points, inefficiencies, and gaps in the service delivery process. By mapping out the entire service experience, organizations can gain valuable insights into the customer's perspective and identify areas for improvement. It enables them to understand how different elements of the service ecosystem interact and impact the overall customer experience. The key elements of a service design blueprint include: 1. Customer Actions: These are the actions performed by the customer at each touchpoint, such as making a reservation, filling out a form, or interacting with a service provider. 2. Frontstage Actions: These are the actions performed by the service provider in direct interaction with the customer, including greeting, guiding, or assisting the customer. 3. Backstage Actions: These are the behind-the-scenes actions that support the service delivery, such as processing orders, preparing materials, or coordinating with other departments. 4. Support Processes: These are the processes and systems that enable smooth service delivery, such as booking systems, CRM software, or inventory management systems. 5. Physical Evidence: This includes all the tangible elements of the service, such as signage, brochures, facilities, or equipment, which contribute to the overall customer experience. By visually representing these components and their interdependencies, the service design blueprint provides a clear understanding of the entire service experience. It helps service designers and organizations identify opportunities for improvements, eliminate bottlenecks, and create seamless and memorable customer experiences.

Service Design Canvas

The Service Design Canvas is a tool used in the field of service design to visually map and explore various aspects of a service. It is a framework that brings together different elements of a service and helps to align the stakeholders and teams involved in its design and delivery. The canvas is divided into nine sections, each representing a different aspect of the service. These sections include the customer journey, the touchpoints, the service concept, the service environment, the service providers, the service processes, the service offerings, the service interactions, and the service measures. In the customer journey section, the canvas helps to identify the different stages or touchpoints that a customer goes through when interacting with the service. This includes both physical and digital interactions. The touchpoints section focuses on the specific points of contact between the customer and the service, such as a website, a call center, or a physical store. It helps to uncover pain points and opportunities for improvement. The service concept section looks at the overall idea or value proposition of the service. It explores the core benefits it offers to the customers and how it differentiates itself from competitors. The service environment section considers the physical and virtual spaces in which the service is delivered. It examines the atmosphere, design, and layout of these spaces to ensure they enhance the overall customer experience. The service providers section looks at the individuals or teams responsible for delivering the service. It considers their skills, knowledge, and attitudes, and how they contribute to the overall service experience. The service processes section focuses on the step-by-step activities and workflows involved in delivering the service. It helps to identify bottlenecks, inefficiencies, and areas for streamlining. The service offerings section looks at the different products, goods, or resources that are part of the service. It helps to define their features, benefits, and how they align with customer needs. The service interactions section considers the different types of interactions that take place between the service provider and the customer. This includes both human interactions and interactions with technology. The service measures section looks at the key performance indicators and metrics that are used to evaluate the success of the service. It helps to define what success looks like and how it can be measured effectively. By using the Service Design Canvas, service designers can gain a comprehensive understanding of the service and its various components. It allows for collaboration, analysis, and iterative improvements, ultimately leading to the creation of more user-centered and effective services.

Service Design Game

Service Design Game is a collaborative and interactive approach used in the field of service design to foster creativity, problem-solving, and co-creation among participants. It is a game-

157

based methodology that helps design teams, stakeholders, and individuals to gain a deeper understanding of the service ecosystem, identify opportunities, and generate innovative solutions. During the Service Design Game, participants are engaged in a series of structured activities and exercises that simulate real-life service scenarios. Through these activities, participants are encouraged to think holistically and empathetically, considering not only the touchpoints but also the behind-the-scenes processes, interactions, and emotions involved in the service experience.

Service Design Handbook

A service design handbook is a comprehensive guide that provides principles, methods, and best practices for designing and improving services. It offers a structured approach to identifying, understanding, and addressing the needs and expectations of users and stakeholders, with the goal of creating valuable and meaningful service experiences. The handbook serves as a valuable resource for service designers, practitioners, and organizations seeking to deliver high-quality services. It offers a range of tools and techniques that can be applied throughout the service design process, from research and analysis to ideation, prototyping, and implementation. The handbook typically covers various aspects of service design, including user research, journey mapping, service blueprinting, co-creation, prototyping, and evaluation. It provides step-by-step instructions and practical examples that help designers and teams navigate each stage of the design process effectively. By following the guidelines and methods outlined in the handbook, designers can gain insights into customer needs and pain points, uncover opportunities for innovation, and develop service solutions that meet those needs in a human-centered and sustainable way. The service design handbook also emphasizes the importance of collaboration and multidisciplinary teamwork. It encourages designers to engage with diverse stakeholders, including users, employees, and partners, to ensure a holistic and inclusive approach to service design. Furthermore, the handbook highlights the significance of iteration and continuous improvement in service design. It encourages designers to test and refine their ideas through prototyping and user feedback, allowing for the development of better services over time. Overall, a service design handbook acts as a comprehensive guide that equips designers and organizations with the knowledge and tools needed to create services that are user-centered, efficient, and deliver meaningful value to users and stakeholders.

Service Design Index

Service Design Index is a quantitative measurement that assesses the performance, effectiveness, and efficiency of service design within an organization. It provides a comprehensive overview of the maturity level and overall quality of service design capabilities. The index is based on various key performance indicators (KPIs) that evaluate different aspects of service design. These KPIs may include customer satisfaction, service delivery time, service reliability, user experience, cost of service design activities, and stakeholder engagement.

Service Design KPIs

Service Design KPIs, or Key Performance Indicators, refer to specific metrics and measurements that are used to evaluate the performance and effectiveness of service design processes and outcomes. These indicators help service designers assess the impact of their design decisions on the overall user experience and identify opportunities for improvement.Service Design KPIs can be divided into different categories, including customer satisfaction, operational efficiency, and financial performance. Customer satisfaction KPIs measure the level of satisfaction and loyalty among service users, and they can be assessed through surveys, feedback forms, or ratings and reviews. These KPIs provide insights into how well the service meets the needs and expectations of its users, allowing designers to identify areas for improvement.Operational efficiency KPIs focus on the effectiveness and efficiency of service delivery processes. They can include metrics such as service delivery time, response time, or the number of errors or complaints. By monitoring these KPIs, designers can identify bottlenecks or inefficiencies in the service delivery process and make adjustments to optimize operations.Financial performance KPIs measure the financial impact of service design efforts. These indicators can include metrics such as revenue growth, cost savings, or return on investment. By tracking these KPIs, designers can demonstrate the value of their work and make data-driven decisions to allocate resources effectively.Service Design KPIs are crucial for ensuring that service design efforts are aligned with business objectives and are driving positive outcomes. By measuring and monitoring these indicators, designers can evaluate the success of their design interventions and make data-driven decisions to continuously improve the service. Additionally, Service Design KPIs can be used to communicate the impact of service design to stakeholders and secure support and resources for future initiatives.

Service Design Operations

Service Design Operations is the management and coordination of the activities and processes involved in designing and delivering services that meet the needs and expectations of customers. It encompasses the planning, implementation, and ongoing evaluation of service design strategies and practices. Service design is a holistic approach to creating and improving services that focuses on understanding and meeting the needs of customers and users. It involves designing service processes, interactions, and touchpoints to deliver a seamless and satisfying experience. Service Design Operations builds on this foundation by providing the framework and structure for managing and optimizing the delivery of services.

Service Design Patterns

Service design patterns refer to established solutions or approaches that are commonly used in the field of service design. These patterns help designers to tackle recurring challenges and solve problems that are frequently encountered when designing services. These patterns are based on best practices and lessons learned from previous service design projects. They provide a set of guidelines and principles that can be applied to different stages of the service design process, from understanding user needs to prototyping and implementation.

Service Design Playbooks

Service Design Playbooks are comprehensive guides that provide a formal framework for designing, implementing, and evaluating services. They offer a structured approach to developing service design solutions that are effective, user-centered, and meet the needs of both the service provider and the end-users. These playbooks typically include a set of guidelines, tools, and techniques that service designers can use throughout the design process. They often cover various aspects of service design, such as understanding user needs, defining service objectives, ideation and prototyping, service delivery, monitoring and evaluation, and continuous improvement.

Service Design Principles

Service design principles are a set of guidelines and concepts that are used in the field of service design to assist designers in creating optimal service experiences. Service design is a multidisciplinary approach that focuses on creating, improving, and innovating services to meet the needs and expectations of both users and providers. There are various principles that can be applied in service design, but here are a few commonly used ones: 1. User-centeredness: The service should be designed with the users in mind. This involves understanding their needs, goals, and behaviors, and creating solutions that are tailored to their specific requirements. 2. Co-creation: The process of service design should involve stakeholders from different perspectives, such as users, employees, and management. By including all relevant parties, it ensures that the service reflects a holistic understanding of the needs and desires of all involved. 3. Holistic approach: Service design takes into account the entirety of the service experience, from the initial contact with the service provider to the post-service relationship. It considers all touchpoints, both physical and digital, to create a seamless and consistent experience. 4. Iterative design: Service design is an ongoing and iterative process. It involves continuous feedback, testing, and improvement, allowing for adjustments and refinements based on real-world usage and user feedback. 5. Service as a system: Services are not isolated entities but rather part of a larger system. Service design principles aim to understand and optimize the interactions and dependencies within the system to ensure a coherent and efficient service experience. 6. Scalability and flexibility: Services should be designed to accommodate growth, changes, and variations in demand. They should be scalable to handle increased volume and adaptable to evolving user needs and expectations. By applying these principles, service designers can create meaningful and valuable service experiences that satisfy the needs of users while also aligning with the goals and capabilities of the service provider. These principles provide a framework for designing services that are efficient, effective, and user-centric.

Service Design Sprints

A Service Design Sprint is a collaborative and time-constrained approach to solving complex challenges in the context of service design. It involves a multidisciplinary team working together for a set period of time, usually between one to two weeks, to research, prototype, and test potential solutions. During a Service Design Sprint, the team follows a structured process that typically consists of five phases: Understand, Define, Ideate, Prototype, and Test. In the Understand phase, the team gains a deep understanding of the problem by conducting user research, mapping out user journeys, and identifying key pain points and opportunities. This phase serves as the foundation for the rest of the sprint. In the Define phase, the team synthesizes their research findings and identifies a specific problem statement to focus on. This helps to ensure that the team's efforts are aligned and that they are working towards a common goal. The Ideate phase is where the team generates a wide range of possible solutions to address the defined problem. This is done through brainstorming and other creative techniques. Once a selection of potential solutions has been identified, the team moves into the Prototype phase. Here, low-fidelity prototypes are created to bring the ideas to life in a tangible and visual way. These prototypes can take various forms, such as sketches, storyboards, or even physical models. The goal is to quickly and cheaply explore different options without investing too much time or resources. Finally, in the Test phase, the team gathers feedback on the prototypes from users or other stakeholders. This feedback is used to refine and iterate on the solutions, ultimately leading to a more robust and user-centered design. The sprint concludes with a set of actionable insights and recommendations for further development and implementation.

Service Design Thinking

Service Design Thinking is a methodological approach that aims to create and improve services by putting the user at the center of the design process. It involves understanding the needs, desires, and behaviors of users in order to design services that are valuable, usable, and enjoyable for them. This approach combines principles and tools from various disciplines, such as design thinking, human-centered design, and user experience design, to create holistic and innovative solutions. Service Design Thinking goes beyond traditional approaches to service design by exploring the entire service ecosystem, including all touchpoints and interactions between the user and the service provider.

Service Design Workbooks

A service design workbook can be defined as a comprehensive tool or document that enables service designers to plan, develop, and implement effective service design strategies and solutions. It serves as a structured and systematic guide that aids in the exploration, analysis, and improvement of various aspects of a service, including its user experience, processes, and interactions. The primary function of a service design workbook is to facilitate collaboration and communication among stakeholders involved in the design process. It helps to align different perspectives, insights, and requirements to create a shared understanding of the service and its objectives. By providing a framework for documenting and organizing information, the workbook ensures that critical details and considerations are not overlooked during the design process.

Service Dominant Logic (SDL)

Service Dominant Logic (SDL) is a conceptual framework that shifts the focus of value creation from products to services. It views services as the primary basis for exchange and sees value as a result of co-creation between the service provider and the customer. This approach recognizes that customers are not passive recipients of value, but active participants in the value creation process. In the context of service design, SDL emphasizes the importance of understanding the needs, preferences, and aspirations of customers. It encourages service designers to co-create value with customers by involving them in the design and delivery of services. This collaborative approach enables service providers to better meet the unique and evolving needs of their customers.

Service Ecology

Service ecology is a concept in service design that refers to the interconnected and interdependent relationships between various services, systems, and stakeholders involved in the delivery and consumption of a service. It recognizes that services do not exist in isolation but are part of a complex ecosystem where different elements influence and shape each other. In service ecology, the focus is on understanding and mapping the different components and their interactions within the service system. This includes not only the visible touchpoints between customers and service providers but also the hidden processes, infrastructures, technologies, and resources that support service delivery. By taking a holistic view of the service ecosystem, designers can identify the dependencies and interdependencies that exist between different elements and anticipate potential impacts and consequences. Service ecology highlights the importance of considering the broader context in which a service operates. This involves analyzing the external factors such as social, cultural, economic, and environmental influences, as well as the internal dynamics within the organization providing the service. By understanding the contextual factors and their potential effects on service delivery, designers can better design and shape services that are more resilient, adaptable, and responsive to changing needs and circumstances. The concept of service ecology also emphasizes the need for collaboration and co-creation among stakeholders. Recognizing that no single entity can control or manage the entire service ecosystem, designers seek to foster collaboration and cooperation between different actors, including service providers, customers, partners, and regulators. This collaborative approach enables the co-design of services that better meet the needs and expectations of all stakeholders and ensures a more sustainable and inclusive service ecosystem. In summary, service ecology is a concept within service design that acknowledges the complex and interconnected nature of services. By understanding the relationships and interactions between different elements within the service ecosystem, designers can create more effective, resilient, and inclusive services that address the needs and aspirations of all stakeholders.

Service Ecosystem Analysis

A service ecosystem analysis is a structured approach used in service design to understand the complex network of interactions between various stakeholders, both human and non-human, that contribute to the creation, delivery, and consumption of a service. It involves examining the relationships, dependencies, and flows of resources, information, and value across the entire service system. This includes identifying the different actors involved, such as customers, employees, suppliers, partners, and competitors, as well as the physical and digital touchpoints they interact with.

Service Ecosystem Mapping

Service Ecosystem Mapping is a service design method that aims to understand and visualize the complex relationships and interactions between various elements within a service system. It involves mapping out the different components and stakeholders involved in the delivery and consumption of a service, as well as identifying the connections and dependencies between them. The process begins by identifying the main actors or entities involved in the service, such as customers, service providers, and supporting organizations. These actors are then mapped onto a visual diagram, often referred to as a service ecosystem map or service blueprint. The map typically consists of interconnected nodes that represent the different actors, along with lines or arrows to indicate the flow of interactions and value exchanges between them. Through the mapping process, the interdependencies and relationships between the various actors become apparent, revealing how they rely on each other to deliver and receive value. This helps to highlight any gaps or inefficiencies in the service system, as well as potential areas for improvement. Furthermore, service ecosystem mapping can also be used to identify the touchpoints or moments of interaction between actors within the service system. By understanding these touchpoints, designers can gain insights into the customer experience and identify opportunities to enhance it. Overall, service ecosystem mapping provides a holistic view of the service system, allowing designers to better understand the complexities and dynamics at play. It helps to identify the various actors, their roles, and the relationships between them, which can inform the design of more integrated and seamless services. By visualizing the service ecosystem, designers can also facilitate communication and collaboration among stakeholders, leading to more effective service delivery and improved customer experiences.

Service Ecosystem

A service ecosystem is a conceptual framework that represents the interconnections and interactions between various entities involved in the delivery of a service. It is a holistic view of the service delivery process, taking into account all the touchpoints, stakeholders, and environmental factors that contribute to the overall service experience. The service ecosystem approach recognizes that a service is not just a transaction between a provider and a customer, but rather a complex network of relationships and resources. It considers the broader context in which the service operates, including the physical environment, technological infrastructure, social dynamics, and regulatory frameworks.

Service Environment Analysis

A service environment analysis refers to the process of assessing and understanding the physical, social, and technological elements that impact the delivery and experience of a service. It involves analyzing the various components and interactions within a service setting in order to identify opportunities for improvement and design interventions that enhance the overall service experience. In service design, the service environment plays a crucial role in shaping customer perceptions, behaviors, and outcomes. By carefully examining the different aspects of the environment, designers can uncover potential barriers or enablers that influence service interactions and customer experiences.

Service Experience Framework

A Service Experience Framework is a conceptual model used in service design to understand, map, and improve the overall experience that customers have while interacting with a service. It provides a structured and holistic approach to analyzing and designing service experiences. At its core, the Service Experience Framework focuses on the customer journey from the initial point of contact with the service until the final interaction or outcome. It considers various touchpoints, interactions, and emotions throughout the entire service process. This framework typically consists of several key elements: 1. Customer Persona: It involves creating a detailed profile of the target customer, including their needs, goals, and behaviors. Understanding the customer persona helps in designing a service experience that aligns with their expectations. 2. Touchpoints: These are the different channels or points of interaction between the customer and the service. Examples of touchpoints include physical locations, websites, mobile apps, call centers, and social media platforms. Mapping touchpoints helps identify opportunities and pain points throughout the customer journey. 3. Customer Interactions: This element focuses on the actual interactions and activities that occur between the customer and the service. It considers both the functional aspects, such as ease of use and efficiency, as well as the emotional aspects, such as empathy and satisfaction. 4. Service Environment: This refers to the physical, digital, and social contexts in which the service is delivered. It includes factors like the physical layout, technology infrastructure, communication channels, and the overall atmosphere of the service environment. 5. Emotional Journey: This element recognizes that customers have emotional responses and expectations throughout their service experience. It involves understanding the range of emotions that customers may feel at different stages and designing strategies to evoke positive emotions and minimize negative ones. By using the Service Experience Framework, service designers can gain a holistic understanding of the customer journey and identify areas for improvement. It helps in identifying pain points, enhancing customer satisfaction, and creating a seamless and memorable service experience.

Service Experience Journey (SEJ)

The Service Experience Journey (SEJ) refers to the process of understanding and mapping the customer's interaction with a service from start to finish. It is a visual representation of the different touchpoints and interactions that a customer goes through when they engage with a service. The SEJ aims to provide a comprehensive view of the entire service journey, including the pre-service, service, and post-service stages. It takes into account the customer's emotions, thoughts, and actions at each stage, with the goal of identifying pain points and areas for improvement. The SEJ is a valuable tool in service design as it helps designers and stakeholders gain a deeper understanding of the customer's perspective. By mapping out the customer's experience, designers can identify moments of truth, critical touchpoints, and potential points of friction. The SEJ can be created using a variety of methods, such as journey mapping, customer interviews, observations, and data analysis. It is important to involve cross-functional teams and stakeholders throughout the process to ensure a holistic view of the service journey. Once the SEJ is created, it can be used to inform service design decisions and identify opportunities for innovation. By gaining insights into the customer's experience, organizations can tailor their services to meet customer needs and expectations. The SEJ is an ongoing process that requires continuous monitoring and refinement. As customer needs and expectations evolve, the SEJ should be updated to reflect these changes. Regularly reviewing and updating the SEJ ensures that the service remains relevant and responsive to customer needs. In conclusion, the Service Experience Journey (SEJ) is a tool used in service design to understand and map the customer's journey from start to finish. It provides a comprehensive view of the customer's experience, helping designers identify pain points and opportunities for improvement. By using the SEJ, organizations can create services that meet customer needs and deliver a positive and memorable experience.

Service Failure Mode And Effects Analysis (FMEA)

Service Failure Mode and Effects Analysis (FMEA) is a comprehensive risk assessment tool used in service design to identify and mitigate potential failures and their impact on service quality. It involves a structured and systematic approach to analyzing potential failure modes, their causes, and the effects they could have on the service delivery process. The main purpose of conducting a Service FMEA is to proactively identify and prioritize potential risks so that appropriate measures can be taken to prevent or minimize service failures. By identifying failure modes and their potential effects, organizations can develop strategies and contingency plans to enhance service reliability, reduce downtime, and improve overall customer satisfaction.

Service Innovation

Service innovation, in the context of service design, refers to the creation and development of new or improved services that meet the evolving needs and expectations of customers. It involves the design and implementation of innovative strategies, processes, and technologies to enhance the delivery and experience of services. Service innovation is driven by a deep understanding of customer needs and involves the identification of opportunities to provide value by addressing those needs in unique and creative ways. This can involve the creation of entirely new services, the modification or improvement of existing services, or the integration of different services to create a more comprehensive offering. Service innovation is not limited to the development of new products or technologies; it extends to the design and delivery of the entire service experience. This includes factors such as the physical environment, customer interactions, communication channels, and the use of digital platforms. By taking a holistic approach to service design, organizations can create seamless and memorable experiences that differentiate them from competitors and foster customer loyalty. Service innovation is a continuous and iterative process that requires organizations to be responsive and adaptable to the changing needs and expectations of customers. It involves a combination of creativity, strategic thinking, and collaboration across different functional areas and stakeholders. Successful service innovation requires organizations to be customer-centric and to prioritize the understanding and anticipation of customer needs. It involves a deep understanding of customer behaviors, preferences, and pain points, which can be gained through research, data analysis, and user testing. In summary, service innovation in the context of service design is the creation and development of new or improved services that provide unique value to customers. It involves a holistic approach to service design, encompassing the entire service experience, and requires organizations to be customer-centric and responsive to changing market conditions.

Service Interface Blueprint

A Service Interface Blueprint is a design tool used in service design to visually represent the interactions between different components of a service. It provides a detailed map of the service system, illustrating how various touchpoints, actors, and resources come together to deliver the desired customer experience. The blueprint consists of several layers that depict both the front-stage and back-stage components of the service. The front-stage layer represents the customer-facing elements, such as physical spaces, digital interfaces, and customer interactions. This layer helps identify the sequence of actions, the role of each touchpoint, and the overall customer journey within the service. The back-stage layer, on the other hand, focuses on the behind-the-scenes operations and supporting processes that enable the service to function effectively. It includes the actors involved in delivering the service, the systems and technologies used, and the internal processes that facilitate the service delivery. This layer helps identify potential gaps or bottlenecks in the service system and allows for improvements to be made to enhance efficiency and effectiveness. By mapping out the service interface blueprint, service designers can gain a holistic view of the service system and identify areas for improvement. It enables them to visualize the service processes, interactions, and dependencies, allowing for a more comprehensive understanding of how the service functions as a whole. This blueprint can also be used as a communication tool, facilitating collaboration and alignment between different stakeholders in the service design process. It provides a common language and visual representation that can be easily understood by all parties involved, fostering a shared understanding of the service system and its potential improvements.

Service Interface Design

A service interface design refers to the process of creating a formal definition for the way in which a service is offered and accessed. It involves carefully designing the interface that allows users or clients to interact with the service, ensuring that it is intuitive, efficient, and meets the needs and expectations of the users. The service interface design plays a crucial role in determining how users will understand and utilize the service. It encompasses various aspects, including the visual layout, navigation, information architecture, and functionality of the interface. The aim is to create an interface that is user-friendly, aesthetically pleasing, and aligns with the overall goals and objectives of the service.

Service Journey Maps

Service Journey Maps are visual representations of the interactions and experiences that customers have with a service throughout their entire journey. They are created in the field of service design to understand and improve the overall customer experience. Service Journey Maps provide a holistic view of the customer's interactions with a service, from the initial contact point to the final resolution of their needs. They focus on capturing not only the direct interactions but also the emotions, thoughts, and expectations that customers may have at each stage of their journey.

Service Level Agreements (SLAs)

Service Level Agreements (SLAs) are formal agreements between service providers and their clients that outline the expected level of service to be provided. These agreements are a key component of service design, as they help define the boundaries and responsibilities of the service provider and ensure a common understanding of the service expectations. SLAs typically include specific metrics and targets that the service provider should meet, such as response time, resolution time, and uptime. These metrics are agreed upon based on the needs and requirements of the client, and they are often measured and reported on regularly to ensure compliance.

Service Mapping

Service Mapping is a crucial step in the process of service design, aimed at identifying, visualizing, and analyzing the interactions and relationships between various components and touchpoints within a service system. By creating a service map, designers can gain a comprehensive understanding of the service system's structure, its components, and how they align with the desired customer experience. It allows for a holistic view of the service, uncovering both the visible and invisible aspects that contribute to its overall functionality. Service Mapping involves mapping out all the touchpoints, processes, resources, and actors involved in delivering a particular service. It provides a visual representation of how different elements of a service interact, enabling designers to identify gaps, redundancies, and opportunities for improvement.

The process of Service Mapping typically begins with gathering data and insights through a combination of research methods, such as interviews, observations, and surveys. The collected information is then analyzed and translated into a visual representation, often using diagrams or flowcharts. Service Maps can take various forms, depending on the specific needs and goals of the design project. They can be high-level maps that provide a broad overview of the service system, or detailed maps that zoom in on specific processes or touchpoints. Regardless of the level of detail, the aim is to capture the complexity and interdependencies of the service ecosystem. By mapping out the service system, designers can identify pain points, bottlenecks, and opportunities for optimization. It allows them to visualize the customer journey, understand different user perspectives, and design interventions that enhance the overall service experience. In conclusion, Service Mapping is a critical tool in service design that helps designers gain insights into the intricacies of a service system. By mapping out the different components and connections, designers can identify areas for improvement and create more seamless, efficient, and customer-centric service experiences.

Service Model Canvas

The Service Model Canvas is a visual tool used in service design to understand and analyze the various components and aspects of a service. It provides a structured framework to develop, describe, and evaluate services. The canvas is divided into nine key building blocks which are interconnected and help in capturing the essential elements of a service. The first block of the Service Model Canvas is the Customer Profile, which identifies the target customers and their characteristics, needs, and preferences. This block helps to define the specific customer segment that the service is designed for. The second block is called Value Proposition, which defines the unique value that the service offers to customers. It outlines the benefits, outcomes, and experiences that customers can expect from using the service. The Channels block represents the various touchpoints and channels through which the service is delivered and customers interact with it. This includes physical locations, digital platforms, customer support, and other communication channels. The Customer Relationship block focuses on the type of relationship the service wants to establish and maintain with its customers. It defines the level of personalization, engagement, and support offered to customers throughout their journey. The Revenue Streams block identifies the different ways in which the service generates revenue. This includes pricing models, payment options, and any additional sources of income related to the service. The Key Activities block outlines the key tasks and activities that are required to deliver the service. It includes activities such as research, design, production, delivery, and ongoing maintenance. The Key Resources block represents the resources required to deliver the service. This includes physical, human, financial, and technological resources that are necessary for the service to function effectively. The Key Partnerships block identifies the strategic partnerships and collaborations that are necessary to deliver the service. This can include suppliers, technology providers, distributors, and other stakeholders. The Cost Structure block represents the cost implications of delivering the service. It includes both fixed and variable costs associated with activities, resources, channels, and partnerships.

Service Modeling

Service modeling is a crucial component of service design that involves the systematic representation and analysis of services to better understand their structure, function, and interactions with various stakeholders. It enables service designers to gain a comprehensive view of the service system and identify areas for improvement or innovation. When designing a service, it is essential to have a clear understanding of its individual components, how they connect, and the overall flow of activities. Service modeling allows designers to translate abstract concepts into tangible representations, such as diagrams or conceptual maps, which facilitate communication and collaboration among different stakeholders.

Service Offering

A service offering refers to a specific combination of products, services, and experiences that are designed and provided by an organization to meet the needs and expectations of its customers. It encompasses the entire range of features, benefits, and value that are delivered to customers in exchange for their payment or participation. Within the context of service design, a service offering is a vital element that guides the design and development process. It serves as the foundation for creating a compelling and differentiated experience for customers, and it plays a crucial role in shaping customer perceptions and satisfaction.

Service Portfolio

A service portfolio is a comprehensive collection and documentation of all services offered by a company or organization. It acts as a strategic tool for service design, development, and management, providing an overview of the various services and helping to align them with the organization's goals and objectives. The service portfolio serves as a single point of reference for all service-related information and enables effective decision-making and communication within the organization. The primary purpose of a service portfolio is to capture and describe the complete range of services provided by an organization, including both existing and planned services. It includes detailed information about each service, such as its description, features, benefits, target audience, delivery process, pricing, and any associated service level agreements (SLAs) or service catalogs. The portfolio also outlines the relationships and dependencies between different services, highlighting any synergies or overlaps. Additionally, the service portfolio helps to prioritize and allocate resources effectively by enabling the organization to assess the value of each service. It allows for the identification of profitable services that contribute to the organization's revenue and profitability, as well as services that may require improvement or discontinuation. This analysis helps in making informed decisions about investments, resource allocation, and service improvement initiatives. Furthermore, the service portfolio ensures alignment between the services and the organization's overall strategy. By mapping each service to the organization's goals and objectives, it facilitates strategic planning and helps to identify opportunities for service innovation and differentiation. The portfolio enables the organization to assess its service capabilities, identify gaps or areas for improvement, and develop a roadmap for future service development and enhancement. In summary, a service portfolio provides a holistic view of an organization's services, enabling effective service design, development, and management. It acts as a repository of service-related information and supports decision-making, resource allocation, and strategic planning. By capturing and documenting the various services offered, the portfolio helps to ensure consistency, alignment, and continuous improvement in service delivery.

Service Prototyping Kits

A service prototyping kit in the context of service design refers to a set of tools, materials, and resources that are used to quickly and effectively create prototypes of service experiences. Service prototyping is a crucial step in the design process as it allows designers to test and iterate on their ideas before fully implementing them. The goal of using a service prototyping kit is to obtain valuable user feedback and insights that can inform design decisions and improve the overall user experience. The components of a service prototyping kit can vary depending on the specific needs of the design project, but typically include a combination of physical and digital tools. Physical tools may include items such as paper, scissors, markers, and post-it notes, which can be used to create low-fidelity prototypes. These prototypes are often quick and inexpensive to produce, allowing for rapid iterations and experimentation. Physical tools also enable designers to engage in hands-on activities, such as role-playing or creating physical models, to simulate the service experience. Digital tools, on the other hand, encompass software applications or platforms that facilitate the creation of high-fidelity prototypes. These tools may include wireframing or prototyping software, which enable designers to create interactive mock-ups of the service experience. Digital tools often provide more realistic representations of the final service and may include features such as user flows, clickable interactions, and simulated data. Additionally, a service prototyping kit may also include resources such as design templates, design thinking methodologies, and user research tools. These resources can assist designers in structuring their prototyping process, generating new ideas, and conducting user research to validate their designs.

Service Prototyping

Service Recovery Strategies

Service Recovery Strategies refer to the set of actions and processes put in place by service providers to effectively address and resolve service failures or customer complaints. These strategies aim to turn a negative customer experience into a positive one, restoring customer trust and satisfaction in the service provider. Service failures can occur in any industry or organization, resulting in dissatisfied customers who may vocalize their frustrations through complaints or negative reviews. Service recovery strategies provide a structured approach for service providers to acknowledge and rectify these failures, with the ultimate goal of retaining customers and maintaining a positive brand image.

Service Safari

Service Safari refers to a research method used in service design to observe and understand the customer experience while interacting with a service. It involves visiting the physical or digital touchpoints of a service and studying how customers navigate through the different stages of their journey. During a Service Safari, designers or researchers act as 'customers' and document their observations, emotions, and reactions as they engage with a service. The goal is to gain insights into the customers' needs, pain points, and expectations, which can then inform the design of better services.

Service Safaris

Service Safaris refer to a method used in service design to observe and analyze existing services in their natural environment. It involves conducting field research to gain a deeper understanding of how services are delivered and experienced. The goal of a Service Safari is to identify opportunities for improvement and generate insights that can inform the design of new or improved services. During a Service Safari, designers and researchers immerse themselves in the service experience as active participants, rather than passive observers. They observe and engage with the service from the perspective of different stakeholders, such as customers, employees, and other relevant actors. This hands-on approach allows them to capture a holistic view of the service, considering both the physical and intangible aspects, and the interactions between various touchpoints.

Service Scenario Planning

Service scenario planning is a methodology used in service design to anticipate and plan for potential future scenarios that may impact a service. It involves examining different trends, events, and factors that could potentially affect the delivery and experience of a service, and devising strategies to adapt and respond to these changes. The process of service scenario planning typically begins with gathering data and insights about the current state of the service and its operating environment. This may involve conducting research, analyzing market trends, and studying customer behavior. The next step is to identify potential future scenarios that might arise, based on various factors such as social, economic, technological, and environmental changes. Once the potential scenarios have been identified, service scenario planning involves mapping out the different pathways that the service could take in each scenario. This includes considering the impact and implications of each scenario on various aspects of the service, such as its value proposition, customer journey, and operational processes. Through service scenario planning, designers can gain a deeper understanding of the potential risks and opportunities that may arise in the future. It allows them to identify potential challenges that the service may face and develop strategies to mitigate these risks. It also enables them to identify new possibilities for innovation and improvement that can be implemented in response to different scenarios. Overall, service scenario planning provides a structured approach to envisioning and preparing for potential future changes in the service landscape. By considering various scenarios and their implications, service designers can develop robust and adaptable service strategies that can withstand uncertainty and change. It helps organizations to proactively plan for the future, rather than simply reacting to unforeseen circumstances.

Service Scenario

A service scenario in the context of service design refers to a detailed description of how a service is performed or experienced by customers. It outlines the specific steps, interactions, and touchpoints that occur during the delivery of a service. The purpose of a service scenario is to provide a comprehensive understanding of the service journey, from the customer's perspective, and to identify opportunities for improvement or innovation. It helps designers and stakeholders visualize the service process, uncover pain points, and generate ideas for enhancing the overall service experience.

Service Scenarios

A service scenario is a tool used in service design to illustrate the interaction between a user and a service. It captures the sequence of actions, decisions, and events that occur throughout the user journey, from initial interaction to the completion of a task or goal. By mapping out service scenarios, designers can better understand the user's experience, identify pain points, and uncover opportunities for improvement. The service scenario typically consists of three main components: the user, the service touchpoints, and the context. The user represents the individual or group who is interacting with the service, while the touchpoints are the different points of contact between the user and the service. These touchpoints can be physical, such as a website or a physical store, or digital, such as an app or a chatbot. The context refers to the specific situation or environment in which the service is being used, including the user's goals, motivations, and constraints.

Service Simulation Tools

Service simulation tools are software applications or models that allow service designers to simulate and test different aspects of a service before it is implemented. These tools help designers understand how a service will function, identify potential issues or challenges, and make necessary adjustments to optimize the service experience for users. Service simulation tools typically offer a range of features and functionalities that support the design process. They enable designers to create virtual representations of the service, including its various touchpoints, processes, and interactions. This allows designers to visualize the service flow and identify any gaps or inconsistencies in the user journey. Furthermore, service simulation tools often provide the capability to simulate different scenarios and user interactions, helping designers explore and evaluate various potential outcomes. This allows designers to assess the impact of different changes or modifications on the service experience and make informed decisions based on the insights gained. These tools may also offer analytical capabilities, allowing designers to collect and analyze data related to the service simulation. This data can be used to gain a deeper understanding of user preferences, behaviors, and needs, and inform the design process accordingly. Service simulation tools are valuable assets in the service design process as they facilitate the identification of potential issues and help designers refine and improve the service concept. By allowing designers to test and iterate their ideas virtually, these tools save time and resources that would otherwise be spent implementing and evaluating services in real-world settings. In conclusion, service simulation tools are software applications or models that enable service designers to simulate and test different aspects of a service before implementation. These tools help designers visualize the service flow, simulate different scenarios, and analyze data to refine and optimize the service experience.

Service Simulation

A service simulation in the context of service design refers to a technique used to create a realistic representation or model of a service experience. It enables designers and stakeholders to envision, test, and refine service interactions, processes, and touchpoints before actual implementation. By simulating a service, designers can gain insights into how different elements of the service work together, identify potential issues or bottlenecks, and make informed decisions to enhance the overall service experience. Service simulations can range from low-fidelity representations using paper prototypes or diagrams to high-fidelity simulations using digital tools and technologies.

Service Strategy

Service Strategy is a key component of service design that focuses on defining and aligning an organization's services with its overall business strategy. It involves understanding the customer's needs and expectations, as well as the organization's capabilities, and then developing a strategic plan to deliver the desired services. The main goal of Service Strategy is to ensure that the organization is offering the right services at the right time and in the most efficient and effective way. This involves conducting market research and analysis to identify current and future customer needs, as well as understanding the competitive landscape and industry trends. Once the customer and market requirements are understood, the organization can then develop a service strategy that outlines how it will meet those needs and differentiate itself from competitors. This includes defining the target market segments, identifying the value proposition of the services, and determining the pricing and positioning strategies. Service Strategy also involves aligning the service offerings with the organization's overall business strategy. This means ensuring that the services support the organization's mission and vision, as well as its goals and objectives. It also involves assessing the organization's capabilities and resources to determine if any changes or enhancements are needed to deliver the desired services. In addition, Service Strategy includes establishing performance metrics and measurement systems to monitor the delivery of services and track customer satisfaction. This allows the organization to continuously improve and optimize its service offerings based on feedback and insights from customers. In conclusion, Service Strategy is a critical component of service design that focuses on defining and aligning an organization's services with its overall business strategy. It involves understanding customer needs, developing a strategic plan, aligning service offerings with the business strategy, and monitoring performance to drive continuous improvement.

Service System Design

Service System Design is a process of creating and organizing the components, activities, and resources required to deliver a service to customers, with the aim of meeting their needs and achieving optimal performance. It involves the strategic planning and arrangement of various elements within a service system, including people, technology, processes, and physical infrastructure, to ensure the efficient and effective delivery of services. The design of a service system starts with understanding the customers' requirements, expectations, and preferences. This customer-centric approach helps identify the key touchpoints and interactions that customers experience throughout their journey with the service. By mapping these touchpoints and interactions, service designers gain insights into the different stages and channels through which services are delivered. Once the customer journey is understood, service system designers focus on designing the processes and activities required to deliver the service. This includes defining the roles, responsibilities, and tasks of the service providers, as well as developing guidelines and protocols for service delivery. The goal is to ensure consistency, reliability, and quality in the service experience, regardless of the channel or point of interaction. In addition to people and processes, service system design also incorporates the use of technology and physical infrastructure. This may involve implementing digital tools and platforms to enhance the customer experience, streamline service delivery processes, and facilitate communication and collaboration among service providers. The design of physical infrastructure, such as service facilities and equipment, is also crucial in supporting the delivery of the service and meeting customers' needs. Service system design is an iterative process that involves continuous improvement and adaptation. It entails monitoring and analyzing customer feedback, performance metrics, and industry trends to identify areas for enhancement and innovation. By regularly evaluating and refining the service system, organizations can ensure their services remain relevant, competitive, and responsive to changing customer demands.

Service System

A service system, in the context of service design, refers to a holistic approach towards designing and delivering services. It involves the coordination of various elements, such as people, processes, technologies, and physical or virtual touchpoints, to create a seamless and satisfying customer experience. The service system encompasses both the frontstage and backstage components of a service. The frontstage includes the visible aspects that customers directly interact with, such as service personnel, digital interfaces, and physical environments. The backstage, on the other hand, involves the behind-the-scenes operations, systems, and resources that support the delivery of the service.

Service Theater

A service theater is a service design technique used to create a staged experience that aligns with a specific service concept or strategy. It involves the use of visual and sensory elements to engage customers and immerse them in a carefully curated environment that reflects the values,

169

identity, and goals of the service provider. The purpose of a service theater is to evoke emotions, create memorable moments, and enhance the overall customer experience. It aims to go beyond functional aspects of service delivery and create a sense of delight, surprise, and wonder. By designing and orchestrating the various touchpoints and interactions within the service theater, service providers can shape the perception and value that customers derive from the service.

Service Touchpoints

Service touchpoints are the various points of interaction or contact between a service provider and its customers throughout the customer journey. These touchpoints can occur both online and offline and play a crucial role in shaping the overall customer experience. In service design, touchpoints are identified and mapped to understand the different moments of interaction a customer has with a service. This includes not only direct interactions, such as customer service calls or face-to-face meetings, but also indirect interactions like website visits, social media interactions, or product reviews. The purpose of identifying and analyzing service touchpoints is to gain insights into the customer's perspective and to improve the overall service experience. Through this analysis, service designers can identify pain points, opportunities, and areas for improvement. By addressing these touchpoints, a company can enhance customer satisfaction and loyalty. Service touchpoints can be categorized into different types based on their nature and significance. These categories include pre-purchase touchpoints (such as advertising, social media presence, and website visits), purchase touchpoints (such as point-of-sale interactions or online order placement), and post-purchase touchpoints (such as customer support, follow-up emails, or loyalty programs). To effectively design and manage service touchpoints, it is important to consider factors such as consistency, convenience, and personalization. Consistency ensures that customers have a seamless experience across different touchpoints, while convenience focuses on making interactions easy and effortless. Personalization involves tailoring touchpoints to meet individual customer needs and preferences. Service touchpoint analysis can be conducted through various methods, including customer journey mapping, service blueprinting, or touchpoint audits. These techniques provide a visual representation of the customer's journey and help identify potential bottlenecks or moments of delight. In conclusion, service touchpoints are critical elements in service design, helping organizations understand and improve the customer experience. By analyzing and optimizing these touchpoints, businesses can create positive interactions and build long-term customer loyalty.

Service Transformation

Service transformation is the process of reimagining and redesigning a service to improve its overall effectiveness, efficiency, and customer experience. It involves a holistic approach to identify and address the underlying issues and challenges within a service, with the goal of delivering a higher level of value to customers. Service transformation typically begins with a thorough analysis of the current service, including its processes, systems, and customer interactions. This analysis helps to uncover areas for improvement and identifies the specific needs and expectations of customers. Based on these insights, a service transformation strategy is developed, which may include changes to the service design, operational processes, technology implementation, and employee training. The design phase of service transformation focuses on creating a service that is customer-centric, seamless, and tailored to meet the unique needs of customers. This often involves mapping out the customer journey and identifying touchpoints where improvements can be made. By optimizing these touchpoints, service providers can streamline processes, reduce customer effort, and enhance the overall customer experience. Service transformation also involves leveraging technology to enable more efficient service delivery and to provide customers with self-service options. This may include implementing customer relationship management (CRM) systems, mobile apps, or other digital tools that enhance convenience and accessibility for customers. Furthermore, service transformation recognizes the importance of employee engagement and empowerment in delivering exceptional service. It involves providing employees with the necessary training, tools, and incentives to deliver a high standard of service. By fostering a culture of continuous improvement and customer-centricity, service providers can ensure that their employees are equipped to deliver value-added service experiences. In conclusion, service transformation is a comprehensive approach to improving a service by addressing its underlying challenges and reimagining its design. By focusing on the needs and expectations of customers and leveraging technology and employee engagement, service providers can enhance their service offerings and deliver a superior customer experience.

Service Visioning

Service Visioning is a process within service design that aims to create a clear and inspiring vision for a service experience. It involves developing a comprehensive understanding of the service and its users, and using this knowledge to envision the ideal future state of the service. The goal of service visioning is to define the desired characteristics, values, and outcomes of the service, and align the design process towards achieving these goals. Service visioning begins with in-depth research and analysis to gather insights about the service, its target users, and their needs. This often involves conducting user interviews, surveys, and observations to gain a deep understanding of user behaviors, motivations, and pain points. The information gathered during this research phase is then synthesized and used to identify key opportunities for improvement and innovation within the service. The next step in service visioning is to develop a set of guiding principles or design principles that will inform the vision for the service. These principles act as a framework for decision-making throughout the design process, ensuring that the service is aligned with its intended values and outcomes. The principles may include elements such as inclusivity, simplicity, personalization, and sustainability, depending on the specific goals and context of the service. Once the guiding principles are established, the service design team engages in a collaborative ideation process to imagine the ideal future state of the service. This typically involves brainstorming, sketching, and prototyping various ideas and concepts that align with the guiding principles. The aim is to create a compelling vision that captures the essence of the desired service experience and inspires both the design team and stakeholders. The final step in service visioning is to distill the vision into a clear and concise statement that can be easily shared and understood by all stakeholders involved in the design process. This vision statement serves as a reference point throughout the design process, guiding the decisions and actions of the team as they work towards bringing the vision to life.

Service Walkthrough

A service walkthrough is a method used in service design to understand and evaluate the user experience and interaction with a service. It involves simulating the journey and touchpoints that a user would go through while using the service, in order to identify any pain points, gaps, or areas for improvement. The walkthrough process typically entails mapping out the entire service experience, from the initial contact with the service to the completion of the desired outcome. This mapping can be done through various means, such as customer journey maps, storyboards, or service blueprints. The aim is to create a visual representation of the service journey, highlighting each step and interaction along the way. Once the service journey is mapped out, stakeholders, including designers, service providers, and even users, can participate in the walkthrough exercise. This involves going through the service journey step-by-step, considering each touchpoint and evaluating its effectiveness and user-friendliness. By mentally putting themselves in the shoes of the user, participants can identify potential pain points, frustrations, or areas of confusion. During the walkthrough, participants analyze various aspects of the service, including quality, efficiency, accessibility, and the overall user experience. They may also evaluate whether the service meets the desired goals and objectives, and whether it aligns with user needs and expectations. This evaluation helps uncover any barriers or obstacles that users may encounter, as well as potential areas for innovation and improvement in the service design. Service walkthroughs provide valuable insights that can drive the enhancement and optimization of services. By identifying and addressing pain points and gaps in the user journey, service providers can improve customer satisfaction, loyalty, and overall service performance. Additionally, these walkthroughs can help identify opportunities for introducing new features or streamlining existing processes, leading to a more seamless and enjoyable user experience.

Service Walkthroughs

A service walkthrough is a technique used in service design to analyze and understand the customer experience when interacting with a service. It involves mapping out the various touchpoints and steps involved in a customer journey, from the initial awareness of the service to the final resolution or outcome. The purpose of a service walkthrough is to gain a holistic understanding of how a service is experienced by customers, as well as to identify pain points, opportunities for improvement, and areas where the service can be enhanced to meet customer needs more effectively. It provides insights into the customer's perspective, emotions, and actions throughout their journey, helping service designers to identify both strengths and weaknesses in the service delivery process. During a service walkthrough, the steps and touchpoints of the customer journey are typically depicted visually, using diagrams or flowcharts. This visualization allows service designers to see the entire journey at a glance, helping them to identify potential bottlenecks, gaps in service provision, or areas where the customer may face difficulties or confusion. Service walkthroughs also involve gathering qualitative and quantitative data about each touchpoint and step in the customer journey. This data can be collected through a variety of methods, such as interviews, observations, customer feedback, or surveys. By analyzing this data, service designers can gain insights into specific pain points or moments of delight for customers, allowing for targeted improvements to be made to the service. The insights gained from a service walkthrough can be used to inform the design and development of the service, ensuring that it is aligned with customer needs and expectations. It can help service designers to identify opportunities for innovation, as well as to prioritize improvements based on their impact on the overall customer experience. In conclusion, a service walkthrough is a technique used in service design to gain a comprehensive understanding of the customer journey and the various touchpoints and steps involved. It helps service designers to identify pain points, opportunities for improvement, and areas where the service can be enhanced to better meet customer needs. By visualizing and analyzing the customer journey, service walkthroughs provide valuable insights that can inform the design and development of the service.

Service Workflow

A service workflow in the context of service design refers to the sequence of activities and tasks that are carried out in order to deliver a service to a customer or user. It outlines the step-by-step process that occurs from the initial request or need for a service, through to the final delivery and potential follow-up activities. The workflow provides a visual representation of the various stages, actions, and possible decision points that are involved in delivering the service. The service workflow typically includes multiple components, such as intake or initiation, planning, execution, and closure. It may also incorporate feedback loops or opportunities for customer input to ensure that the service meets their needs and expectations. Within each stage of the workflow, specific tasks or actions are identified, along with their associated inputs and outputs. This helps to ensure that all necessary resources and information are available at each step, and that the service is delivered efficiently and effectively. For example, in the intake or initiation phase, the workflow may include activities such as capturing the customer's request, assessing its feasibility and impact, and assigning appropriate resources. In the planning phase, tasks may involve defining the scope and objectives of the service, identifying potential risks or constraints, and developing a detailed plan or schedule. The execution phase encompasses the actual implementation of the service, including tasks such as performing the required actions or procedures, monitoring progress, and addressing any issues or problems that arise. Finally, in the closure phase, the workflow may include activities such as obtaining customer feedback, documenting lessons learned, and formally closing out the service. Overall, the service workflow serves as a valuable tool for service designers and providers to understand and optimize the process of delivering a service. It helps to ensure consistency and quality, streamline operations, and improve the overall customer experience.

ServiceBlue

ServiceBlue is a service design framework that focuses on creating meaningful and valuable experiences for users through the intentional design of services. It aims to align the goals and needs of both the service provider and the user to create a mutually beneficial relationship. With ServiceBlue, the design process starts by understanding the context and environment in which the service operates. This includes identifying the stakeholders, their roles, and their relationships within the service ecosystem. By understanding the dynamics of the system, designers can better identify opportunities and challenges for improvement. The next step in the ServiceBlue framework is to deeply empathize with the users and gain a deep understanding of their needs, desires, and pain points. This is done through various research methods such as user interviews, observation, and analysis of user behavior. By putting themselves in the shoes of the users, designers can ensure that the services they create are relevant, accessible, and enjoyable. Once the user needs are understood, designers can ideate and brainstorm potential solutions. This involves generating a range of ideas, both radical and incremental, to address the identified user needs. By using techniques such as brainstorming, idea mapping, and prototyping, designers can explore different possibilities and evaluate their potential effectiveness. After generating a set of potential solutions, the next step is to develop and test prototypes. This allows designers to quickly iterate and gather feedback from users and stakeholders. By involving users in the testing process, designers can refine the service concepts and ensure that they truly meet the needs and expectations of the target audience. Once the prototypes have been validated, the final step in ServiceBlue is to implement and launch the service. This involves designing the service blueprint, which outlines the touchpoints, interactions, and processes involved in delivering the service. By considering the entire customer journey, including pre-service, in-service, and post-service interactions, designers can create a seamless and consistent experience for users.

ServiceNow

ServiceNow is a cloud-based platform that provides a comprehensive set of tools and features for designing, managing, and improving services within an organization. It offers a systematic approach to service design by enabling teams to collaborate, automate workflows, and streamline processes. Service design in the context of ServiceNow refers to the practice of designing and optimizing services to meet the needs and expectations of customers. It involves understanding customer requirements, defining service offerings, and mapping out the entire service journey from request to resolution.

Shadowing

Shadowing in the context of service design refers to the practice of observing and documenting the experiences and behaviors of individuals who are using a service. This research technique involves closely following and documenting the actions, emotions, and interactions of users as they engage with a service, typically in their natural environment. The purpose of shadowing is to gain a deep understanding of the user's perspective and uncover insights into their needs, preferences, and pain points. By immersing oneself in the user's world and capturing their experiences first-hand, designers can develop a more holistic view of the service and identify areas for improvement or innovation.

Shaping Tomorrow

Shaping Tomorrow is a service design tool aimed at analyzing and predicting future trends and potential challenges in order to develop strategies and solutions for businesses and organizations. The platform provides a structured and systematic approach to understanding the factors that shape the future and helps users make informed decisions by identifying and exploring emerging trends, risks, and opportunities. It combines expert insights, research, and data analysis to create a comprehensive view of the future landscape.

Silent Card Sorting

Silent Card Sorting is a research method commonly used in service design to gain insights into how users categorize and prioritize information. This method involves individuals sorting a set of cards representing elements or concepts related to a specific service or process without any verbal discussion or guidance from a facilitator. During Silent Card Sorting, participants are given a collection of cards that contain information or ideas related to the service being designed. These cards can include different elements such as features, tasks, content, or user roles. The participants are then instructed to categorize and group the cards based on their understanding and perception of the relationships between the elements. The key feature of Silent Card Sorting is the absence of verbal communication among participants. This approach eliminates potential biases that may arise from group dynamics or dominant individuals influencing the sorting process. By removing verbal interaction, it allows individuals to focus solely on their own thought process and priorities when organizing the cards. After completing the sorting activity, participants may be asked to provide labels or names for the categories they have created. This additional step helps in understanding the mental models and terminology used by users to navigate and comprehend the service being studied. The collected data from Silent Card Sorting is typically analyzed to identify larger patterns, themes, or clusters that emerge from the participants' sorting behavior. It provides designers with insights into how users perceive relationships between different elements of a service, enabling them to make informed decisions about information architecture, menu organization, or process flows. Silent Card Sorting is a powerful research method as it allows for individual, reflective thinking, reducing the influence of social pressure or conformity. Its non-verbal nature makes it particularly useful in cross-cultural research or when dealing with participants who may have difficulty expressing their thoughts verbally. By fostering a more introspective and personal approach to information organization, Silent Card Sorting helps designers gain a deeper understanding of users' mental models and preferences.

Situational Analysis

Situational analysis, in the context of service design, refers to the process of gathering and analyzing relevant information about the current situation or context in which a service operates. It involves assessing various factors such as the needs and expectations of users, the competitive landscape, the organizational capabilities, and any external influences or constraints that may impact the service. The purpose of conducting a situational analysis is to gain a comprehensive understanding of the existing conditions and dynamics that surround the service. This knowledge serves as the foundation for making informed decisions and developing effective strategies to improve or design a service that meets the needs of its users and stakeholders.

Six Sigma

Six Sigma is a disciplined, data-driven approach to improving service design and operational performance. It focuses on identifying and eliminating defects or errors that occur in the service delivery process, ultimately aiming to reduce variation and improve overall customer satisfaction. The key principles of Six Sigma are based on statistical analysis and measurement, as well as a strong customer-centric approach. It involves a systematic, step-by-step approach known as DMAIC (Define, Measure, Analyze, Improve, Control), which guides service designers in identifying and addressing issues in their processes.

Six Thinking Hats

The Six Thinking Hats is a popular decision-making and problem-solving technique used in the field of service design. Developed by Edward de Bono, the concept is based on the idea that individuals have different thinking styles or perspectives that can be used to approach a problem or decision. Each thinking style is represented by a different colored "hat," and by consciously switching between these hats, teams can ensure a comprehensive exploration of all angles and possibilities. The six hats each represent a different mode of thinking: - The White Hat represents objective and neutral thinking, focusing on facts, data, and information. It is used to gather all available information and analyze it without making any judgments. - The Red Hat represents emotional thinking, allowing individuals to express their feelings, intuitions, and gut reactions without the need for justification. It encourages a more subjective approach to the problem or decision at hand. - The Black Hat represents critical thinking and the identification of potential risks, weaknesses, and obstacles. It allows individuals to point out flaws, potential problems, and areas of concern without being overly optimistic. - The Yellow Hat represents positive thinking and optimism, focusing on the benefits, opportunities, and advantages of a particular idea or solution. It helps to generate positive and constructive suggestions. - The Green Hat represents creative thinking and the generation of new ideas, alternatives, and possibilities. It encourages brainstorming and free association of ideas, without the need for immediate evaluation or judgment. - The Blue Hat represents meta-cognitive thinking and overall control of the thinking process. It is used to facilitate the discussion, set the agenda, and ensure that the rules of the Six Thinking Hats technique are followed. By consciously switching between these different hats, individuals and teams can look at a problem or decision from multiple perspectives, improving the quality of analysis, creativity, and decision-making. Each hat provides a specific framework for thinking, which prevents individuals from getting stuck in one mode and allows them to find innovative solutions and make well-rounded decisions. The Six Thinking Hats technique is widely used in service design processes to help teams explore different angles, consider all relevant factors, and make more effective, informed, and balanced decisions.

Sketch

Service design is a multidisciplinary approach that focuses on the development and improvement of services. It involves understanding the needs and goals of both the service provider and the service user, and then creating solutions that effectively and efficiently meet those needs. Service design takes into account various factors, such as the context in which the service is delivered, the interactions between the service provider and the user, and the overall experience of using the service. The primary goal of service design is to create service experiences that are user-centered, holistic, and seamlessly integrated. This involves conducting research and analysis to gain insights into the needs, motivations, and behaviors of the service users. By understanding their perspectives and expectations, service designers can identify pain points, uncover opportunities for improvement, and develop innovative solutions that address these issues.

SketchFlow

SketchFlow is a service design tool that facilitates the development and visualization of user experiences for digital products and services. It is a software application that enables designers to create interactive prototypes, gather feedback, and iterate on their designs. Designed specifically for user-centered design and service design processes, SketchFlow helps designers and stakeholders collaborate effectively during the design phase. The tool allows designers to quickly sketch out their ideas and transform them into interactive wireframes and prototypes, which can be tested with users to validate and refine the design concept. With SketchFlow, designers can create and link multiple screens, define interactions and transitions between them, and add annotations and comments to provide additional context. This enables stakeholders to understand the flow and functionality of the final product, making it easier to provide feedback and make informed design decisions. One of the key features of SketchFlow is its ability to simulate user interactions, allowing designers to create realistic and interactive prototypes. This helps in simulating the user experience and testing the usability of the design. By capturing user feedback and behavior, designers can identify areas for improvement and make necessary changes to enhance the user experience. SketchFlow also offers collaboration capabilities, allowing multiple team members to work on the same project simultaneously. This promotes teamwork and reduces the time and effort required for coordination between team members. Overall, SketchFlow is a valuable tool for service designers as it provides a platform to visually conceptualize, test, and refine design ideas. Its interactive and collaborative features support the iterative nature of the service design process, enabling designers to create user-centered solutions that meet the needs and expectations of their target audience.

Smaply Journey

A Smaply Journey is a fundamental tool used in service design to map out the entire customer experience from their initial encounter with a product or service to their ongoing interactions and eventual departure. It provides a visual representation of the customer's journey, highlighting all touchpoints, emotions, and pain points they encounter along the way.By using a Smaply Journey, service designers can gain a deep understanding of the customer's perspective and identify areas for improvement or enhancement. It allows designers to visualize the complete end-to-end experience, enabling them to identify key moments of truth and areas of opportunity to enhance customer satisfaction and loyalty.

Smaply Touchpoint

Smaply Touchpoint is a service design tool that enables organizations to identify, analyze, and visualize the various interactions and touchpoints between customers and their products or services. It is a web-based platform that helps service designers, marketers, and analysts to map and understand the customer journey, ensuring a better understanding of customer needs, expectations, and pain points. With Smaply Touchpoint, users can create visual representations of the customer journey by mapping out the different touchpoints and interactions that customers have with a company at various stages. These touchpoints can include both online and offline interactions, such as website visits, social media interactions, phone calls, emails, physical store visits, and more. The tool allows users to add detailed descriptions, images, and notes to each touchpoint, providing a comprehensive view of the customer experience.

Smaply

Smaply is a web-based software tool that supports service design processes. It offers a collaborative and visual platform for service designers to map and analyze customer experiences, create personas, and design customer journeys. Smaply allows service designers to create and manage various types of service blueprints, including customer journey maps, stakeholder maps, and touchpoint maps. These maps help to understand the interactions between customers, front-stage employees, and backstage processes in a service system. The software enables designers to easily visualize and communicate complex service systems in a user-friendly way. It allows them to create visual representations of customer journeys, incorporating different touchpoints, channels, and emotions. These maps help designers identify pain points, moments of truth, and areas for improvement within the service system. With Smaply, service designers can also create and manage customer personas, which represent typical users of a service. Personas help designers understand the needs, motivations, and expectations of different customer segments. By integrating personas into the mapping process, designers can create more tailored and personalized services. Furthermore, Smaply supports collaboration and teamwork by allowing multiple users to work on the same project simultaneously. Designers can invite colleagues, stakeholders, and clients to contribute and provide feedback on the service designs. The software also provides features for commenting, version tracking, and exporting maps in various formats. In conclusion, Smaply is a powerful tool for service designers, providing a visual and collaborative platform for mapping and analyzing customer experiences. It helps designers understand the complexities of service systems, identify areas for improvement, and create more user-centered services.

Smart Prototyping

Smart Prototyping refers to a service design approach that allows for the rapid creation of physical and digital prototypes utilizing smart technologies and methods. It involves the iterative process of designing, testing, and refining prototypes in order to develop innovative solutions and deliver enhanced user experiences. As a part of service design, Smart Prototyping enables designers and developers to simulate the user journey and interaction with a product or service. Through the use of various smart technologies, such as Internet of Things (IoT) devices, sensors, and connected systems, designers can collect valuable data and insights on user behavior and preferences. This data-driven approach allows for the creation of prototypes that closely resemble the final product or service, resulting in more accurate and valuable user feedback.

Smartlook

Smartlook is a service design tool that offers a comprehensive solution for businesses to improve their online user experiences. It provides real-time analysis of user behavior on websites and mobile apps, allowing businesses to understand how users interact with their platforms. With Smartlook, businesses can track user sessions and generate heatmaps to identify the most engaging areas of their websites or apps. This information helps businesses pinpoint any usability issues and make data-driven decisions to enhance their user experience.

Snaplytics

Snaplytics is an innovative service designed to provide comprehensive analytics and management solutions for businesses and individuals using the popular social media platform, Snapchat. This service is specifically aimed at helping users gain insights into their Snapchat performance, enhance their content strategies, and increase their overall engagement and reach within the platform. With Snaplytics, users have access to a range of valuable features and tools that enable them to analyze and track their Snapchat metrics effectively. These metrics include reach, engagement, views, and screenshots, among others. By closely monitoring these key performance indicators, users can gain a better understanding of their audience's preferences and behavior, allowing them to refine their content and maximize their Snapchat presence.

Social Design

Social design in the context of service design refers to the intentional and systematic approach of creating and improving social services that meet the needs and aspirations of various stakeholders within a society. It involves the application of design thinking methods, tools, and principles to address complex social issues and challenges, and to develop innovative and sustainable solutions. Social design is centered around the belief that design has the power to shape and transform social systems, structures, and behaviors for the betterment of society as a whole.

Social Listening

Social listening, in the context of service design, refers to the process of monitoring and analyzing online conversations and discussions related to a brand, product, or service. It involves actively listening to what customers are saying across various social media platforms, blogs, forums, and other online channels, in order to gain insights and understand their needs and preferences. By listening to customer conversations, service designers can gather valuable information about customer experiences, opinions, and sentiments. This information can then be used to identify areas of improvement, address customer pain points, and make data-driven decisions to enhance the overall customer experience. Social listening allows service designers to stay connected with customers and understand their evolving expectations, which is crucial for designing services that meet their needs and anticipate future demands.

Social Media Listening Tools

Social media listening tools are software applications or services that are designed to monitor, track, and analyze conversations and activities happening on various social media platforms. These tools enable businesses and organizations to gather valuable insights and information about their target audience, competitors, industry trends, and overall online reputation. With social media becoming an integral part of people's lives, it has become essential for businesses to have a strong online presence and actively engage with their audience. However, keeping track of all the conversations, mentions, and interactions across multiple social media platforms can be a daunting task. Social media listening tools simplify this process by providing a centralized platform where businesses can monitor and analyze their presence on social media. These tools typically utilize advanced algorithms and machine learning techniques to scan social media platforms for relevant keywords, hashtags, and brand mentions. They collect and organize the data, providing businesses with actionable insights and real-time analytics. By tracking customer sentiment and identifying key influencers, businesses can make informed decisions to improve their products, services, and marketing strategies. Moreover, social media listening tools allow businesses to measure the impact of their social media campaigns, measure brand awareness, and monitor their competitors' activities. These tools provide detailed reports and visualizations, helping businesses to understand and interpret the data in a meaningful way. The insights gained from social media listening tools can be used in various areas of service design. For example, businesses can identify customer pain points and tailor their services to meet their needs more effectively. By understanding customer preferences and expectations, businesses can design and deliver personalized experiences that foster customer loyalty. In conclusion, social media listening tools play a crucial role in service design by providing businesses with valuable insights from social media conversations. They enable businesses to monitor and analyze their online reputation, track competitors, and make informed decisions to improve their services. These tools empower businesses to optimize their social media strategies and deliver exceptional experiences to their customers.

Speed Dating

Speed Dating is a service design concept aimed at facilitating quick and efficient matchmaking between individuals seeking romantic connections. This concept involves a structured event where participants rotate through a series of short, timed interactions with potential partners. The purpose of these interactions is to quickly assess compatibility and interest, helping participants identify individuals they would like to pursue further connections with.

Spotify Model

A Spotify Model is a service design concept that focuses on delivering personalized music streaming experiences to users. It is built on a digital platform that leverages data analytics, algorithms, and user feedback to curate and recommend music based on the individual preferences and behaviors of each user. The Spotify Model encompasses various elements that contribute to its success in providing a seamless and enjoyable music streaming service. One key element is the extensive music library, which includes a wide range of genres, artists, and songs from different periods and cultures. This allows users to explore and discover new music that aligns with their taste and interests.

Stakeholder Analysis

Stakeholder Analysis is a service design technique that involves the identification, categorization, and analysis of individuals or groups who have a direct or indirect interest in a service or project. The purpose of stakeholder analysis is to understand the needs, expectations, and viewpoints of these stakeholders in order to inform the design and delivery of a service. The stakeholder analysis process typically involves several key steps. Firstly, stakeholders are identified and categorized based on their level of influence and interest in the service. This helps to prioritize stakeholders and determine their significance in the design process. Stakeholders can include internal staff, customers, partners, suppliers, regulators, and other external parties. Once stakeholders are identified, the next step is to gather detailed information about each stakeholder group. This includes understanding their goals, motivations, and concerns related to the service. It may also involve analyzing their attitudes, preferences, and behaviors in order to gain a deeper understanding of their role in the service ecosystem. During stakeholder analysis, it is important to consider the potential impact of each stakeholder on the design and delivery of the service. This includes assessing the level of power and influence that stakeholders hold, as well as any potential risks or conflicts that may arise. By understanding the power dynamics and potential conflicts among stakeholders, service designers can proactively address any issues and ensure that the design process is inclusive and effective. The insights gained from stakeholder analysis are used to inform the design and implementation of the service. By understanding the needs and expectations of stakeholders, service designers can make informed decisions and prioritize features and functionalities that will deliver the greatest value to stakeholders. This helps to ensure that the service meets the diverse needs of all stakeholders and contributes to their overall satisfaction and success.

Stakeholder Engagement

Stakeholder engagement in the context of service design refers to the process of involving and collaborating with individuals or entities who have a vested interest or influence in the service being designed. These stakeholders can include customers, employees, management, community members, and any other parties affected by the service. The purpose of stakeholder engagement is to ensure that their perspectives, needs, and expectations are incorporated into the design and delivery of the service. By actively involving stakeholders in the design process, the service designer can gain valuable insights, improve understanding of the current situation, identify potential issues, and develop effective solutions that meet the needs of all stakeholders.

Stakeholder Mapping

Stakeholder Mapping, in the context of service design, refers to a visual representation of the various individuals, groups, or organizations that have an interest in or are affected by a particular service or system. It is a strategic tool used to identify, analyze, and understand the relationships between stakeholders and the service being designed. The purpose of stakeholder mapping is to gain insights into the needs, expectations, and influence of each stakeholder in order to effectively engage and manage their involvement throughout the service design process. By mapping stakeholders, service designers can identify potential conflicts, align priorities, and ensure that the final service solution meets the needs of all relevant stakeholders.

Stakeholder Maps

Stakeholder Maps are a tool used in service design to visually represent the relationships and connections between different stakeholders involved in a service or process. They provide a comprehensive overview of the various individuals, groups, organizations, and entities that have an interest or influence in the service being designed. The purpose of creating a stakeholder map is to gain a clear understanding of the different stakeholders and their roles, responsibilities, and perspectives. It helps service designers identify potential conflicts, dependencies, and opportunities for collaboration among stakeholders, which can inform the design and delivery of the service.

Stormboard

Stormboard is a web-based collaborative platform that enables businesses and teams to ideate, organize, and plan their projects and processes in a visually engaging and interactive way. It is specifically designed for service design, which involves the creation and optimization of services to meet customer needs and improve user experiences. With Stormboard, users can easily create and share virtual sticky notes, which serve as the building blocks of their service design projects. These sticky notes can contain text, images, and even videos, allowing teams to express their ideas and concepts in a visually appealing manner. The platform also provides a variety of templates and customizable frameworks to help structure the design process. Collaboration is a key aspect of service design, and Stormboard facilitates this by allowing multiple team members to work on the same project in real-time. Users can leave comments, give feedback, and make updates directly on the virtual sticky notes. This fosters a collaborative and iterative approach, where ideas can be refined and developed collectively. Stormboard also offers various features that enhance the service design process. Users can create and manage action items, assign tasks, and set due dates to ensure that projects stay on track. The platform also includes voting and prioritization tools, which enable teams to gather feedback and make data-driven decisions. In addition, Stormboard provides robust data visualization capabilities. Users can generate charts, graphs, and reports to better understand and communicate their service design findings. This feature helps teams identify trends, analyze customer feedback, and evaluate the effectiveness of their service offerings. Overall, Stormboard is a comprehensive and user-friendly platform for service design. Its collaborative nature, visual interface, and diverse set of features make it an invaluable tool for businesses and teams looking to enhance their service design processes and create innovative and customer-centric services.

Storyboarding

Storyboarding is a crucial technique used in service design to visually represent and outline the sequence of events, interactions, and touchpoints that take place within a service experience. It is a way of visual storytelling that allows designers to communicate and iterate on their ideas in a tangible and accessible format. At its core, a storyboard is a series of sketches or illustrations arranged in a chronological order, accompanied by brief descriptions or annotations. It provides a step-by-step narrative of different stages and key moments that occur during a service interaction, helping service designers and stakeholders better understand the overall service experience.

Storymapping

A storymap in the context of service design is a visual tool used to map out the user journey and experience within a service. It is a structured way to outline the different steps, touchpoints, and interactions that a user goes through when using a service. The storymap is typically created by first identifying the key user personas or customer segments that will be using the service. Each persona represents a specific type of user with their own goals, needs, and motivations. The storymap then follows the user journey by mapping out the sequence of events that occur from the user's perspective.

Storytelling Workshops

Storytelling workshops in the context of service design are interactive sessions or courses that focus on teaching individuals or teams how to effectively tell stories to enhance the design of a service. These workshops usually involve practical exercises, group discussions, and guidance from experienced facilitators. The goal of storytelling workshops in service design is to help participants develop the skills and knowledge needed to effectively communicate their ideas, insights, and solutions in a compelling and memorable way. By mastering the art of storytelling, designers are better able to engage stakeholders, generate empathy, and inspire action.

Storytelling

Storytelling in the context of service design refers to the practice of using narratives to convey information, engage users, and communicate the value of a service. It involves crafting and sharing stories that help users understand and connect with a service, its purpose, and its benefits. Storytelling is a powerful tool in service design as it allows designers and stakeholders to effectively communicate complex ideas, insights, and concepts in a way that is relatable and memorable. By using narratives, designers can create a shared understanding among stakeholders, build empathy with users, and inspire innovative solutions.

Structured Brainstorming

Structured brainstorming, in the context of service design, is a collaborative approach that encourages participants to generate and organize ideas in a systematic and effective manner. This method is used to explore and generate innovative solutions to complex problems or challenges related to the design and improvement of services. During a structured brainstorming session, participants are encouraged to freely share their ideas and thoughts without judgment or criticism. This creates a safe and open environment that fosters creativity and the exploration of new possibilities. The facilitator of the session guides and moderates the discussion, ensuring that all voices are heard and that the process remains focused and productive.

Structured Interviewing

Structured interviewing is a method used in service design to gather information from participants in a systematic and standardized manner. It involves asking a set of predetermined questions to elicit specific information and insights related to the design of a service. This approach ensures consistency in the data collection process and allows for a more objective analysis of the responses. During a structured interview, the interviewer follows a predefined script of questions and prompts, often called an interview guide. These questions are carefully crafted to address the research goals and objectives of the service design project. They may cover a wide range of topics, such as user needs, expectations, pain points, preferences, and feedback on existing services. The interview process typically begins with an introduction, where the interviewer explains the purpose of the interview, assures the participant of their confidentiality and anonymity, and obtains their consent to participate. The structured interview then proceeds with a series of closed-ended and open-ended questions designed to gather specific information from the participant. Closed-ended questions are those that require a simple and direct response, such as yes or no, rating scales, or multiple-choice options. These types of questions are useful for collecting quantitative data and gaining insights into participants' preferences or satisfaction levels with certain aspects of the service. Open-ended questions, on the other hand, encourage participants to provide detailed and qualitative responses. These questions often begin with phrases like "Tell me about..." or "Describe your experience with..." They allow participants to express their thoughts, opinions, and emotions more freely, providing valuable insights into their needs, challenges, or suggestions for service improvement. By using a structured interviewing approach, service designers can collect a rich and well-organized set of data that can inform the design and refinement of services. The standardized nature of the process ensures that all participants are asked the same questions, reducing bias and enabling comparisons between responses. The insights gained from structured interviews can help identify patterns, trends, and areas for improvement, ultimately leading to the creation of more user-centered and effective services.

Structured Walkthroughs

Structured Walkthroughs refer to a systematic process employed in service design to evaluate and improve the usability and effectiveness of a service. It involves a comprehensive examination of the service from start to finish, identifying potential flaws and areas of improvement. A Structured Walkthrough typically involves a multidisciplinary team of experts and stakeholders who collaboratively review the service design, functionality, and user experience. This process aims to highlight any potential issues or gaps in the service and generate actionable recommendations for improvement.

Subject Matter Expert (SME) Workshops

A Subject Matter Expert (SME) Workshop in the context of service design refers to a collaborative session where individuals with specific expertise and knowledge within a particular domain come together to share insights, exchange ideas, and make informed decisions to address complex service-related challenges or opportunities. These workshops typically involve a diverse group of individuals, including industry professionals, key stakeholders, and subject matter experts who possess deep knowledge and understanding of a specific subject area or discipline. The purpose of the workshop is to leverage the expertise of these individuals to gain valuable insights and identify potential solutions or improvements for the design and delivery of services.

SurveyMonkey

SurveyMonkey is an online survey platform that allows individuals and organizations to create and distribute surveys to gather feedback and data from a targeted audience. As a service design tool, SurveyMonkey enables users to design, administer, and analyze surveys efficiently and effectively. Its user-friendly interface and customizable survey templates make it accessible even to individuals with limited technical expertise.

Surveys And Questionnaires

Surveys and questionnaires are research tools used in the field of service design to gather information and insights from users or customers. These tools are designed to collect data in a systematic and structured manner, allowing service designers to understand people's needs, preferences, and experiences. A survey is a method of data collection that involves asking a predefined set of questions to a sample of individuals. Surveys can be conducted in various formats, such as online, through email, telephone, or in-person interviews. The questions in a survey can be closed-ended (e.g., multiple choice, rating scales) or open-ended (e.g., free text responses), depending on the type of information sought. A questionnaire, on the other hand, is a specific type of survey that typically consists of a series of written questions. Similar to surveys, questionnaires can be administered through different channels and can include both closed-ended and open-ended questions. Questionnaires are often preferred when researchers want to collect standardized data from a large number of respondents. Both surveys and questionnaires are valuable tools in service design as they provide designers with valuable insights into the needs, expectations, and perceptions of users and customers. By using these research instruments, service designers can gather quantitative and qualitative data to inform the design and improvement of services. Surveys and questionnaires help service designers in several ways. Firstly, they allow designers to collect demographic information about the respondents, such as age, gender, and occupation, which can help in understanding different user segments and tailoring services to specific groups. Secondly, these tools enable designers to gather feedback on various aspects of the service, such as usability, satisfaction, and perceived value. This feedback can identify pain points and areas for improvement, guiding designers in making informed design decisions. In conclusion, surveys and questionnaires are important research tools in service design, offering a structured approach to collect data from users and customers. These tools provide valuable insights into user needs and preferences, aiding service designers in creating user-centered and impactful services.

Sustainability Assessment

A sustainability assessment in the context of service design is the process of evaluating the environmental, social, and economic impacts of a service throughout its lifecycle. It involves the identification and analysis of potential risks, opportunities, and trade-offs associated with the service, aimed at ensuring its long-term viability and minimizing negative impacts on the planet and society. During a sustainability assessment, various aspects are considered, including energy consumption, waste generation, emissions, resource use, social equity, and economic viability. The assessment covers the entire lifecycle of the service, from its inception or development, through its implementation and operation, to its eventual disposal or termination.

System Mapping

System Mapping is a visual representation technique used in service design to analyze and

181

understand the interactions, relationships, and flows of a complex system. It illustrates the various components, processes, and actors involved in delivering a service, highlighting their interdependencies and the overall functioning of the system. A System Map provides a holistic view of a service ecosystem, capturing both the internal and external elements that contribute to its functioning. By mapping out the entire system, including the different touchpoints, channels, and stakeholders, it helps designers identify strengths, weaknesses, and opportunities for improvement. The primary purpose of System Mapping is to gain insight into the mechanics and dynamics of a service system. It allows designers to visualize the sequential and parallel processes, interactions, and feedback loops within the system, facilitating a comprehensive understanding of how various components work together to deliver the intended outcomes. System Mapping typically involves the use of diagrams, flowcharts, or other visual representations to depict the structure and connections of the system. These visuals make it easier to identify bottlenecks, inefficiencies, duplication of efforts, or gaps in the service delivery, enabling designers to propose targeted improvements. The process of creating a System Map involves conducting extensive research, engaging with stakeholders, and collecting data on the service ecosystem. This information is then organized and visualized in a clear and coherent manner to highlight the relationships, dependencies, and complexities of the system. System Mapping is a valuable tool in service design as it helps uncover the underlying mechanisms of a service system. By providing a comprehensive overview of the system's structure and functioning, it enables designers to make informed decisions, design more effective interventions, and develop solutions tailored to address the identified challenges or opportunities.

System Usability Scale (SUS)

The System Usability Scale (SUS) is a widely used questionnaire-based tool in service design that measures the usability of a system or service. It provides a standardized approach to assess the user's perception of the usability and user experience (UX) of a product or service. SUS consists of 10 statements that measure the perceived usability of a system or service. These statements are designed to capture the user's overall satisfaction, learnability, efficiency, and ease of use. The scale uses a Likert-type response format, where participants rate their agreement or disagreement on a 5-point scale ranging from "Strongly Disagree" to "Strongly Agree". After completing the questionnaire, the responses are scored and aggregated to calculate a final SUS score. The score ranges from 0 to 100, with a higher score indicating better usability. The calculation involves transforming the individual ratings into numeric values and adjusting for odd and even responses to ensure consistency in interpretation. The SUS questionnaire is flexible and can be administered in various ways, such as in-person interviews, online surveys, or remote user testing. It can be applied at different stages of the service design process, including the evaluation of prototypes, beta versions, or fully developed systems. The SUS has proven to be a reliable and valid tool for assessing the usability of systems and services across a wide range of domains. Its simplicity makes it easy to administer, and its standardized approach allows for comparisons between different products or services. The SUS score provides a valuable metric for service designers to identify areas for improvement, track changes over time, and benchmark against competitors. Overall, the System Usability Scale is an essential tool in service design that helps to evaluate and enhance the usability and user experience of systems and services. Its standardized questionnaire and scoring system provide valuable insights into the user's satisfaction and perception, enabling designers to make informed decisions and iterate on their designs.

Task Analysis

Task analysis is a systematic approach used in service design to understand and document the steps and activities involved in completing a specific task or process. It involves breaking down a task into smaller, more manageable components to identify the actions, decisions, and interactions required to accomplish the desired outcome. The main purpose of conducting a task analysis is to gain insight into the user's behavior, needs, abilities, and preferences within the context of the service being designed. By carefully examining each step of the task, service designers can identify pain points, inefficiencies, and opportunities for improvement. This analysis helps them make informed decisions about optimizing the service experience to better meet user needs and expectations.

Task Analytics

Task Analytics refers to the systematic collection, analysis, and interpretation of data related to the performance and usability of tasks within a service design. It aims to provide insights into how users interact with a service, identify bottlenecks and areas for improvement, and optimize the overall user experience. Through the use of various analytics tools and techniques, Task Analytics allows service designers to gather quantitative and qualitative data on user behavior, task completion rates, time spent on each task, errors encountered, and user satisfaction levels. This data can be collected through methods such as user surveys, user testing, clickstream analysis, heatmaps, and session recordings. Once the data is collected, it is analyzed to uncover patterns, trends, and user preferences. Service designers can use this information to identify pain points in the user journey, understand user needs and expectations, and make informed decisions to enhance the service. For example, if analysis reveals that users are spending a significant amount of time on a particular task or encountering frequent errors, designers can prioritize improvements to simplify the process or address the underlying issues. Task Analytics also plays a vital role in measuring the impact of service design changes. By comparing data before and after implementing design changes, designers can assess the effectiveness of their interventions and validate the improvements made. This iterative approach allows for continuous refinement and optimization of the service based on user feedback and behavior. In conclusion, Task Analytics is a valuable tool in service design that enables designers to gather and analyze data, understand user behavior, identify areas for improvement, and optimize the user experience. By leveraging insights obtained through Task Analytics, designers can create services that are intuitive, efficient, and user-centric.

The Five Whys

The Five Whys is a problem-solving technique used in service design to identify the root cause of a particular issue or problem. It involves asking "why" multiple times, usually five times, in order to reach the underlying cause of the problem. This technique is based on the idea that by asking "why" repeatedly, we can peel back the layers of symptoms and surface-level causes to uncover the fundamental cause that is leading to the problem. By addressing this root cause, we can implement more effective solutions and prevent the problem from recurring.

Think Aloud Testing

Think Aloud Testing is a qualitative research method used in service design to understand the user's thought process and decision-making while interacting with a product or service. It involves observing and recording the user's verbalized thoughts, opinions, and reactions as they navigate through a specific user journey or task. During Think Aloud Testing, participants are asked to verbalize their thoughts continuously, expressing their likes, dislikes, confusion, expectations, and any other relevant opinions or insights. This helps service designers gain valuable insights into the user's cognitive load, usability issues, emotional responses, and overall user experience.

Think-Aloud Testing

Think-Aloud Testing is a research method used in service design to gain insights into the thoughts and decision-making processes of users as they interact with a service or product. It involves asking users to verbalize their thoughts, perceptions, and reactions while performing tasks or experiencing a service. During Think-Aloud Testing, participants are encouraged to express their thoughts and feelings out loud, providing a continuous stream of feedback in real-time. This technique allows designers and researchers to understand the user's mental model, uncover usability issues, and identify areas for improvement in the service design.

Touchpoint Analysis

Touchpoint analysis is a method used in service design to identify and understand the various points of interaction between a customer and a service provider. These interactions, or touchpoints, can occur through a wide range of channels such as websites, mobile apps, physical stores, call centers, social media, and email. The goal of touchpoint analysis is to map out and evaluate these points of contact to gain insight into the customer experience and identify opportunities for improvement. During a touchpoint analysis, designers focus on both pre-purchase and post-purchase touchpoints, as well as those that occur during the actual service delivery. This holistic approach helps to capture the customer journey and examine the different touchpoints that shape the overall experience. By analyzing each touchpoint, designers can identify pain points, areas of confusion, or moments of delight. This analysis provides valuable information for optimizing the service experience and enhancing customer satisfaction.

Touchpoint Optimization

Touchpoint optimization is a strategic approach used in service design to improve the interactions and experiences between customers and a company or organization. It involves identifying and analyzing the various touchpoints, or points of contact, that customers have with a brand throughout their journey, and then implementing changes to optimize these touchpoints for a more seamless and positive customer experience. The goal of touchpoint optimization is to enhance customer satisfaction, increase customer loyalty, and ultimately drive business growth. By identifying and improving touchpoints, companies can better understand their customers' needs, reduce friction and barriers in the customer journey, and deliver a more personalized and memorable experience. There are several steps involved in touchpoint optimization. The first step is mapping out the customer journey and identifying all the touchpoints along the way. This could include physical interactions, such as visiting a store or calling customer service, as well as digital touchpoints like using a website or mobile app. Once the touchpoints have been identified, the next step is to analyze each touchpoint to understand the customer's experience and identify areas for improvement. This can be done through methods such as customer feedback surveys, usability testing, and data analysis. By gathering insights from customers and analyzing the data, companies can identify pain points, gaps, and areas of opportunity in the customer journey. After analyzing the touchpoints, the next step is to prioritize and implement changes to optimize them. This could involve simplifying processes, improving communication channels, personalizing interactions, or providing additional support and resources. The changes should be designed to enhance the overall customer experience and align with the company's brand values and goals. Finally, touchpoint optimization is an ongoing process. It requires continuous monitoring and evaluation to ensure that the changes implemented are effective and to identify any new areas for improvement. By continuously refining and optimizing touchpoints, companies can create a seamless and consistent experience that builds customer loyalty and drives business success.

Trello

Trello is a web-based project management tool that facilitates collaborative work and organization. It is designed to help individuals and teams manage tasks, projects, and workflows efficiently. The core feature of Trello revolves around the use of boards, lists, and cards. A board represents a project or a workspace, where users can create multiple lists to signify different stages or categories within the project. Each list contains a set of cards, which represent individual tasks or items to be completed. Trello's interface is simple and intuitive, with a drag-and-drop functionality that allows users to easily move cards between lists or reorder them within a list. This visual approach makes it easy to track the progress of tasks and identify bottlenecks or areas that may require attention. Within each card, users can add detailed notes, checklists, due dates, attachments, and labels to provide more context and information. They can also assign cards to specific team members, enabling easy delegation and accountability. Users can collaborate with team members by leaving comments on cards and tagging relevant individuals, fostering communication and coordination. In addition to boards, lists, and cards, Trello offers several features that enhance project management and organization. Users can create custom labels to categorize cards, filter and search for specific tasks, and set notifications to receive updates on card activity. Trello also allows integration with other popular productivity tools and apps, such as Google Drive, Slack, and Dropbox, enabling seamless workflow and data sharing. Overall, Trello provides a user-friendly and flexible platform for managing tasks and projects. It offers a visual and collaborative approach to project management, promoting transparency, efficiency, and collaboration among team members. Whether used by individuals, small teams, or large organizations, Trello is a versatile tool that can streamline work processes and improve productivity.

Triading

Triading refers to a process in service design where three parties collaborate to exchange, create, and enhance value through the design and delivery of services. The three parties involved in triading typically include the service provider, the service recipient, and a third-party entity that plays a facilitating or mediating role. Triading is characterized by a dynamic and iterative exchange of ideas, experiences, and insights between the three parties involved. It aims to ensure that services are co-created based on a deep understanding of the service recipient's needs, expectations, and aspirations. Triading goes beyond a traditional customer-provider relationship and seeks to build a collaborative partnership that fosters innovation and continuous improvement.

TryMyUI

TryMyUI is a service design platform that helps businesses evaluate the usability and user experience (UX) of their digital products or services. The platform connects businesses with a diverse panel of real users, who perform specific tasks on the product or service while providing feedback in the form of verbal comments and written responses. Through TryMyUI, businesses can gain valuable insights into the strengths and weaknesses of their digital offerings from a user's perspective. The service is particularly useful during the early stages of product development or when making significant updates to an existing product, as it allows businesses to identify potential issues and make improvements before the product reaches a wider audience.

UXCam

UXCam is a service design tool that enables businesses to optimize their mobile app user experience by providing in-depth analytics and visual recordings of user interactions. By implementing UXCam, companies gain a better understanding of how users interact with their app, allowing them to make data-driven decisions to improve user satisfaction and ultimately drive business performance. The tool captures various metrics, including heatmaps, session recordings, and user journeys, which provide valuable insights into user behavior and pain points.

Usability Testing

Usability testing is a method of evaluating a service or product by testing it with representative users to determine its ease of use, efficiency, and user satisfaction. It is a crucial step in the service design process as it provides insights into how users interact with the service and identifies any usability issues or areas of improvement. During usability testing, participants are given specific tasks to complete while using the service. Their interactions and feedback are observed and recorded by the design team. This testing approach focuses on understanding the user's perspective and allows for iterative improvements to be made based on their needs and preferences.

UsabilityHub

UsabilityHub is a service design tool that focuses on improving the usability and user experience of digital products and services. It provides a platform for designers and researchers to conduct user testing, gather feedback, and make informed design decisions. With UsabilityHub, designers can create and run various types of usability tests, such as first-click tests, preference tests, and five-second tests. These tests help identify any issues or obstacles users may encounter when interacting with a website, app, or prototype. By collecting data and feedback from a target audience, designers can gain valuable insights into how to optimize their designs for improved usability.

User Experience (UX) Metrics

User Experience (UX) Metrics refer to the quantitative and qualitative measures used to evaluate the effectiveness of a service design in meeting user needs and achieving business goals. These metrics help designers and stakeholders understand how well the service is performing and identify areas for improvement. Quantitative metrics provide numerical data about user behavior and interaction with the service. These metrics can include measures such as conversion rates, click-through rates, time spent on task, and error rates. Quantitative metrics are useful for identifying patterns and trends in user behavior, as well as evaluating the impact of design changes on user engagement and satisfaction. Qualitative metrics, on the other hand, capture subjective feedback and insights from users. These metrics can be gathered through methods such as user interviews, surveys, and usability testing. Qualitative metrics can provide a deeper understanding of user needs, preferences, and pain points, helping designers uncover usability issues and prioritize design improvements. Both quantitative and qualitative metrics are essential for measuring the user experience of a service design effectively. By analyzing these metrics, designers can gain actionable insights and make informed decisions to improve the service's usability, efficiency, and overall user satisfaction. Measuring UX metrics is a continuous process that should be integrated into the service design cycle. By setting specific goals and defining relevant metrics at the beginning of a project, designers can track the progress towards achieving those goals throughout the design process. Regularly reviewing and analyzing UX metrics enables designers to make data-driven design decisions, identify areas for optimization, and evaluate the impact of design changes on the user experience.

User Flow

A user flow is a visualization or representation of the steps a user takes to achieve a specific goal or complete a task within a service or system. It provides an overview of the user's journey, highlighting the sequence of actions they need to perform and the possible paths they can take. The user flow is typically depicted as a series of interconnected steps or screens, showing the progression from one stage to another. It illustrates the flow of information, actions, and decisions made by the user, as well as any feedback they receive.

User Interface (UI) Design

User interface (UI) design in the context of service design refers to the artistic and functional arrangement of visual elements and interactive components that enable users to effectively interact with a digital or physical service. It involves the careful consideration and implementation of various design principles to create an intuitive and user-friendly experience. The primary goal of UI design is to optimize the usability and convenience of a service by ensuring that users can easily navigate and accomplish their tasks. It encompasses the visual aesthetics, layout, and overall structure of the interface, as well as the behavior and responsiveness of its elements. UI design aims to enhance the user's perception of the service, establish trust, and foster positive engagement.

User Interviews

An user interview is a research method used in the field of service design to gather insights and understand the needs, motivations, and behaviors of users. It involves conducting one-on-one conversations with individuals who are representative of the target user group or population. The purpose of user interviews is to obtain qualitative data that helps designers and researchers gain a deeper understanding of the users and their experiences. This information can then be used to inform the design and development of products, services, or experiences that are tailored to their specific needs.

User Needs Analysis

A User Needs Analysis is a method used in service design to gather and understand the specific requirements of users for a particular product or service. It involves conducting research and gathering data to identify and prioritize user needs, goals, and pain points. The goal of a User Needs Analysis is to ensure that the final product or service is designed and developed in a way that meets the needs and expectations of the target users. By understanding what the users want and need, designers can make informed decisions on how to improve the user experience, increase customer satisfaction, and ultimately create a successful product or service.

User Research

Service design is a user-centered approach that involves the creation and improvement of services to meet the needs of both customers and providers. It is a multidisciplinary approach that combines various methods and tools to understand, design, and deliver services that are efficient, effective, and enjoyable. Service design focuses on understanding and addressing the

186

entire service experience, from the initial point of contact to the final outcome. It takes into account not only the tangible aspects of a service, such as the physical environment and interactions, but also the intangible elements, such as emotions and perceptions.

User Stories

User stories are concise, informal descriptions of a feature or functionality of a service, written from the perspective of an end user or customer. They serve as a communication tool between the various stakeholders involved in the design and development process, ensuring that everyone has a clear understanding of the user's needs and expectations. User stories typically follow a specific format, known as the "As a, I want, So that" format, which captures the who, what, and why of a user's request. The "As a" part of the user story identifies the user or customer who is making the request. This could be a specific role or persona, such as a customer, administrator, or manager. The "I want" part of the user story describes the specific feature or functionality that the user is asking for. It should be written in clear and concise language, focusing on the desired outcome or benefit rather than the technical implementation. The "So that" part of the user story explains the reason or objective behind the user's request. It provides context and helps the development team understand the user's motivations and the impact the requested feature will have on their experience. User stories are typically written on index cards or sticky notes during collaborative workshops or meetings. They are then organized and prioritized in a backlog, which acts as a repository of all the requested features or functionalities. The development team can then use these user stories as a basis for planning and estimating the work required to deliver them. By using user stories, service designers can ensure that the focus remains on the needs and expectations of the end users or customers. They provide a clear and concise way to capture and communicate user requirements, facilitating collaboration and alignment among all stakeholders. User stories enable iterative and incremental development, as they can be reprioritized and refined based on user feedback and changing business needs. Overall, user stories are a valuable tool in service design, helping to ensure that the resulting service meets the needs and expectations of the end users, while also providing a clear vision for the development team. They promote a user-centered design approach and facilitate effective communication and collaboration among all stakeholders involved in the process.

User-Centered Design (UCD)

User-Centered Design (UCD) is an approach that focuses on the needs, wants, and preferences of users when designing services. It places the user at the center of the design process, ensuring that the service meets their expectations and is easy to use. In UCD, designers gather insights about the target users through various research methods, such as interviews, observations, and surveys. This helps them understand the users' goals, tasks, and context of use. By empathizing with the users, designers can gain a deeper understanding of their needs and design solutions that address these needs effectively. Once the user insights are collected, the design team can begin the ideation and prototyping phase. They generate multiple design concepts, evaluating each against the user requirements. The chosen concept is then refined and translated into a prototype, allowing users to interact with and provide feedback on the service. This iterative process helps identify any usability issues or areas for improvement early on. Throughout the design process, UCD emphasizes the importance of usability. Usability testing is conducted to evaluate the effectiveness, efficiency, and satisfaction of the service. User feedback is considered valuable in optimizing the service to align with user expectations and preferences. UCD also recognizes that users' needs and preferences may evolve over time. Therefore, post-launch monitoring and evaluation of the service is crucial. User feedback and data analytics help designers identify areas for enhancement and ensure the service continues to meet user requirements. By following UCD principles, service designers can create services that are tailored to the user's specific needs and provide a positive user experience. This approach fosters user satisfaction, loyalty, and engagement, ultimately leading to the success and sustainability of the service.

User-Centered Design

User-Centered Design, in the context of service design, refers to a design approach that focuses on crafting services that meet the needs and expectations of the intended users. It involves

187

taking into account user insights, goals, behaviors, and preferences throughout the design process to ensure the resulting service aligns with their needs and provides a positive, effective, and enjoyable user experience. The essence of User-Centered Design lies in understanding the users' needs, desires, and perspectives. This involves conducting user research, such as interviews, surveys, and observation, to gain insights into their motivations, behaviors, and pain points. These insights inform the design process by guiding decisions on service features, interactions, and interfaces. The iterative nature of User-Centered Design allows for continuous improvement and refinement based on user feedback and testing. Prototypes and mock-ups are created and tested with users, allowing designers to observe and understand how users interact with the service and identify areas for improvement. User-Centered Design encourages collaboration and co-creation between designers, stakeholders, and users. By involving users in the design process, designers can gain empathy for their needs and preferences, leading to more informed and effective design decisions. Ultimately, the goal of User-Centered Design is to create services that are intuitive, enjoyable, and valuable to the users. By putting the user at the center of the design process, designers can ensure that the service meets their expectations, addresses their pain points, and fulfills their goals, resulting in increased user satisfaction, engagement, and loyalty.

User-Centered Evaluation

User-centered evaluation is a systematic approach to gathering and analyzing feedback from users to assess the effectiveness and usability of a service design. It is a method used in service design to ensure that the service meets the needs and expectations of its users. The evaluation process involves collecting data and insights from users through various research methods, such as interviews, surveys, and observations. During the evaluation, the focus is on understanding the experiences, preferences, and challenges of users when interacting with the service. This includes examining the user's journey through the service, identifying pain points or areas of improvement, and capturing their overall satisfaction. The collected data is then analyzed to identify common patterns, trends, and areas for improvement. User-centered evaluation helps service designers to understand the users' needs and perspectives, enabling them to make informed decisions and iterate on their designs. It provides valuable insights into the usability, accessibility, and overall user experience of the service. By involving users in the evaluation process, designers can gain a better understanding of how the service is perceived and used in real-world scenarios. The evaluation process typically follows a cyclical approach, where feedback and insights gathered from users are used to inform design decisions and improvements to the service. This iterative process ensures that the service evolves based on real user feedback and aligns with their expectations. Overall, user-centered evaluation is a fundamental part of service design, as it allows designers to validate and refine their solutions based on user needs and expectations. By involving users in the evaluation process, designers can create more user-friendly and effective services that meet the needs of their target audience.

User-Centered Research

User-Centered Research is a fundamental practice in service design that focuses on understanding the needs, behaviors, and preferences of users to inform the creation and improvement of services. It involves gathering and analyzing qualitative and quantitative data directly from users to gain insights and make more informed design decisions. This research approach involves various methods and techniques to collect and interpret data, including interviews, observations, surveys, and usability testing. By engaging with users in their natural environments or in controlled lab settings, designers can gain a deep understanding of their experiences, motivations, and pain points when interacting with a service. The goal of user-centered research is to uncover user needs and expectations, as well as identify any barriers or constraints they may encounter when using a service. It helps designers empathize with users and gain insights into their context, allowing for the creation of more relevant and meaningful service experiences. Through user-centered research, designers can generate valuable insights that drive the design process. By involving users throughout the design lifecycle, from initial concept development to iterative prototyping and testing, designers can ensure that the final service meets user needs and aligns with their goals. The findings from user-centered research can be used to inform various aspects of service design, including service offerings, features, interactions, and touchpoints. By understanding users' goals, motivations, and expectations,

188

designers can make informed decisions about the design and delivery of services. In conclusion, user-centered research is an essential practice in service design that aims to uncover user needs, behaviors, and preferences. By engaging directly with users and gathering data, designers can gain valuable insights that inform the design and improvement of services.

UserReport

A UserReport refers to a tool or process used in service design to gather insights and feedback from users, with the aim of improving the overall user experience and meeting customer needs. It is an essential component of customer-centric and user-centered design approaches. The UserReport typically involves the collection of user feedback, opinions, and observations regarding the service or product being offered. This feedback can be gathered through various methods such as surveys, questionnaires, interviews, usability testing, and direct observation of user interactions. The collected data can be both qualitative and quantitative in nature, allowing for a comprehensive understanding of user attitudes, behaviors, and preferences. The purpose of using a UserReport in service design is to identify areas of improvement, uncover pain points, and gather insights that can inform the design and development of a service. By actively involving users in the design process, organizations can ensure that their services are better aligned with user expectations and deliver value-added experiences. The UserReport helps to bridge the gap between the service provider and the end-users, fostering a more collaborative and user-centered design approach. Once the data from the UserReport is collected and analyzed, it can be used to generate actionable insights and recommendations. These insights can highlight specific areas where there is room for improvement, potential innovations, and emerging trends. This information can be used by service designers, product managers, and other stakeholders to inform decision-making, prioritize design changes, and refine service offerings. In conclusion, a UserReport is a valuable tool in service design, enabling organizations to gather user feedback and insights that inform the design process. It helps to ensure that services are user-centered, align with customer expectations, and deliver enhanced user experiences.

Validately

Validately is a service design platform that enables companies to gather feedback and insights from users to inform and improve their products and services. It provides a range of tools and services that facilitate the testing and validation process, allowing businesses to make data-driven decisions and iterate on their designs. The platform offers various methods for collecting user feedback, such as remote usability testing, moderated interviews, surveys, and card sorting exercises. These methods can be conducted remotely, which allows for a diverse pool of participants and eliminates geographic constraints. Validately also provides tools for capturing user behavior and interaction patterns, enabling businesses to gain deeper insights into user preferences and needs. One of the key features of Validately is its usability testing capabilities. The platform allows companies to create and customize tasks for participants to complete, which can simulate real-life scenarios and interactions with the product or service. Participants' interactions and feedback are recorded, providing valuable insights into usability issues and areas for improvement. In addition to usability testing, Validately offers tools for conducting moderated interviews, which allow researchers to have real-time conversations with participants and probe deeper into their thoughts and experiences. These interviews can be conducted remotely, making it convenient for both parties and reducing logistical constraints. Validately also provides a platform for surveys, which can help businesses gather quantitative data and measure user satisfaction and preferences. Surveys can be easily designed and distributed, and the platform offers features for analyzing and visualizing survey data. Overall, Validately is a comprehensive service design platform that offers a range of tools and services for gathering user feedback and validating design decisions. It provides businesses with the means to make informed decisions based on data and insights, allowing for iterative improvement of products and services.

Value Chain Analysis

A value chain analysis in the context of service design is a systematic process of identifying and analyzing the activities and resources involved in the creation and delivery of a service, with the aim of understanding how value is generated throughout the service lifecycle. The value chain analysis begins by identifying the primary activities and support activities that are necessary for delivering the service. Primary activities include activities such as marketing, sales, and customer service, while support activities include activities such as procurement, human resources, and technology support. By examining each of these activities, service designers can gain a holistic view of the entire service delivery process. Once the activities have been identified, the next step is to analyze how value is created at each stage of the service lifecycle. This involves assessing the inputs, processes, and outputs of each activity to understand how they contribute to the overall value of the service. For example, in the marketing activity, the inputs may include market research and customer segmentation, while the processes may involve advertising and promotion, and the outputs may include increased brand awareness and customer acquisition. By conducting a value chain analysis, service designers can identify areas where value is being created or lost, and make informed decisions about how to improve the overall value proposition of the service. This could involve optimizing existing activities, redesigning processes, or introducing new technologies or partnerships. In conclusion, a value chain analysis is a valuable tool in the service design process as it provides a structured framework for understanding and improving the value creation process within a service. By examining the activities and resources involved in delivering a service, service designers can identify opportunities for enhancing value and delivering a superior service experience to customers.

Value Chain Mapping

Value Chain Mapping, in the context of service design, refers to the process of identifying and visualizing the various activities and interdependencies involved in the creation and delivery of a service. It involves mapping out the flow of value through different stages of a service, from the initial customer request to the final delivery or outcome. The value chain is a strategic tool used to analyze and improve the efficiency and effectiveness of a service. By mapping the value chain, service designers can gain a comprehensive understanding of how value is created and delivered, as well as identify potential areas for improvement.

Value Network Analysis

Value Network Analysis is a systematic approach used in service design to identify, analyze, and understand the relationships and interactions between various stakeholders involved in the delivery of a service. It aims to map out the network of actors, resources, activities, and value exchanges that contribute to the creation and delivery of value to customers. In the context of service design, a value network can be seen as a web of relationships and interactions between service providers, customers, partners, suppliers, and other stakeholders. Each stakeholder within the network plays a crucial role in the value creation process, and their actions and contributions have an impact on the overall value experienced by the customer. The primary goal of Value Network Analysis is to gain a holistic understanding of how value is created, exchanged, and consumed within the network. By mapping out the various actors and their interdependencies, service designers can identify potential bottlenecks, inefficiencies, or opportunities for improvement in the value creation process. Value Network Analysis typically involves the following steps: - Identifying and mapping the actors within the network, including service providers, customers, partners, and suppliers. - Analyzing the relationships and interactions between the actors, such as dependencies, collaborations, conflicts, or power dynamics. - Examining the resources and capabilities that each actor brings to the network, including knowledge, expertise, technology, or physical assets. - Investigating the activities and processes involved in the value creation process, including how resources are mobilized and utilized. - Understanding the value exchanges that occur within the network, such as monetary transactions, information sharing, or co-creation of value with customers. Through Value Network Analysis, service designers can uncover insights that help optimize the design and delivery of services. It provides a visual representation of the complex relationships and dependencies within the network, facilitating strategic decision-making and collaboration among stakeholders to enhance the overall value proposition for customers.

Value Proposition Design

A value proposition is a statement or a set of statements that conveys the unique benefits and value that a service provides to its customers. It defines the distinct advantages and outcomes that differentiate the service from its competitors and attract customers. Value proposition design is a methodological approach that helps service designers create and refine their value propositions. It involves understanding the needs, wants, and pain points of the target customer segment and aligning them with the value the service offers. This design process aims to articulate the value proposition in a clear and compelling manner, ensuring that it resonates with the customer and addresses their specific needs.

Value Proposition

The value proposition, in the context of service design, refers to the unique combination of benefits and value that a service offers to its customers. It is a clear statement that outlines why a customer should choose a particular service over competitors. A value proposition highlights the specific problems or needs that the service is addressing and describes the benefits that customers will receive from using the service. It communicates the value that the service brings to customers by addressing their pain points and providing solutions. In service design, a value proposition is an essential component of designing a successful service. It helps to differentiate the service from others in the market and to attract and retain customers. A well-defined value proposition will clearly articulate the unique selling points and benefits of the service. To create an effective value proposition, service designers need to understand the target customers and their needs. This involves conducting extensive research to gain insights into customer behaviors, preferences, and pain points. By understanding customer needs, service designers can tailor the value proposition to address those needs and provide a compelling reason for customers to choose the service. In addition to addressing customer needs, a value proposition also takes into consideration the competitive landscape. It outlines how the service stands out from the competition and why customers should choose it over alternatives. This could involve highlighting key features, unique experiences, cost savings, or other value-added benefits that differentiate the service. A well-crafted value proposition should be clear, concise, and easy to understand. It should focus on the benefits and value that customers will experience rather than simply describing the features of the service. By effectively communicating the unique value that the service offers, a value proposition helps to attract and retain customers, ultimately leading to the success of the service.

Verint

Verint is a vendor that specializes in service design, which involves creating and refining customer experiences across various touchpoints and channels. Service design aims to improve service delivery, enhance customer satisfaction, and ultimately drive business success. Verint's approach to service design is based on a comprehensive understanding of customer needs and expectations. Through in-depth research and analysis, Verint helps organizations identify pain points and opportunities for improvement in their service offerings. This includes examining the entire customer journey, from initial contact to post-purchase support.

Video Ethnography

Video ethnography is a research method used in the field of service design to gain a deep understanding of users' needs, behaviors, and experiences by capturing and analyzing video footage of their interactions with a service or product. With video ethnography, researchers observe and record real-life situations to uncover insights that may be missed through traditional research methods, such as surveys or interviews. By capturing users' actions, gestures, facial expressions, and verbal and nonverbal communication, video ethnography provides rich, detailed data that can inform the design and improvement of services.

Virtual Reality Prototyping

Virtual reality prototyping is a process specifically applied in the field of service design, wherein virtual reality technologies are utilized to simulate and test service experiences before they are fully developed and implemented. It involves creating realistic virtual environments that allow designers, stakeholders, and users to interact and experience the proposed service offering in a highly immersive and interactive manner. This prototyping method offers several advantages over traditional prototyping techniques. Firstly, it enables designers to visualize the service concept in a more tangible and realistic way, helping them refine and iterate on the design more effectively. By experiencing the service prototype in a virtual environment, designers can get a better sense of how users would interact with the service and identify any issues or challenges that may arise. Moreover, virtual reality prototyping allows for real-time user feedback and engagement, enabling designers to gather insights from users early in the design process. This feedback can then be harnessed to inform further iterations and improvements, enhancing the overall user experience. The immersive nature of virtual reality also stimulates a more emotional and visceral response from users, providing valuable insights into how the service can evoke certain feelings or emotions. Virtual reality prototyping has proven to be particularly valuable in the service design field, as it helps bridge the gap between conceptual ideas and their real-world implementation. By enabling designers to test and validate service concepts in a virtual environment, potential issues or shortcomings can be identified and addressed prior to the costly and time-consuming development phase. It also ensures that the final service offering meets the needs and expectations of the target users, enhancing the chances of successful adoption and customer satisfaction.

Visio

Visio is a software tool developed by Microsoft that is widely used for service design. It provides a platform for creating diagrams and visualizations that help in understanding, documenting, and communicating complex service systems and processes. Service design involves the creation and improvement of services with a focus on user experience and customer satisfaction. It encompasses the design of not only the tangible components of a service, such as physical products and infrastructure, but also the intangible aspects, such as processes, interactions, and emotions. Effective service design requires a holistic understanding of the service system and its various components, and Visio plays a crucial role in facilitating this understanding.

Visual Design

Visual design, in the context of service design, refers to the planning and creation of aesthetically appealing visual elements that are used to communicate and enhance a service experience. It involves the use of various techniques and principles to craft a visually cohesive and engaging interface that effectively conveys the brand message and provides a positive user experience. Visual design plays a crucial role in service design as it helps to establish a strong visual identity and create a unified and consistent look and feel across all touchpoints of a service. By leveraging color, typography, layout, imagery, and other design elements, visual design establishes a visual language that communicates the service's values, personality, and functionality. Effective visual design ensures that the service interface is visually appealing, easy to navigate, and guides users through their interactions seamlessly. It aims to create a balance between aesthetics and usability, creating a visually pleasing experience that is also intuitive and user-friendly. Through visual design, important information and key service features can be highlighted and emphasized, making them more noticeable and memorable for users. It also helps in organizing and presenting information in a logical and easily understandable manner, improving comprehension and reducing cognitive load. By using visual hierarchy, contrast, and visual cues, visual design guides users' attention to important elements, helping them to achieve their goals efficiently within the service. Furthermore, visual design contributes to the overall brand perception and differentiation. By creating a visually distinctive and consistent brand presence, visual design reinforces the brand's values, identity, and positioning. It helps to establish a strong emotional connection with users, fostering trust, recognition, and loyalty towards the service. In summary, visual design in service design is the strategic and intentional crafting of visual elements that enhance a service experience. It encompasses the use of various design principles and techniques to create a visually appealing, intuitive, and memorable interface that communicates the brand message, guides users, and fosters strong brand perception and differentiation.

Visual Facilitation

Visual facilitation is a technique used in service design to create clear and concise visual representations of complex ideas, concepts, and processes. It involves the use of visual tools, such as diagrams, sketches, and illustrations, to visually communicate and facilitate understanding among stakeholders involved in service design projects. The main goal of visual facilitation is to simplify complex information and make it more accessible and engaging for all participants. By using visual elements, the facilitator can capture and synthesize the key points and insights discussed during workshops, meetings, or brainstorming sessions. This helps to ensure that all participants have a shared understanding of the problem, solution, or design challenge at hand.

Visual Thinking

Visual thinking is a cognitive process that involves using visual elements and techniques to generate, organize, and communicate information. In the context of service design, visual thinking is a valuable tool for understanding and designing the user experience. When designing services, it is important to consider the multiple touchpoints and interactions that users have with the service. Visual thinking helps designers to map out and visualize these touchpoints, allowing for a holistic understanding of the service experience. By visually representing the user journey, designers can easily identify pain points and areas for improvement.

Web Analytics

Web Analytics refers to the measurement, collection, analysis, and reporting of website data to understand and optimize its performance. It involves the use of various tools and methodologies to track and interpret user behavior, demographics, and interactions on a website. As a service design tool, Web Analytics provides valuable insights into how users engage with a website, enabling designers to make informed decisions and improvements. It helps in understanding user needs, preferences, and pain points, enabling the design team to create user-centric experiences and optimize the overall service.

Wireflows

Wireflows are a visual representation of the sequence of screens or pages that a user will navigate through while interacting with a digital service or application. They are an important tool in service design, providing a detailed overview of the user's journey and the different interactions they will have with the service. Wireflows typically consist of a series of wireframes or screen mockups, organized in a logical flow that represents the user's path from start to finish. The wireframes show the layout, structure, and content of each screen, while the connecting arrows or lines illustrate the user's movement from one screen to the next.

Wireframing

Wireframing is a preliminary design technique used in the context of service design. It involves creating simple, visual representations of the layout and structure of a service or product, focusing on its core functionality and user interactions. Wireframes are typically created during the early stages of the design process as a means of communicating and iterating on ideas. They serve as a blueprint or a skeletal framework that helps designers, stakeholders, and developers align their understanding of the service and its various components.

Wizard Of Oz Testing

Wizard of Oz testing is a service design technique that involves simulating the behavior of an automated system or service using human operators instead of actual software or hardware. The term "Wizard of Oz" alludes to the hidden manipulation and control performed by a human operator, similar to the iconic character in the novel and movie. This technique is used to gather user feedback and evaluate the user experience of a service before investing in the development of a complete system. The purpose of Wizard of Oz testing is to test the feasibility, usability, and effectiveness of a service concept or design by mimicking its intended functionality, even if the underlying technology is not yet fully implemented.

Woopra

Woopra is a service design tool that enables organizations to gather, analyze, and interpret data to enhance the design and performance of their services. It offers a comprehensive suite of features and insights to understand customer behavior, improve user experiences, and measure service effectiveness.Woopra allows businesses to track and monitor various customer touchpoints across multiple channels, such as websites, mobile apps, email campaigns, and social media. By collecting and consolidating data from these different sources, it provides a holistic view of customer interactions and engagement with the services offered.

Work Domain Analysis

A work domain analysis is a systematic approach used in service design to gain a comprehensive understanding of the context, activities, and interactions that occur within a particular work domain. It involves studying the various elements, such as processes, tasks, roles, and environmental factors, that contribute to the overall functioning of a specific service or system. The primary objective of a work domain analysis is to identify and analyze the key characteristics and requirements of the work domain in order to inform the design of a service or system that is effective, efficient, and user-friendly. This analysis helps designers understand the existing workflows, challenges, and opportunities within the work domain, and enables them to make informed decisions about how to design and improve upon the service or system being developed.

Workflow Analysis

A workflow analysis is a systematic examination of the sequence of activities and processes that make up a particular service. It involves documenting and understanding how tasks are performed, who is responsible for each task, and how information flows between different steps or individuals. The goal of a workflow analysis in the context of service design is to identify areas for improvement and to optimize the efficiency and effectiveness of the service. By mapping out the current workflow, service designers can identify bottlenecks, redundancies, and opportunities for automation or streamlining. This analysis allows for the identification of pain points and areas where the service can be redesigned to better meet the needs of its users.

Workplace Observation

A workplace observation is a systematic process of gathering information about the activities, interactions, and overall dynamics within a specific workplace environment. It involves closely observing employees, their behaviors, and the physical layout of the workspace to better understand how the organization operates and how it can be improved. Through workplace observations, designers can identify potential areas of improvement, highlight existing challenges, and gather insights to inform the development of service design strategies. By studying the interactions between employees, customers, and the physical environment, designers can gain a deeper understanding of how the service is currently delivered and experienced.

Workshops

A workshop in the context of service design refers to a collaborative and interactive session conducted with the aim of generating innovative ideas, solving problems, and improving the overall customer experience in a service. It brings together stakeholders, designers, users, and other relevant parties to brainstorm, prototype, and co-create solutions. During a service design workshop, participants engage in various activities and exercises that foster creative thinking, empathy, and a deep understanding of customer needs and pain points. These activities often include brainstorming sessions, user journey mapping, persona development, service blueprinting, role-playing, and prototyping.

XMind

XMind is a service design tool that helps in the creation and visualization of service blueprints, customer journey maps, and other design artifacts. It provides a platform for designers to collaborate, ideate, and iterate on service design projects. With XMind, designers can map out the end-to-end customer experience, understand touchpoints and interactions, and identify pain points and opportunities for improvement. The tool offers a range of features and functionalities that support the service design process, including: - Templates: XMind provides a wide collection of templates specifically designed for service design, such as service blueprints, customer journey maps, personas, and stakeholder maps. These templates provide a starting point for designers and enable them to quickly create professional-looking visualizations. - Mind mapping: XMind's core feature is its mind mapping capabilities. Designers can easily create mind maps to organize and structure their ideas, concepts, and information related to the service being designed. This enables a holistic understanding of the service and its various components. - Collaboration: XMind allows for real-time collaboration, enabling designers to work together on service design projects. Multiple team members can simultaneously create and edit service design artifacts, facilitating teamwork and ensuring everyone's input is captured. - Integration: XMind integrates with other tools commonly used in the service design process, such as design prototyping tools and project management platforms. This seamless integration streamlines the design workflow and makes it easier to connect the dots between different stages of the service design process. - Export and sharing: Designed artifacts can be easily exported in various formats, including PDF, PNG, and Microsoft Office formats. This allows designers to share their work with stakeholders, present it in meetings, or incorporate it into reports and presentations. In summary, XMind is a powerful tool for service designers to facilitate the creation, collaboration, and visualization of service design artifacts. It provides a comprehensive set of features and functionalities that support the entire service design process, from ideation to implementation.

Zendesk

Zendesk is a software platform that offers customer service and support solutions for businesses. It provides a centralized system for managing customer inquiries, support tickets, and communication channels, allowing businesses to streamline and improve their customer service operations. Through its user-friendly interface, Zendesk enables businesses to handle customer interactions efficiently. It offers various features such as ticketing, live chat, knowledge base, and customer self-service portals. These tools enable businesses to provide seamless customer support across multiple channels, including email, social media, phone, and chat.

Zero-In

Zero-In is a service design approach that focuses on aligning a company's offerings with the needs and wants of their target customers. It involves thoroughly understanding the customer journey and designing the service experience to create value for both the customer and the company. The Zero-In process starts with conducting extensive research to gain insights into the target customers, their behaviors, preferences, and pain points. This research helps identify the gaps and opportunities for improvement in the current service offering. The next step is to define the desired future state of the service, taking into consideration the needs, desires, and expectations of the customers. Once the future state is defined, the Zero-In approach involves ideation and co-creation workshops to generate innovative ideas and solutions for bridging the gaps and enhancing the service experience. These workshops bring together cross-functional teams, including design experts, employees, and even customers, to collaboratively brainstorm and design new service concepts. After the ideation phase, prototypes are developed and tested with real customers to gather feedback and refine the service concepts. This user-centered approach ensures that the service design is optimized to meet the specific needs and preferences of the target customers. Finally, the Zero-In approach involves implementing the refined service concepts, continuously monitoring and evaluating their performance, and making adjustments based on feedback and insights gained from the customer experience. This iterative process allows for continuous improvement and ensures that the service design remains aligned with the evolving needs and expectations of the customers.

Zoho CRM

Zoho CRM is a cloud-based customer relationship management (CRM) software that helps businesses effectively manage their customer interactions and sales processes. It provides a comprehensive set of tools and features designed to streamline and automate various aspects of customer relationship management, including lead management, pipeline management, contact management, and sales tracking. With Zoho CRM, businesses can easily capture and organize leads from various sources, such as websites, email campaigns, and social media. The software allows users to track and analyze leads, assign lead ownership, and nurture leads through targeted marketing campaigns. It also enables businesses to manage their sales pipeline effectively, providing visibility into the status of each deal and tracking progress against sales targets. Zoho CRM offers a centralized database for storing and managing customer information, including contact details, interactions, purchase history, and support tickets. It allows businesses to segment their customer base and create targeted marketing campaigns based on specific criteria, such as buying behavior or demographics. The software also provides tools for managing customer support and service requests, with features like ticket management, case tracking, and knowledge base management. In addition to customer management, Zoho CRM offers integration with various third-party applications and services, such as email marketing tools, e-commerce platforms, and accounting software. This allows businesses to centralize their customer data and streamline their business processes across different systems.

Zoomph

Zoomph is a service design platform that focuses on providing comprehensive tools and solutions to enhance social media engagement and audience insights for businesses and organizations. With its user-friendly interface and extensive features, Zoomph enables users to actively manage, analyze, and leverage social media data to create personalized experiences and optimize their overall digital marketing strategies. At its core, Zoomph aims to revolutionize the way brands engage with their target audience by empowering them with real-time data and actionable insights. Through its advanced analytics, Zoomph allows users to monitor and track social media conversations, measure the impact of campaigns, and identify the most influential voices in their respective industries. By understanding the preferences, behaviors, and sentiments of their audience, businesses can tailor their communication strategies to effectively connect and resonate with their target market.

Zurb

Zurb is a service design company that focuses on helping businesses create exceptional user experiences through effective design and development solutions. Zurb offers a range of services including design consulting, user research, prototyping, and front-end development. Zurb's service design approach involves understanding the needs and preferences of the target users and creating tailored solutions that meet those needs. The company employs a user-centered design methodology, which places the end-user at the center of the design process. This approach ensures that the final design solution is intuitive, user-friendly, and meets the specific goals of the business. With a team of experienced designers and developers, Zurb is able to provide end-to-end service design solutions. The company conducts thorough user research to gain insights into user behaviors, attitudes, and motivations. This research informs the design process and helps in creating user interfaces that are visually appealing, easy to navigate, and provide a seamless user experience. Zurb also emphasizes the importance of rapid prototyping in service design. By quickly creating and testing prototypes, the company is able to gather valuable feedback from users and make iterative improvements to the design. This iterative process ensures that the final design solution meets the user's needs and generates positive outcomes for the business. Furthermore, Zurb offers front-end development services, ensuring that the design concepts are effectively translated into functional websites or digital products. The company's front-end development team is skilled in using modern web technologies and adheres to industry best practices, resulting in well-performing and responsive digital experiences. In summary, Zurb is a service design company that combines user-centered design, research, prototyping, and front-end development to deliver exceptional user experiences. Their approach focuses on understanding user needs, creating intuitive designs, and iterating based on user feedback. Through their comprehensive service design solutions, Zurb helps businesses achieve their goals and improve customer satisfaction.

Zygote Body

Zygote Body is a digital service designed to provide an interactive and educational experience for users to explore and learn about the human anatomy. It allows users to visualize and navigate through a detailed 3D model of the human body, enabling them to study the structure and function of various organs, systems, and tissues. The service is based on the concept of a "zygote," which refers to the fertilized egg cell that gives rise to a new individual. In this context, Zygote Body represents the initial stage of human development, symbolizing the beginning of a journey to understand the intricate aspects of the human body.

196

www.ingramcontent.com/pod-product-compliance
Lightning Source LLC
LaVergne TN
LVHW041204050326
832903LV00020B/454